ICON READER

# Geoffrey Chaucer

## The General Prologue to The Canterbury Tales

EDITED BY J.-A. GEORGE

Consultant editor: Nicolas Tredell

**ICON BOOKS**

Published in 2000 by Icon Books Ltd.,
Grange Road, Duxford, Cambridge CB2 4QF
e-mail: info@iconbooks.co.uk
www.iconbooks.co.uk

Distributed in the UK, Europe, Canada, South Africa and Asia by the
Penguin Group: Penguin Books Ltd., 27 Wrights Lane, London W8 5TZ

Published in Australia in 2000 by Allen & Unwin Pty. Ltd.,
PO Box 8500, 9 Atchison Street, St. Leonards, NSW 2065

Editor's text copyright © 2000 J.-A. George

The author of the editor's text has asserted her moral rights.

No part of this book may be reproduced in any form, or by any means,
without prior permission in writing from the publisher.

Consultant editor: Nicolas Tredell
Managing editor: Duncan Heath
Series devised by: Christopher Cox
Cover design: Simon Flynn
Typesetting: Wayzgoose

ISBN 1 84046 170 5

Printed and bound in Great Britain by
Biddles Ltd., Guildford and King's Lynn

# Contents

**INTRODUCTION**     7

Addresses the lasting popularity of *The General Prologue*, discusses the poem in relation to *The Canterbury Tales* as a whole and fixes it within the wider chronology of Chaucer's work. The contents of the six chapters of this Guide are also outlined.

**CHAPTER ONE**     11

**'Of Engelond to Caunterbury they Wende': 1368–1880**

Examines the early tributes to Chaucer's 'greatness' made by fellow poets. We begin in 1368 with that of Eustache Deschamps and end with Matthew Arnold's *homage* of 1880. A chronology of the first editions of Chaucer's poems is provided in this chapter, as are extracts from Thomas Tyrwhitt's analysis of *The General Prologue*, found in the Preface to his own 1775–78 edition of the poet's work.

**CHAPTER TWO**     22

**'Tales of Best Sentence and Moost Solaas': 1892–1949**

Charts the influence of early editors of Chaucer such as F.J. Furnivall and Walter Skeat, and Thomas R. Lounsbury's tribute to The Golden Age of the Editors is quoted as evidence of their centrality. Continuing interest in Chaucer by other writers is signalled in extracts from the work of T.S. Eliot and Virginia Woolf. Extracts from commentaries on *The General Prologue* by Fredrick Tupper, Henry Barrett Hinckley, G.L. Kittredge and Muriel Bowden are also provided.

**CHAPTER THREE**     46

**'So as it Semed me': The 1950s and 1960s**

Begins with the work of J.S.P. Tatlock and how the 1950s saw a genuine and sustained flourishing of professional Chaucer criticism. An extract from Kemp Malone on *The General Prologue* follows, and the focus of the chapter then shifts to consider E.T. Donaldson's seminal 'Chaucer the Pilgrim', an article that was to influence later generations of scholars' ideas about the narrator's position and voice in the poem. Rosemary Woolf's re-examination of the Chaucerian 'I' in relation to Chaucer's style and methods of satire is also extracted, as are pieces by J.V. Cunningham and Robert M. Jordan. The chapter ends with another highly influential study, D.W. Robertson's *Preface to Chaucer*.

CHAPTER FOUR  65

'Th'estaat, th'array, the Nombre, and eek the Cause': The 1970s

The emergence of interest in Sociology as a discipline and its application to Chaucer studies is demonstrated in extracts from R.T. Lenaghan's 'Chaucer's *General Prologue* as History and Literature'. The main focus of this chapter, however, is Jill Mann's *Chaucer and Medieval Estates Satire: The Literature of Social Classes and the General Prologue to the Canterbury Tales*, a ground-breaking study which raised important questions about the form of *The General Prologue*. The notion of 'Renaissance Chaucer' is then explored through the work of Alice Miskimin. Extracts from analyses of the poem by Charles A. Owen, Jr. and Loy D. Martin follow, and the chapter concludes with a detailed look at Donald R. Howard's major contribution to our understanding of the relationship of *The General Prologue* to *The Canterbury Tales* as a whole.

CHAPTER FIVE  88

'What Nedeth Wordes Mo?': The 1980s

Explores what Alastair J. Minnis has called the 'new wave' of Chaucer criticism, beginning with the work of H. Marshall Leicester, Jr. and his re-defining of Donald R. Howard's notion of 'unimpersonated artistry' as 'impersonated artistry' and how this relates to the utterance of particular Canterbury pilgrims. An extract from an article by Barbara Nolan offers us another look at the structure of *The General Prologue* and this is followed by Elton D. Higgs's piece on Chaucer's social conscience and how this is demonstrated in the order of the pilgrim portraits in *The General Prologue*. Terry Jones's radical re-assessment of the portrait of Chaucer's Knight is also set against Higgs's thesis. The final extracts in this chapter are from Judith Ferster's exploration of the themes of literary and political authority in *The General Prologue*.

CHAPTER SIX                                                               119

'She was a Worthy Womman al hir Lyve': The 1990s

Looks largely at four feminist and/or gender-based readings of *The General Prologue*: Elaine Tuttle Hansen and Priscilla Martin offer readings of the portraits of the Wife of Bath and the Prioress, Monica E. McAlpine analyses the enigmatic Pardoner, David Aers takes on the Host and Jane Chance provides an innovative analysis of Chaucer's use of myth and how it exposes the sexual politics at work in *The General Prologue*.

APPENDIX                                                                  155

A table of the relative popularity of Chaucer's poems at different times

NOTES                                                                     157

SELECT BIBLIOGRAPHY                                                       166

ACKNOWLEDGEMENTS                                                          174

INDEX                                                                     176

## A NOTE ON REFERENCES AND QUOTATIONS

All quotations from *The General Prologue* have been amended to accord with the version of the text found in *The Riverside Chaucer* edition of 1987.

In any quotation, a row of three dots indicates an editorial ellipsis within a sentence or paragraph, and a row of six dots (that is, two ellipses) indicates an editorial omission of a paragraph break, or of one or more paragraphs.

# INTRODUCTION

*T*HE GENERAL PROLOGUE to *The Canterbury Tales* is one of, if not the most, widely read of Chaucer's works. Taught in schools and universities around the world, and the constant subject of academic books, essays and articles down the years, its centrality to the English literary canon has never been in dispute. Indeed, the extreme popularity of the poem makes the remit of a Guide such as this one very challenging as the amount of critical material available seems almost infinite. This situation has led the editors of the *Variorum* edition of Chaucer's works, for example, to comment on 'the extraordinary amount of interpretative commentary published on particular passages, lines, and words in the *General Prologue*'.[1] The sheer bulk of criticism on offer is not the only problem, however, for the *Variorum* editors also maintain that its very nature presents certain difficulties: 'Whereas it is possible – and fruitful – to trace the developing interpretation of one of *The Canterbury Tales*, it is more difficult to apply this approach to the *General Prologue*, since most interpretative writing on it deals with particular, and relatively short, passages from the text rather than with the text as a whole.'[2] The reader of this Guide may find this in part to be the case, but abundant examples of longer works devoted to more extended passages of *The General Prologue* shall also be provided in the following pages. A happy balance was aimed at here and, it is hoped, achieved.

We must also remember that *The General Prologue* is but one part of a much larger work. As a result, it should come as no surprise that the relationship between it and *The Canterbury Tales* as a whole is an important topic of critical debate. In other words, just how 'autonomous' is the *Prologue*? Coupled with this is the question of its composition in relation to that of the various tales told by the pilgrims en route to Canterbury. One possible, and widely accepted, answer is provided by Larry D. Benson, editor of *The Riverside Chaucer* (where the authoritative text of *The General Prologue* used in this Guide is to be found), in his discussion of the overall chronology of Chaucer's works:

■ . . . . . . the scholar intent upon establishing the relative dates of Chaucer's work must consider matters of style and his increasing

THE GENERAL PROLOGUE

mastery of his craft. This is a difficult matter, since Chaucer's literary accomplishments are so varied that it may be said that he never "developed" in the manner of many writers. He was the most restlessly experimental of poets, constantly trying, and mastering, then abandoning but sometimes later returning to genres, metrical forms, styles, and subject matter. Stylistic comparison for the purposes of determining chronology is thus rendered very difficult indeed. Yet, applied with care, stylistic analysis can help to determine the relative dates of composition.

By such means scholars have developed a chronology of Chaucer's work about which there is, given the nature of the problem, a surprisingly broad consensus. Opinion is not unanimous, however, and the chronology given below represents only a general agreement . . .

. . . . . . 1388–92: *The General Prologue* and the earlier of *The Canterbury Tales; A Treatise on the Astrolabe* ((1391–92), with additions in 1393 or later).

1392–95: Most of *The Canterbury Tales*, including probably the "Marriage Group".

1396–1400: The latest of the *Tales*, including probably The Nun's Priest's Tale, The Canon Yeoman's Tale (though part of the latter is probably earlier), and the Parson's Tale; and several short poems, including Scogan, Bukton, and the Complaint to His Purse.[3] □

Dolores Warwick Frese, in her book *An Ars Legendi for Chaucer's Canterbury Tales*, offers an alternative chronology based upon her analysis of the relationship between the final version of *The General Prologue* and *Tales* that 'follow' and her thoughts on the reader's own experience(s) of this relationship:

■ . . . . . . I am suggesting that Chaucer's "General Prologue" to the *Canterbury Tales* was composed in its final form after all the "Tales" were written and assigned, save only the "Canon's Yeoman's Tale" . . . Thus, any attentive first reading of the "Prologue" yields rich descriptive pleasure and nuanced versions of anticipation and surprise that always attend subtle literary characterization. But a second or subsequent reading of the "General Prologue", after a reading of all the "Tales", adds to these mimetic pleasures the repeated conversion of such characteristically descriptive data into new registers of meaning whereby the featured detail revises its very mode of signification. Now transcending the category of mere description, such detail will typically bear witness to the numinous meaning of some extended portion of the larger text to which it has become imaginatively assimilated. In such instances, these renegotiated textual signs come to assume the character of poetic stigmata. We see them breaking forth

# INTRODUCTION

with fresh, vivid traces of sympathetic connection to an entire body of meaning whose prior existence supersedes and constitutes the very ground of being for such phenomenally realized acts of imagination.[4] □

Part of the reason for the existence of such a huge volume of critical material devoted to *The General Prologue* has to do, of course, with the fact that Chaucer's work attracted the attention of other writers, as well as that of the more general reading public, almost from its very inception. Thus, we have more than six hundred years of criticism available to us. Accordingly, the first chapter of this Guide covers the admittedly vast period from 1368–1880; 1368 being the year of the first recorded tribute to Chaucer (by his French contemporary Eustache Deschamps), and 1880 the date in which fellow English poet Matthew Arnold published his enthusiastic tribute to him. What this chapter attempts to foreground is the fact that before the twentieth century most of the interest in Chaucer's poetry was generated, as might be expected prior to the dawn of 'proper' literary criticism, by other poets, antiquarians or the first editors of his work. This chapter will also demonstrate that many of these early responses to Chaucer did not set out to praise a specific poem (though when a poem *is* singled out for recognition it is, more often than not, *The General Prologue*); rather, they presented a more impressionistic analysis of his 'greatness'. Thus, the majority of the extracts here are not solely devoted to *The General Prologue*. Instead, their main purpose is to establish the foundations for the criticism that followed later.

The second chapter of this Guide finds a narrowing of the chronological focus, covering as it does a mere sixty-year period from 1892–1949. During this time, as shall be seen, writers (especially the likes of T. S. Eliot and Virginia Woolf) are still eagerly engaging with Chaucer's poetry, but the seeming monopoly editors once had in the field of Chaucer studies begins to give way to more modern notions of literary criticism. The publication in 1948 of Muriel A. Bowden's *A Commentary on the General Prologue to the Canterbury Tales* is in many ways a crucial testament to this. The various scholarly gazes highlighted in this chapter are also firmly fixed on *The General Prologue*. The following chapter of this Guide, as one might predict, takes on the 1950s and 1960s and looks largely at the work of some of the most important American critics of Chaucer such as J. S. P. Tatlock, Kemp Malone, E. Talbot Donaldson and D. W. Robertson. Donaldson's invention of the figure of 'Chaucer the Pilgrim' in 1954 was to influence, as shall be seen, much of the later criticism of *The General Prologue*. During these two decades the idea of Chaucer's modernity was also beginning to be explored. Accordingly, this issue is dealt with by several of the critics highlighted in this chapter.

The final three chapters of this Guide are devoted, respectively, to the 1970s, 1980s and 1990s – a chapter a decade attesting to the accelerating volume of Chaucer criticism produced during the last quarter of the twentieth century. Structuralist, socio-political, postmodern and feminist approaches to *The General Prologue* are, among a host of others, offered up in the variety of extracts presented in these chapters. Chapter six is unique in that it is the only chapter devoted exclusively to one particular critical school: in this case, feminist and gender-based readings of *The General Prologue*. By the time the reader completes this final chapter, s/he may very well arrive at the same conclusion about the criticism devoted to *The General Prologue* as John Dryden famously did about the poem itself: 'Tis sufficient to say, according to the proverb, that here is God's plenty.'[5]

CHAPTER ONE

# 'Of Engelond to Caunterbury they Wende': 1368–1880

THE VERY first commentaries on Chaucer tended to be of a rather general nature and, as a result, specific and detailed critical engagement with *The General Prologue* was relatively rare until the twentieth century. Indeed, before the eighteenth century more attention seems to have been paid to Chaucer's tragic love poem *Troilus and Criseyde* than to *The Canterbury Tales* or any of its component parts. As Caroline F. E. Spurgeon has pointed out in her invaluable reference work *Five Hundred Years of Chaucer Criticism and Allusion, 1357–1900* (1925): 'Up to 1700 the number of references to *Troilus* are more than double those made to *The Canterbury Tales* (as a whole), and they are over three times as many as those to the *General Prologue*.'[1] (The Appendix on pages 155–6 reproduces Spurgeon's table of the relative popularity of Chaucer's poems at different times to set against this observation.) An additional factor to consider here is that most of the early responses to Chaucer were found in prefaces and notes to editions of his work, the most notable of these editions being those by William Caxton (1478 and 1484), Wynkyn de Worde (1498), William Thynne (1532), John Stowe (1561), Thomas Speght (1598 and 1602), John Urry (1721), Thomas Morell (1737) and Thomas Tyrwhitt (1775/78 and 1798).[2] Tyrwhitt's not fully favourable observations on Caxton's effort are worth noting here: 'It is therefore much more to the honour of our meritorious countryman William Caxton, that he chose to make *The Canterbury Tales* one of the earliest productions of his press, than it can be to his discredit, that he printed them very incorrectly.'[3]

Aside from these early editors, who else was commenting on Chaucer and steadily consolidating his place in literary history? To a large extent, this question is answered by David Williams in his student-friendly book *The Canterbury Tales: A Literary Pilgrimage* (1987):

THE GENERAL PROLOGUE

■ The very first recorded tribute to Chaucer is by his French contemporary Eustache Deschamps, who, about 1368, pays the English poet an elegant compliment in which he describes Chaucer as a Socrates in philosophy, a Seneca in morals, and an Ovid in poetry. Such descriptions not only help us understand the kind of reputation Chaucer had in his own day but also suggest that by the fourteenth century there existed an international school of poetry very conscious of the importance of art and ready to make bold claims for its theoretical foundation.

In his own time Chaucer's work was already a model for other artists, and Chaucerian "schools" grew up soon after his death. *The Canterbury Tales* in particular was imitated, and several poets of the fifteenth century expanded the original work by adding to it tales of their own creation. The so-called Scottish Chaucerians included King James I of Scotland, who, while imprisoned in England, wrote verse influenced by Chaucer.

An important fact not always given sufficient emphasis in discussion of Chaucer is that he is the first native English literary authority, and the extent of his authority is unequaled in English literature. This is due, in part, to Chaucer's own awareness of the importance of his canon, his entire literary production, in forming a beginning to a larger, ever-growing English literary canon. Again and again Chaucer reflects upon the state of his art and authorship; this conscious tradition-making seems to have found a response in later poets.

Chaucer is repeatedly referred to in the fifteenth and sixteenth centuries as "Master" by aspiring and established writers alike. In his *Apology for Poetry* (1595), Sir Philip Sidney firmly established Chaucer (along with Gower) as the wellspring of English poetry: "I know not whether to marvel more, either that he in that misty time could see so clearly, or that we in this clear age walk so stumblingly after him." Edmund Spenser, in *The Shepheardes Calendar* (1579), finds advantage in describing himself as the literary descendant of Chaucer. Shakespeare, who never mentions Chaucer, was clearly influenced by his predecessor's work, especially by *Troilus and Criseyde* and the *Canterbury Tales*.[4] ☐

In the extract cited above, Williams identifies the broad range of responses to Chaucer voiced during the fifteenth and sixteenth centuries; as later chapters of this Guide will show, several of these responses continue to be relevant to more specific readings of *The General Prologue*. Of particular note here is the idea of Chaucer as 'the first *native English* [italics mine] literary authority', his constant reflection 'upon the state of his art and authorship' and the debate over the exact nature of Chaucerian morality. Though Deschamps in the late 1360s may have lauded Chaucer as a

'Seneca in morals', Ann Thompson points out in *Shakespeare's Chaucer* (1978) that this opinion was not universal:

■ His [Chaucer's] reputation as a 'moral' writer had a . . . surprising and insecure basis. It is one thing for Speght to sprinkle the margins of his second edition with little hands pointing to notable 'sentences', but another for John Foxe to call Chaucer 'a right Wiclevian' in his *Ecclesiastical History* (1570)[5] and to see him as an outspoken critic of Rome. The reason for the latter opinion lies in the ascription to Chaucer of the large quantity of apocryphal material printed under his name, some of it, like *The Plowman's Tale* (first published in William Thynne's edition of 1542) and *Jack Upland* (first published by Speght in 1602) of a distinctly radical and anti-clerical nature. On the basis of such spurious works Speght indulged in the 'autobiographical fallacy', or hypothetical assumptions about the poet's life, offering his readers a Chaucer who had to flee abroad after favouring 'some rashe attempt of the common people', and whose *Canterbury Tales* were of a distinctly political cast, showing 'with such Art and cunning . . . the state of the Church, the Court and Country' that the author was 'admired and feared' by all.

On the other hand, writers were becoming critical of Chaucer's morality, and the traditional defence of 'decorum' (i.e., appropriateness of tale to narrator) used by Chaucer himself [in *The General Prologue*] was only grudgingly admitted, if at all. Sir John Harrington accused Chaucer of 'flat scurrilitie' in his *Apologie for Poetrie* in 1591,[6] and *Greene's Vision* of 1592 opposed merry Chaucer to moral Chaucer by presenting the former giving encouragement to Greene with the words, 'If thou doubtest blame for thy wantonnes, let my selfe suffice for an instance, whose Canterburie tales are broad enough before, and written homely and pleasantly, yet who hath bin more canonised for his workes than Sir Geffrey Chaucer?'[7] . . . . . . for the Elizabethans, . . . [Chaucer's] reputation as a learned and moral writer rested on very shaky ground and was already subject to scepticism and challenge. Yet it is apparent from all the references to him that despite everything he was widely read and enjoyed . . . [8] □

Both Williams and Thompson in the critical passages given above address the issue of Chaucer's influence on the poets (and at least one king) who sprang up after him. That, as Williams notes, '*The Canterbury Tales* in particular was imitated' is illustrated to good effect in Judith H. Anderson's recent essay 'Narrative Reflections: Re-envisaging the Poet in *The Canterbury Tales* and *The Faerie Queene*'.[9] In the introduction to this piece – which is found in chapter five of Theresa M. Krier's edition *Refiguring Chaucer in the Renaissance* (1998) – Anderson states her wish to relate

## THE GENERAL PROLOGUE

'Spenser to Chaucer'. She then identifies one of the key elements of *The General Prologue*, the role of the narrator (another subject to which later chapters of this Guide will return):

■ I do so [i.e., attempt to relate Spenser to Chaucer] first because a narrative voice or narrator is one of the most conspicuous features of Chaucer's writing and one that has dominated much interpretation of it in the past half-century; and second because Spenser's assertion of poetic affinity with what he termed Chaucer's "owne spirit".[10] □

Using Thynne's 1532 edition of Chaucer's *Works*, Anderson provides a close reading of (and 'minimal modern punctuation' for[11]) lines 725–38 of *The General Prologue*, a largely poststructuralist analysis heavily influenced by H. Marshall Leicester's 1990 publication *The Disenchanted Self: Representing the Subject in the Canterbury Tales* (discussed in chapter six of this Guide):

■ A number of characteristics of the General Prologue invite comparison with *The Faerie Queene* [Spenser's nationalistic epic poem of the 1580s], among them its movement from seemingly assured categories and symbols to an increasingly uncertain and self-reflexive awareness of its own construction, an awareness figured first in the narrator's unsteady valuations of the pilgrims and then in his anxiety as he approaches his rendering of the tales themselves:

> But firste I pray you, of youre curtesy
> That ye ne arette it nat my folly
> Thogh that I playnly speke in this matere
> To tellen you her wordes and eke her chere[,]
> Ne thogh I speke her wordes properly[;]
> For this ye knowen as wel as I[:]
> Who shal tellen a tale after a manne
> Her mote reherce as nye as euere he canne
> Euerych word, if it be in his charge[,]
> Al speke he neuer so rudely ne large[,]
> Or els he mote tellen his tale vntrewe
> Or feyne thynges, or fynde wordes newe[–]
> He may nat spare al tho he were his brother[;]
> He mote as wel saye o worde as another

Surely, this narrator protests too much. Again and again, and then yet again, he signals a conclusion, only to continue spinning his apologetic wheels – in fact, for several lines more than I've cited. In order to account for his behavior, we can posit a poet genuinely uncertain about the acceptability of the tales he is about to report; or, recalling the persistence of irony in the *General Prologue*, we can envision a poet who really isn't worried at all but still wants to cover himself in case others are, poking fun, while he's about it, at the convention of the willing reporter's dubiously sincere apology; or we can combine these two figures into a poet who communicates duplicitously through the guise of a narrative persona and therefore both gets to have his worry and to distance himself from it; or, in a final poststructural maneuver, we can forget about the poet altogether and, taking a further plunge into textuality, describe the text as the site of awareness, a self-reflexive construct figured in an ironized speaker, a text in this case effectually becoming the conscious subject.[12] On numerous occasions, the same interpretative choices play themselves out in *The Faerie Queene* . . . [13] ☐

Following on from this extract, we find Anderson embarking upon a twofold discussion encompassing both the 'concrete particularity and fictive complexity of portraits [especially here the Monk, Parson and Summoner] in Chaucer's Prologue'[14] and a complex reading of 'the primary narrators of both Chaucer and Spenser'[15] based in part, upon Don H. Bialostosky's description of 'intertextual dialogics'.[16] In the final pages of the essay, she returns to the subjects of narrative voice and Chaucer's influence on Spenser: 'Spenser seems to me an incredibly astute student of Chaucer's work, and variously throughout *The Faerie Queene* he – or rather, his narrative voice or attitude – slips ambiguously, duplicitously into a mask or into the techniques of impersonation.'[17]

More than a century after the composition of *The Faerie Queene*, another English writer, an equally 'astute student of Chaucer's work' and one who, like Spenser before him, 'suggest[s] the continuous appeal of Chaucer'[18] emerged and, some have claimed, launched Chaucer criticism for real. John Dryden is considered to be at the forefront of the 'transformation of Chaucer studies and Chaucer books [taking] place in the eighteenth century'[19] largely due to the comments he makes about Chaucer, *The Canterbury Tales* and *The General Prologue* in particular, in his 'Preface' to *Fables, Ancient and Modern* (1700). In this 'Preface', Dryden emphasises 'the general and continuing truth of Chaucer's characterisation [as found in *The General Prologue*]'[20] and, according to Joseph A. Dane in his book *Who is Buried in Chaucer's Tomb?: Studies in the Reception of Chaucer's Book* (1998), this 'truth' is established in the following manner:

■ Dryden thus considers the *Canterbury Tales* from first to last as a drama, one cut off from the large, unreadable, gothic book in which (for Dryden) those tales had appeared. The central organizing principle becomes one of character: first the fictional characters and finally the character of the author himself. Just as a character's words and actions are reflections of the fictional character itself, so is the fictional character in turn a reflection of the author who creates that character.[21] ☐

Here, now, are Dryden's own words to set against the extract above:

■ It remains that I say something of Chaucer in particular . . . . . . In the first place, as he is the father of English poetry, so I hold him in the same degree of veneration as the Grecians held Homer or the Romans Virgil. He is a perpetual fountain of good sense . . . . . . He must have been a man of a most wonderful comprehensive nature, because as has been truly observ'd of him, he has taken into the compass of his *Canterbury Tales* the various manners and humors (as we now call them) of the whole English nation, in his age. Not a single character has escap'd him. All his pilgrims are severally distinguish'd from each other; and not only in their inclinations, but in their very physiognomies and persons . . . The matter and manner of their tales, and of their telling, are so suited to their different educations, humors, and callings, that each of them would be improper in any other mouth. Even the grave and serious characters are distinguish'd by their several sorts of gravity: their discourses are such as belong to their age, their calling, and their breeding; such as are becoming of them, and of them only. Some of his persons are vicious, and some virtuous; some are unlearn'd, or (as Chaucer calls them) lewd, and some are learn'd. Even the ribaldry of the low characters is different: the Reeve, the Miller, and the Cook are several men, and distinguish'd from each other, as much as the mincing Lady Prioress and the broad-speaking gap-tooth'd Wife of Bath. But enough of this: there is such a variety of game springing up before me, that I am distracted in my choice, and know not which to follow. 'Tis sufficient to say, according to the proverb, that here is God's plenty. We have our forefathers and great-grandames all before us, as they were in Chaucer's days; their general characters are still remaining in mankind, and even in England, tho' they are called by other names than those of monks and Friars, and Canons, and Lady Abbesses, and Nuns: for mankind is ever the same, and nothing lost out of nature, tho' everything is alter'd.[22] ☐

Dryden's use here of the phrase 'the father of English poetry' to describe Chaucer, coupled with his opinion that the pilgrims presented in *The General Prologue* portraits are representative of 'the whole English nation' lend credence to David Williams's claim that Chaucer 'is the first *native English* [italics mine] literary authority' (see p. 12 of this Guide). Views such as this, in turn, inform a nationalist reading of *The General Prologue*. Especially relevant to this type of reading is the following extract from Thomas A. Kirby's comprehensive essay 'The General Prologue', found in chapter twelve of Beryl Rowland's edition *Companion to Chaucer Studies* (1968; revised 1979):

> ■ Chaucer's world is a real world, but there are frequent hints of the ideal world as well. Most readers will probably agree with Raymond Preston [in *Chaucer*, 1952. rpt. 1968, p. 168] that the "*Prologue* gives us a 'real' England, and rather more than we should get in a fourteenth-century group. We can also see, in a glimpse, an ideal England, not so people could dream about it after dinner, but in order that they might desire it." Then, quoting lines 15–6 ("And specially from every shires ende . . . "), he concludes:
>
>> The consciousness of nationality was new and exciting; . . . [ellipsis is Kirby's] I cannot read these two lines without a certain emphasis. They have their relation to the contemporary preaching about St. Thomas of Canterbury, St. Thomas of yngelonde. And if we desire this *Yngelonde*, the Engelond that is always "Now and in England," then the opening of Chaucer's *Prologue* contains even more than Englishmen going towards Augustine's Canterbury, and trying to find, in the art of *felaweshipe*, the good life; it contains also the water of life quenching the drought, it contains death and resurrection, Lent and Easter, a new Spring that may come to all pilgrims. (pp. 168–9)[23] □

A fuller analysis of 'the consciousness of nationality' displayed in *The General Prologue* is provided in chapter five of this Guide, where Elton D. Higgs's pertinent article 'The Old Order and the "Newe World" in *The General Prologue* to *The Canterbury Tales*' (1982) is discussed.

Aside from Dryden's 'Preface', the other significant Enlightenment reading of *The General Prologue* appears in another 'Preface', that of Thomas Tyrwhitt's 'small-format edition'[24] (with unwieldy title) – *The Canterbury Tales of Chaucer* (to which is added an essay on his Language and Versification, and an introductory discourse together with notes and glossary) – of 1775–78. Tyrwhitt tackles, like Dryden before him, the characters of the pilgrims and announces that they 'are as various as, at that time, could be found in the several departments of *middle* life; that is, in fact, as various as cou[l]d, with any probability, be brought together, so as to form one company, the highest and the lowest ranks of society being necessarily excluded'.[25] Whilst Tyrwhitt obviously harkens back to Dryden here, he also implicitly touches upon the subject of Estates Satire in *The General Prologue*. This is a subject crucial to any study of *The General Prologue* and shall be returned to in later chapters of this Guide.

As well as musing upon the nature of the characters of *The General Prologue*, Tyrwhitt also offers his thoughts on the wider relationship

## THE GENERAL PROLOGUE

between *The General Prologue* and *The Canterbury Tales* as a whole, concluding that 'The General Plan of the *Canterbury Tales* may be learned in a great measure from the Prologue, which Chaucer himself has prefixed to them'.[26] He continues, a little later, on another note:

■ A second point, intended to be defined in the Prologue, is the *number of the company*; and this too has its difficulties . . . It must be observed, however, that in this list there is one very suspicious article, which is that of the *three Preestes*. As it appears evidently to have been the design of Chaucer to compare his company of individuals of different ranks, in order to produce a greater variety of distinct characters, we can hardly conceive that he would, in this single instance, introduce *three*, of the same profession, without any discriminating circumstances whatever.[27] □

The enigma of the *'three Preestes'*, one of 'a number of inconsistencies'[28] to be found in *The General Prologue*, was to trouble later critics as well. Charles A. Owen, Jr., for example, in *Pilgrimage and Storytelling in the Canterbury Tales* (1977) returns to this thorny problem and attempts to explain it in relation to his theory of the overall development of *The Canterbury Tales*:

■ . . . Further evidence of the way Chaucer worked comes with the lines:

Another Nonne with hire hadde she,
That was hir chapeleyne, and preestes thre. [ll. 163–4]

The priests become the single "Nonnes Preest" named Sir John (B 3999) when the Host calls on him; and though the Second Nun and the Nun's priest both tell tales, neither has the portrait one might expect from the narrator's assurance that he will tell "al the condicioun/Of ech of hem" (A 37–8). The "wel nyne and twenty" Chaucer tells us he met at the Tabard work out to be thirty or thirty-one, depending on whether we count in Chaucer or not.
. . . . . . This theory for the development of the Prologue . . . can be summarized as follows:
I. 1387?–1388: Portraits of fourteen of the pilgrims and the joint portrait of the five guildsmen were composed; the Nun, the three priests, and the five churls were simply listed without being described, the priests being differentiated from one another by name. Rhymes connected the Yeoman and the Prioress, the names of the priests and the Merchant, the Cook and the Shipman, and the Plowman and the list of churls.
II. Ca. 1396: Chaucer substituted the Monk and the Friar for two of

the priests, composed their portraits (linked by rhyme), and inserted them in the appropriate place, using the name of the third priest for the Friar in order to preserve the rhyme Huberd-berd, but leaving the line mentioning the three priests to be altered when he composed portraits of the Nun and the Nun's Priest. During this period he was also writing the descriptions of the five churls. It was probably in this period that he composed the introductory lines for the portraits (A35–42), in which he says he is going to tell us about each of the pilgrims.[29] ☐

Owen returns, at the end of his volume, to the issues of incompleteness and inconsistencies in *The General Prologue* and ultimately concludes that 'The pilgrimage, incomplete though Chaucer's record of it is, has form for its readers. Lacking any simple interpretation, it has a multitude of meanings and levels of meanings'.[30]

One final point raised by Tyrwhitt must needs be mentioned here, and that is his comment about the exact nature of the realism of *The General Prologue*. Sir Arthur T. Quiller-Couch, in *The Age of Chaucer* (1926), has wryly and famously remarked on this matter: 'Let us not inquire too deeply how far every word [spoken on the pilgrimage] was audible to the whole thirty [pilgrims] as they clattered and splashed along.'[31] Though some believe this to be the last (if not the most dismissive) word on the subject, the question persists and, as shall be seen throughout the course of this Guide, pervades much of the criticism generated by *The General Prologue*. It is no wonder, then, that it crept into Tyrwhitt's commentary as well when he suggests that Chaucer, in an attempt to make the opening of *The Canterbury Tales* seem more 'real', intended 'in the first lines of the Prologue, to mark with some exactness the *time* of his supposed pilgrimage'.[32] Tyrwhitt then moves on to a related issue, the possibility that the pilgrimage described in *The General Prologue* may have been based upon a real spiritual journey to Canterbury. Offering a modicum of hope to his readers who want to believe in this literary pilgrimage's historical authenticity, Tyrwhitt writes:

■ Those who are disposed to believe the Pilgrimage to have been real, and to have happened in 1383, may support their opinion by the following inscription, which is still to be read upon the Inn, now called the Talbot, in Southwark. "This is the Inn where Sir Jeffrey Chaucer and the twenty-nine Pilgrims lodged in their journey to Canterbury, Anno 1383." Though the present inscription is evidently of a very recent date, we might suppose it to have been propagated to us by a succession of faithful transcripts from the very time; but unluckily there is too good reason to be assured, that the first inscription of this sort was not earlier than the last century.[33] ☐

## THE GENERAL PROLOGUE

Though Tyrwhitt, as we have seen, had remarked earlier in his 'Preface' that establishing *'the number of the company'* was not without its 'difficulties', he lets the Inscription's confident assurance that there were 'twenty-nine Pilgrims' on the road to Canterbury pass without comment. Also allowed to escape unremarked is Chaucer's elevation to the status of a knight ('Sir Jeffrey Chaucer').

In the nineteenth century, 'interestingly enough, it is for different reasons that Chaucer maintains his position of prestige within the [English literary] tradition'.[34] David Williams, in the work already cited in this chapter, elaborates upon this statement in the following manner:

■ Chaucer's naturalness and freedom from contrivance is what many of the Romantic poets admire in his work. Keats, for example, imitates the poetry and language of the *Canterbury Tales* to evoke a "medieval" tone in "The Eve of St. Mark." William Blake, in his illustration of the *Canterbury Tales* [from 1809], provides a kind of visual interpretation of the poem that is typically nineteenth century. Coleridge [in the *Table Talk* entry for 15 March, 1834] not only extravagantly praises Chaucer but also specifically prefers Chaucer to Shakespeare, for reasons of Romantic ideology. "The sympathy of the poet with the subjects of his poetry is particularly remarkable in Shakespeare and Chaucer; but what the first effects by a strong act of imagination and mental metamorphosis, the last does without any effort, merely by the inborn kindly joyousness of his nature. How well we seem to know Chaucer! How absolutely nothing do we know of Shakespeare!"[35] □

S.T. Coleridge's 'Romantic ideology' may have caused him to look kindly upon the 'joyousness' of Chaucer's nature but, as has been shown, the question of 'merry' versus 'moral' Chaucer was not always resolved in the poet's favour and the debate continued to surface during the Victorian period. The poet and critic Matthew Arnold, for example, in his general introduction to *The English Poets* (1880), concedes that examples of 'Chaucer's virtue' can be found, but for him the charm soon departs – especially when Chaucer is compared to the mediaeval Italian poet Dante (1265–1321). At this moment, Arnold partially subverts a nationalist reading of Chaucer; this is especially true when he avows that no 'poet in the England of that stage of growth' (i.e., the fourteenth century) could compete with Dante.[36] Like Coleridge, however, Arnold subscribes to the notion of what we might alliteratively define as 'Humanist/Humane/Human Chaucer', a view signalled in the lines I have italicised in the following extract and one largely drawn from the Chaucer of *The General Prologue*:

■ If we ask ourselves wherein consists the immense superiority of Chaucer's poetry over the romance-poetry – why it is that in passing from this to Chaucer we suddenly feel ourselves to be in another world, we shall find that his superiority is both in the substance of his poetry and the style of his poetry. *His superiority in substance is given by his large, free, simple, clear yet kindly view of human life, – so unlike the total want, in the romance-poets, of all intelligent command of it. Chaucer has not their helplessness; he has gained the power to survey the world from a central, a truly human point of view.* We have only to call to mind the Prologue to *The Canterbury Tales*. The right comment upon it is Dryden's: "It is sufficient to say, according to the proverb, that *here is God's plenty.*"

And again: "He is a perpetual fountain of good sense." *It is by a large, free, sound representation of things, that poetry, this high criticism of life, has truth of substance; and Chaucer's poetry has truth of substance.*[37] □

Though Arnold determines in the extract above that there is much in Chaucer's poetry (especially *The General Prologue*) to commend, he concludes his discussion of the poet on a decidedly critical and prevaricating note: 'To our praise, therefore, of Chaucer as a poet there must be this limitation; he lacks the high seriousness of the great classics, and therewith an important part of their virtue.'[38] Luckily for Chaucer, however, the critics of the next century did not take this dismissal as the last word on the poet. Quite the contrary, for Chaucer criticism burgeoned and became ever more sophisticated as the twentieth century advanced and, as the following chapters of this Guide will demonstrate, much of the critical attention was focused on *The General Prologue*.

CHAPTER TWO

## 'Tales of Best Sentence and Moost Solaas': 1892–1949

IT WAS stated in the previous chapter of this Guide that 'most of the early responses to Chaucer were found in prefaces and notes to editions of his work' (p.11). The Golden Age of the Editors continued well into the nineteenth century, as Thomas R. Lounsbury confirms in his introduction to his comprehensive *Studies in Chaucer: His Life and Writings* of 1892. The extract that follows also acknowledges the phenomenon of Chaucer's rapidly expanding readership during this period:

■ About twenty-five years ago, a small volume containing nearly four thousand lines of Chaucer's poetry, with notes and a glossary, was issued from the Clarendon Press of Oxford University. It met at the outset with a respectable but by no means rapid sale. But on the title-page, which bears the date of 1886 – the last year of this particular edition which I have chanced to see – the number printed up to that time stands recorded as sixty-six thousand. Since then the work has been revised and reissued. The whole number published has now undoubtedly mounted to many thousands more, and the circulation of the book in its new form is not unlikely to have already overtaken and even gone beyond the figures just mentioned.

Though this has been the most successful of all, it is nevertheless but one of several works of a similar character that have appeared during the last quarter of a century. Every year, indeed, adds to their number in a steadily increasing ratio. Editions of the poems of Chaucer, in whole or in part, are coming out constantly in England, in Germany, and in America. It is well within bounds to say that he has been more read during the past twenty years than during the previous two hundred. If this indicates nothing else, it shows the existence of a large class to whom Chaucer is something more than a name. A generation which could scarcely be spoken of as knowing him at all has been supplanted by a generation with which he is becoming a familiar and favorite author.[1] □

One of these major editions was that of Walter Skeat, whose seven-volume edition of Chaucer's works appeared in 1894–97. It is thanks to the pioneering work of scholars such as Skeat, as well as those more generally alluded to by Lounsbury above, that we now have 'a reasonably accurate text [of Chaucer's poetry] to read and some knowledge of fourteenth-century pronunciation'.[2] We also know because of them ' . . . the extent of his [Chaucer's] borrowing, his dependence on other books'[3] – or, to take a more modern approach, we know something about the inter-textuality of Chaucer's poetry.

Aside from commenting on the various editors of Chaucer, Lounsbury also addresses a number of issues of specific relevance to *The General Prologue*, two of which we shall consider here. Firstly, there is his theory about the portrait of the Knight. The Knight, the first figure to be described in *The General Prologue*, is a character much debated by scholars. Some have suggested that his is one of the few truly idealised pilgrim portraits (along with the Parson and his brother the Plowman); others have strenuously countered this claim.[4] The other question often raised about the Knight (and, indeed, several of the other pilgrims who appear in *The General Prologue* such as the Wife of Bath and the Host) is whether or not Chaucer based him upon a real, living individual; in the nineteenth century, the future king Henry IV was put forward as a possible candidate. In the extract which follows we find Lounsbury's strenuous refutation of this suggestion:

■ Henry of Lancaster also [like Chaucer's Knight] started on a pilgrimage to Jerusalem, though he got no farther than Rhodes. It is possibly noteworthy that while the future king was absent from England on these expeditions, Chaucer either lost or gave up the positions under the government to which he had succeeded in 1389. We cannot assume that this is anything more than a mere coincidence, especially as during this last-mentioned year John of Gaunt [Henry's father] had returned to the country on the summons of the king [Richard II]. But if the fortunes of the House of Lancaster had any influence upon the poet's, it would almost inevitable [*sic*] tend to make him idealize the character of the man who was destined in the course of nature to be its representative, and in whose future his own would be more or less involved. No one will indeed pretend that the portrait drawn in the prologue of the Knight – who is specially celebrated as fighting for the Christian faith – can have been designed even remotely as a representative of the deeds of Henry IV. The event in which the former is described as sharing happened before the latter was born. Still, it is conceivable that in the portrayal of the character Chaucer may have had in mind the son of his patron, upon whom had been fixed, long before he came to the throne, the hopes of the party discontented with the profligacy and misgovernment of Richard II. The view can only be taken for what it is worth. In the matter of positive evidence there is nothing in favor of it that is entitled to the name.[5] □

In volume three of his *Studies in Chaucer*, under the heading 'Chaucer as Literary Artist: Relation of Art to Morality', Lounsbury moves on to consider another point of extreme relevance to *The General Prologue*, the relationship between the teller and the tale. He writes:

■ The quasi-apology which Chaucer in the General Prologue makes to a certain class of his critics for the character of some of his stories gives us a clear insight into his ideas about the proper relation of art to morals. If it proves nothing else, it disposes of the theory that in his production he acted merely from creative impulse which had about it no element of critical reflection. He must, he says, tell his tale "after his man;" that is he must tell the kind of tale the particular person introduced was sure to tell, and must tell it in the way it was told. So to do was not 'villainy' on his part; that is, conduct belonging to a villein but unbecoming a gentleman. It was proper regard for the truth of nature, and therefore of the truth of art. If the personage whose story is recounted follow his instincts in speaking "rudeliche and large" – that is, coarsely and broadly – there are but two courses open to the author. He must report the words precisely as they were uttered, or else substitute for them either new words or new matter of his own. But if he adopt the latter line of conduct, he is not faithful to the duty he has assumed. He is not telling the tale truly; that is, as it would have been told by the character to whom it was assigned.[6] □

The rhetoric employed in the preceding extract is typical of its time, especially in its correlation of that Victorian object of admiration, The Gentleman, with Chaucer and his conduct as a 'proper' writer. Similar language was utilised even earlier in the century by F.J. Furnivall in his *A Temporary Preface to the Six-Text Edition of Chaucer's Canterbury Tales, Part I (Attempting to Show the True Order of the Tales and the Days and Stages of the Pilgrimage, Etc. Etc.)*, published in 1868.[7] In the rather eccentric temporary preface to this work Furnivall outlines the reasons for the central role he took in the creation, also in 1868, of The Chaucer Society.[8] He presumes to speak, in a rousing patriotic tone, for 'England's upper and middle classes': 'I am bound to confess that my love for Chaucer – and he comes closer to me than any other poet, except Tennyson – would not by itself have made me give up the time and trouble I can ill afford to bestow on this task; but when an American, who had done the best bit of work on Chaucer's words, asked, and kept on asking, for texts of our great English poet, could an Englishman keep on refusing to produce them?'[9] The American in question here is F.J. Child (1825–1896), a distinguished professor at Harvard University. Child, along with G.L. Kittredge (1860–1941), J.M. Manly (1865–1940), J.S.P. Tatlock (1876–1948), Robert Kilburn Root (1877–1950) and John Livingstone Lowes (1867–1945), was part of the group of early American critics who, in the words of Sheila Sullivan, took 'Chaucer for their own and [have made] his debt to American scholarship . . . vast'.[10]

Furnivall's *A Temporary Preface to the Six-Text Edition of Chaucer's Canterbury Tales, Part I* contains, aside from an eccentric preface, a section entitled *A few Notes on the Prologue* in which Furnivall quotes in full 'The greatest gain of late times to [the study of] the Prologue [which is] clearly Mr. Skeat's showing that Chaucer's *Ram* of line 8 is not the blunder for the *Bull* that [Thomas] Tyrwhitt and his followers supposed it to be; but is quite right'.[11] In the following extract, then, we find Walter Skeat refuting one of the conclusions reached by Thomas Tyrwhitt in his work on Chaucer (see chapter one of this Guide) and offering instead his famous reading of a much contested line of *The General Prologue*:

■ Every reader who has ever opened a Chaucer must remember the opening lines of the Prologue, where the poet speaks of the showers of April, and has the lines –

>'the yonge sonne
>Hath in the Ram his halfe-course i-ronne.'

But this passage has never been explained up to the present moment, and I therefore think that many . . . readers would be glad that it *can* be explained so as to be perfectly consistent and correct.

Tyrwhitt saw the difficulty of speaking of the sun being in the *Ram* in the month of *April*, and therefore has proposed to read *Bole*, i.e., *Bull*. But the MSS. [manuscripts] are here against him.

The exact day of April to which Chaucer refers is most probably the 17th, as will be shown presently. Where then was the sun on the 17th of April at that time? The answer is affected by the precession of the equinoxes, which may be accounted for by considering the change of style; with sufficient accuracy, that is, for our present purpose.

The difference between the old and new styles, which now amounts to twelve days, amounted in Chaucer's time to only eight days. Hence the sun, on the 17th of April, 1386, would be very nearly where he is now on the 25th of April – i.e., in the fifth degree of Taurus. This can be verified by Chaucer's own words, for he says in his

Treatise on the Astrolabe, in a passage which Tyrwhitt appositely quotes, that the vernal equinox, or first degree of Aries, corresponded in his time to the 12th of March; from which it follows, by the use of an astrolabe ['An instrument formerly used to take altitudes, and to solve other problems of practical astronomy', *OED*] that on the 17th of April (old style) he would be in the fifth degree of Taurus, as already calculated. But this is not the *actual* and *visible*, but only the *theoretical* and *supposed* position of the sun. This is best explained by the following quotation from Milner's *Gallery of Nature*, p. 149:

> The effect [of the precession of the equinoxes] has been to separate the asterisms [a cluster of stars] from their denominational signs, so that . . . the *constellation of Aries* is in the *sign of Taurus*, &c.

And, in fact, a glance at a modern celestial globe shows that the meridian of the eleventh degree of Taurus (which is *now* where the fifth degree was *then*) passes near the star . . . Arietis, which is *exactly the central star of the constellation of the Ram*. Hence it appears that Chaucer is perfectly and most accurately correct.[12] ☐

Skeat's close reading of line eight of *The General Prologue*, though celebrated by Furnivall and his contemporaries, may seem arcane to the modern reader of Chaucer. With its recourse to the astrolabe and Milner's *Gallery of Nature*, however, it perfectly exemplifies 'the nineteenth-century transfer of scientific concepts to the study of literature'.[13] It also presents the view which began to gain ground during this period that a 'true' reading of any of Chaucer's poems could only be arrived at through close scrutiny of the extant manuscripts. Indeed, The Chaucer Society itself was established by Furnivall 'to do honour to Chaucer, and to let lovers and students of him see how far the best unprinted manuscripts of his works differed from the printed texts'.[14]

During the time period covered in this chapter, scholars would also turn their attentions to the twenty-three miniature portraits of Chaucer and the Canterbury pilgrims found in the Ellesmere manuscript, now housed in the Huntington Library in California (this early fifteenth-century codex is one of only six illustrated copies of *The Canterbury Tales*, though there are approximately eighty surviving manuscripts of the actual poem). In 1924, for example, Edwin Ford Piper published his article 'The Miniatures of the Ellesmere Chaucer' in *The Philological Quarterly* and concluded herein that the pilgrims' portraits 'represent an interpretation based upon study – careful study of the *General Prologue*, the links [between the *Tales*], the *Tales*'.[15] More recent scholarship by critics such as Charles A. Owen, Jr. and Martin Stevens has supported Piper's thesis. Owen, in 1991, stated that ' . . . the illuminated portraits [in the

Ellesmere manuscript] at the beginning of each tale, showing as they do an intelligent reading of the *Prologue* and a critical appreciation of the importance of the frame story, give the ms. [manuscript] its prime distinction'.[16] Stevens, writing in the early 1980s, believed that ' . . . the Ellesmere miniatures are unique early efforts to present faithful textual illustrations and, further, that they serve an important practical function in binding the *GP* [*General Prologue*] to the text of the tales'.[17]

It is clear that careful study of the Ellesmere manuscript soon provided scholars with another way of unlocking the interpretative secrets of *The General Prologue* and its lively cast of storytellers. In 1915, Frederick Tupper attempted to further our understanding of these characters and their inter-relationships in 'The Quarrels of the Canterbury Pilgrims'. In this article, Tupper identifies these 'three chief quarrels' as being between the Friar and Summoner, Manciple and Cook and Miller and Reeve.[18] With recourse to a Shakespearean analogy, he views these skirmishes as being at least partly generated by the characters' hypocrisy and, ultimately, believes they form the basis of the 'class-satire' found in *The General Prologue* and other parts of *The Canterbury Tales*. In the extract that follows, Tupper also cites, as many have done before and since, the *Romance of the Rose* as one of the sources of *The Canterbury Tales*:

■ The literary *motif* of clash between precept and practice is in no way Chaucer's monopoly. The painter of vice, heavily tarred with his own stick, has always been the butt of the satirist.

. . . False-seeming of the *Roman de la Rose* (11423f.) doubly anticipates Chaucer's Pardoner by preaching against abstinence, though he loves good dishes and bright wine, and by exalting poverty, though his bags overflow with coin . . . The Canterbury Pilgrims show, like Ophelia's ungracious pastors, "the steep and thorny road to heaven" and tread themselves "the primrose path of dalliance".

. . . . . . All this by way of necessary preamble to our present theme, "The Quarrels of the Canterbury Pilgrims". No phase of that fourteenth-century journey displays more amply Chaucer's regard for class-satire and his frequent combination of this with the ironical illustration of the sins of each social order than the clashes between the representatives of traditionally unfriendly vocations. Though the contests between Friar and Summoner, Manciple and Cook, Miller and Reeve are, each and all, demonstrably typical of their respective classes, yet only in the case of the first of these encounters has the conventional character of the class-feud won the attention of scholarly readers; and even here much that is significant has escaped its meed [reward] of comment.[19] □

Whilst Tupper alludes to the originality of his argument in the final lines of this passage, he also simultaneously clues us in to what is *not* original about the characterisations of certain of the Canterbury pilgrims. That these 'contests', or quarrels, are 'demonstrably typical' is a good example of how Chaucer, as a poet of the Middle Ages, was not primarily driven by the need for innovation. What Umberto Eco has said about mediaeval aesthetics applies equally to literary production of the period: it 'was filled with repetitions, regurgitations'.[20]

The extent to which Chaucer depended on 'other books' when he sat down to write *The General Prologue* was a topic much discussed in the early part of the twentieth century. This is seen, for example, in Tupper's allusion to the *Romance of the Rose* above. A much more detailed discussion of source studies, however, is found in Henry Barrett Hinckley's *Notes on Chaucer: A Commentary on the Prolog and Six Canterbury Tales* of 1907. One of Hinckley's major areas of study here is the framing device of *The General Prologue* and its possible literary antecedents. Though he admits that this is an extremely large subject to tackle ('Examples of the custom of framing tales are altogether too numerous in Europe to permit enumeration'[21]) he isolates in the same paragraph 'three cases especially interesting' to the student of *The General Prologue*:

■ (1). The *Confessio Amantis* of Gower. Gower was a fellow-countryman and a contemporary of Chaucer, and the question how far either of the poets influenced the other, and whether they ever compared notes or worked together, is very interesting, though, in large part, probably insoluble.

(2). The *Decameron* of Boccaccio. Tyrwhitt (p. xlix) remarked: 'The Canterbury Tales are a work of the same nature with the Decameron, and were, in all probability, composed in imitation of it.' For a long time this was the received opinion . . . [but I am inclined to think that] The resemblances between the *Canterbury Tales* and the Decameron seem not to be such as indicate imitation of the latter by the former; but to be due either to the two writers having used the same or cognate literary sources . . .

(3). The *Novelle* of Giovanni Sercambi of Lucca. Here we have a series of tales told by a number of pilgrims traveling all over Italy with the special object of avoiding through spiritual purification the pestilence with which Lucca was at that time visited. The pilgrimage, like Chaucer's, is likely to have been an historical fact, and is represented as taking place in 1374. One of the company is chosen president (*preposto*) and performs functions not unlike those of Chaucer's Host of the Tabard. The tales are told sometimes on the road and sometimes in the cities where the company halts . . . . . . The resemblance between Chaucer and Sercambi is extremely interesting. Among minor details observe Chaucer's probable allusion to the pestilence in v. 18 ['That hem hath holpen when that they were seeke']. **Nevertheless it is altogether probable that the resemblance is mere coincidence, due to the two writers having had a similar experience. Sercambi, though an important person in the political history of Lucca, was hardly known at all for his *Novelle* until the 19th century. Chaucer can hardly have seen the MS. of his work . . .**

**As a picture of various kinds of English folk Chaucer's *Prolog* was preceded by and resembles the *Prolog* to Langland's *Vision of Piers the Plowman*. Langland was a man of genius, yet his *Prolog* is artistically so far inferior to Chaucer's as to be almost negligible. Chaucer's *Prolog*, on the other hand, is a consummate masterpiece. As a compact picture of society in a given age, poetically executed, I know but of a single masterpiece that challenges comparison, and that is the description of Achilles in the 18th Book of the *Iliad*. I will merely record my opinion that the *Prolog* is, on the whole, the finer work of literary art.**

**Just how far Chaucer's pilgrims were idealized at the promptings of the poet's genius we shall never know. But certain circumstances show that he drew, partly, at least, from actual models; that some, if not all, of his pilgrims are portraits from life. The 'mormal' on the Cook's shin, for example, adds nothing to the artistic excellence of the picture. Like the wen in Sir Peter Lely's portrait of Cromwell, it serves merely for purposes of identification. Chaucer mentioned it only because it was something he actually saw.**

**The date at which the *Prolog* was written is, in all probability, between 1384 and 1388.**[22] □

Hinckley, unpromisingly some might say, dismisses two of his 'cases' as improbable and one as 'insoluble'. He does, however, identify a host of subjects that are, as chapter one of this Guide has already shown, highly relevant to the study of *The General Prologue*: How much was Chaucer influenced by the work of his countrymen and contemporaries (Gower and Langland)? Is the pilgrimage depicted in *The General Prologue* 'likely to have been an historical fact'? What is the date of its composition? The question Hinckley raises of the indebtedness to the *Decameron* of *The Canterbury Tales*, and, even more precisely, of *The General Prologue*, has continued to be the subject of debate and has been admirably summarised by N. S. Thompson in *Chaucer, Boccaccio and the Debate of Love: A Comparative Study of the Decameron and The Canterbury Tales* (1996):

■ Did Chaucer know the *Decameron*? This question has been asked many times and with increasing frequency. Almost certainly, if Chaucer did know Boccaccio's great collection of tales, its universality could hardly have failed to influence the creation of *The Canterbury Tales*, even if questions of 'how'? and 'in what ways?' immediately follow the hypothesis. When Chaucerian scholars first began to investigate connections between the two texts, they found several broad correlations:

> the use of a frame narrative
>
> the use of narrators
>
> the use of a 'director' of narrative ('king' or 'queen' in the *Decameron*; the Host in the *Canterbury Tales*)
>
> a broad similarity of subject matter and several shared narratives.[23]
>
> But the general trend in favour of influence seemed to end in 1916 with a study by H.M. Cummings [*The Indebtedness of Chaucer's Works to the Italian Works of Boccaccio*], who concluded there was no 'source' in Boccaccio's work, a view which seemed to find favour at the time and was later repeated with unfailing regularity. More recently, scholars have been more open on the subject and mention of the *Decameron* has become admissible again.[24]
>
> ...... the *Decameron* and the *Canterbury Tales* do have an obvious similarity. They are both framed collections of interconnected popular narratives whose intercalary [inserted or interpolated] material is as important as the narratives themselves. Furthermore, both works have rightly become 'classics' for the freshness and vitality of the human dimension and perspective which they bring to the still largely spiritual aspirations of Western Europe in the last phase of the Middle Ages. In so doing, they paved the way for future literary developments, especially by creating a new space for popular fiction.
>
> ...... what has struck me is that both collections reflect many shared themes and preoccupations, ranging from similar narrative material, to literary techniques, to the question of the purpose of fiction ...[25] □

Thompson neatly summarises some of the ways in which the *Decameron* may have impacted on *The General Prologue*, especially when he speaks of the role of the Host and the use of the frame narrative. The extract above, with its mention of H.M. Cummings's 1916 publication, also returns us firmly to the main period covered in this present chapter. Around the same time, 1914 to be exact, George Lyman Kittredge (one of the American critics mentioned above) delivered a series of celebrated lectures on Chaucer at Johns Hopkins University in the United States. These talks were eventually published under the title *Chaucer and his Poetry* (1915). The following passage, taken from chapter five of this book, begins by refuting the notion that a firm source can be identified for *The Canterbury Tales*. One of Hinckley's conclusions is supported, however, for Kittredge acknowledges that 'The most tantalizing of all the parallels . . . is Sercambi's *Novelle*, for which the frame is likewise a pilgrimage'.²⁶ Thus, another voice joins the debate on this important topic:

■ There has been a rather active discussion, for more than a hundred years, concerning the probable source of Chaucer's scheme of the Canterbury Pilgrimage. The result is a *non liquet* [not proven]. Several possible models have been pointed out, and others are turning up continually. The *pros* and *cons* in every case have been argued with learning and ingenuity. So far as I can see, however, the advocates of each new source, though they have found it easy to demolish the arguments of their predecessors, have not been quite so successful in constructing acceptable theories of their own. There is, then, no single collection of tales to which we can point, with any confidence, as that which gave Chaucer the hint.

. . . . . . Before the idea of a pilgrimage occurred to him, Chaucer had twice undertaken to compose a series of tales. The results lie before us in the Tragedies, afterwards assigned to the Monk, and the Legend of Cupid's Saints, otherwise known as Good Women [i.e., *The Legend of Good Women*]. Both works exhibit, in the most striking fashion, the orderly habits of mediaeval literature.²⁷ □

After introducing the subject of the 'infinite variety' of the 'form and subject' of *The Canterbury Tales*, Kittredge responds to Dryden's reading of Chaucer discussed earlier in this Guide. In this section, Kittredge introduces his famous analysis of the poem as a 'Human Comedy', advances a theory of Chaucer's 'genius' commonly found in the criticism of this period and earlier, and explains why it is necessary to resist viewing *The General Prologue* as a self-contained poem. Derek Brewer, in *Chaucer: The Critical Heritage* (1978), has remarked of the extract which follows that Kittredge takes 'up a well-established tradition . . . [and] argues for an underlying structural principle for "The Canterbury Tales" . . . and by means of what he calls "straightforward interpretation" reads "The Canterbury Tales" as a fully dramatic piece of a realistic kind, a self-enclosed fiction like a novel':²⁸

■ I am much deceived if Dryden is not . . . treading on the verge of the proposition that the Canterbury Tales is, to all intents and purposes, a Human Comedy. Certainly he is calling our attention to something that distinguishes Chaucer's work from every collection of stories that preceded it. It was much, as we have seen, that Chaucer had the judgment, among the infinite doings of the world, to select a pilgrimage, and to parcel out his tales to the miscellaneous company that met at the Tabard on the way to Canterbury. It was more, far more, that he

THE GENERAL PROLOGUE

had the genius to create the Pilgrims, endowing each of them with an individuality that goes much beyond the typical. If we had only the Prologue, we might, perhaps, regard the Pilgrims as types. The error is common, and venial. But we must not stop with the Prologue: we must go on to the play. The Pilgrims are not static: they move and live. The Canterbury Pilgrimage is, whether Dryden meant it or not, a Human Comedy, and the Knight and the Miller and the Pardoner and the Wife of Bath and the rest are the *dramatis personae*. The Prologue itself is not merely a prologue: it is the first act, which sets the personages in motion. Thereafter, they move by virtue of their inherent vitality, not as tale-telling puppets, but as men and women. From this point of view, which surely accords with Chaucer's intention, the Pilgrims do not exist for the sake of the stories, but *vice versa*. Structurally regarded, the stories are merely long speeches expressing, directly or indirectly, the characters of several persons. They are more or less comparable, in this regard, to the soliloquies of Hamlet or Iago or Macbeth. But they are not mere monologues, for each is addressed to all the other personages, and evokes reply and comment, being thus, in a real sense, a part of the conversation.

Further, – and this is a point of crucial significance, – the action of the plot, however simple, involves a great variety of relations among the Pilgrims. They are brought together by a common impulse, into a casual and impermanent association, which is nevertheless, for the time being, peculiarly intimate. They move slowly along the road, from village to village and inn to inn, in groups that are ever shifting, but ever forming afresh. Things happen to them . . .

. . . . . . Chaucer's contemporaries were quite aware of the dramatic nature of the Pilgrimage and the significance of the Pilgrims as characters in a comedy . . . [*The Canterbury Tales* are] a micro-cosmography, a little image of the great world.[29] □

Kittredge goes on to locate the pilgrims and the pilgrimage motif firmly within a socio-historical framework and explains why the figures of the Host and the Knight are central to this type of analysis:

■ Travel, as everybody knows, is for the time being a mighty leveller of social distinctions, particularly when its concomitants throw the voyagers together while at the same time isolating them from the rest of the world . . . . . . Now, an organised company of Pilgrims – and Chaucer's Pilgrims had effected an organization at Harry Bailley's inn – were brought together in a[n] . . . intimacy, which was made especially close by the religious impulse that actuated them all in common. We must not be skeptical about the genuineness of this impulse, merely because some of the Pilgrims are loose fish, or because they do not always act and speak with propriety. If we let this consideration much affect us, it must be either because we are uninstructed in mediaeval manners, or because we apply our own religion to life in a deplorably wooden fashion. This score and a half of Englishmen and Englishwomen were fulfilling the vow they had made to St. Thomas in sickness or danger or misfortune. However diverse their stations in life, their moral codes, or the sincerity of their religion in general, – and in all these points there is variety so rich as almost to bewilder, – here they were at one. The saint had helped them, and they were gratefully doing their duty in return.

But the occasion was not only religious, it was social. Listen to the Host, who has entertained hundreds of such companies at the Tabard Inn:

> Ye goon to Caunterbury – God yow speede,
> The blisful martir quite yow youre meede!
> And wel I woot, as ye goon by the weye,
> *Ye shapen yow to talen and to pleye;*
> For trewely, confort ne myrthe is noon
> To ride by the weye doumb as a stoon; [*GP*, ll. 769–74]

The occasion, then, was both religious and social; and the various Pilgrims, knowing that all men are equal in God's sight, were not indisposed to sink their differences of rank for the nonce [occasion], so far, at least, as to laugh and talk together without stand-offish punctillo of rigid etiquette.

 ... ... The Host, as we know, is the appointed leader. He nominates himself for the office, as many a good politician has done before and since, but not until after supper, when his social qualities have been fully tested. He is well fitted for the office – a fine large man, handsome after his florid fashion, merry, afraid of nobody – "of manhod hym lakkede right naught" [*GP*, l. 756] – loud-voiced and free-spoken. It is not by accident that Chaucer calls him a fair burgess as there is in Cheap; for London was an *imperium in imperio* [force in power], and the citizens were persons of importance, not merely in their own eyes, but in the estimation of all orders and even of the king. Chaucer himself, who was always in politics, – would that we had his political autobiography! – is a first-rate example of a "king's man," a sort of courtier who was also a burgher by descent and in actuality. Once a Londoner, always a Londoner, no matter what else you might become.

 ... ... Yet, despite the Host's autocracy, the ruler of the company is actually the Knight. It is he that asserts himself whenever the cause requires and appeals to the controlling forces of the social world.[30] □

In the 1920s, *The General Prologue* once more attracted the interest of a poet. This time the poet was T. S. Eliot and he used it as the source for the opening lines of his ground-breaking poem *The Waste Land* (1923):

■ April is the cruellest month, breeding
  Lilacs out of the dead land, mixing
  Memory and desire, stirring
  Dull roots with spring rain.[31] □

Eliot's use of Chaucer inspired, in turn, a series of comparative analyses that were kick-started by the critic Hugh Kenner. In *The Invisible Poet: T.S. Eliot* (1959), Kenner claims that in Eliot we find 'a denial of Chaucer'[32] as Eliot fails to mimic the tone of the initial four lines of *The General Prologue*:

■ Whan that Aprill with his shoures soote
  The droghte of March hath perced to the roote,
  And bathed every veyne in swich licour
  Of which vertu engendred is the flour. □

Christopher Ricks, however, in *T.S. Eliot and Prejudice* (1988), offers this alternative reading of Chaucer's meaning here:

■ . . . Hugh Kenner may say of *The Waste Land* that it 'opens with a denial of Chaucer', and Cairns Craig [in *Yeats, Eliot, Pound and the Politics of Poetry*, 1982] speak of 'Eliot's inversion of Chaucer in the first line of *The Waste Land*'. But Chaucer's lines are less unequivocal than this would suggest, for they do not present April as the kindest month; the energies of April, of its weather and of its incitements to a longing which will not be entirely fulfilled, are not sentimentalized by Chaucer. Moreover, for every poem about April which can be offered (so that the preconception here be one about April), a counter-poem about sad November can be offered (so that the preconception be about cruel months). And since the words are the very opening, we lack that sufficiency of established context which will often secure us.[33] □

Two years after the publication of *The Waste Land*, novelist Virginia Woolf published *The Common Reader* (1925). In this work she included her 'eagle view of the Chaucer landscape',[34] a chapter on 'The Pastons and Chaucer'. Here, Woolf explains why Chaucer had an 'advantage over the moderns' (and, implicitly, why some of the Modernists were so fascinated by him); because his 'England was an unspoilt country'.[35] This image of the 'virgin land' is central to Woolf's reading of Chaucer as a poet. It is also invaluable when considering the 'Spring opening' of *The General Prologue* and the role of Nature in the poem as a whole:

## 'TALES OF BEST SENTENCE AND MOOST SOLAAS': 1892–1949

■ . . . . . . He [Chaucer] has pre-eminently that story-teller's gift, which is almost the rarest gift among writers at the present day. Nothing happens to us as it did to our ancestors; events are seldom important; if we recount them, we do not really believe in them; we have perhaps things of greater interest to say . . . For the story-teller, besides his indescribable zest for facts, must tell his story craftily, without undue stress or excitement, or we shall swallow it whole and jumble the parts together; he must let us stop, give us time to think and look about us, yet always be persuading us to move on. Chaucer was helped to this to some extent by the time of his birth; and in addition he had another advantage over the moderns which will never come the way of the English poets again. England was an unspoilt country. His eyes rested on a virgin land, all unbroken grass and wood except for the small towns and an occasional castle in the building. No villa roof peered through Kentish tree-tops, no factory chimney smoked on the hill-side. The state of the country, considering how poets go to Nature, how they use her for their images and their contrasts even when they do not describe her directly, is a matter of some importance. Her cultivation or her savagery influences the poet far more profoundly than the prose writer. To the modern poet, with Birmingham, Manchester, and London the size they are, the country is the sanctuary of moral excellence in contrast with the town which is the sink of vice. It is a retreat, the haunt of modesty and virtue, where men go to hide and moralise. There is something morbid, as if shrinking from human contact, in the nature worship of Wordsworth, still more in the microscopic devotion which Tennyson lavished upon the petals of roses and the buds of lime trees. But these were great poets. In their hands, the country was no mere jeweller's shop, or museum of curious objects to be described, even more curiously, in words. Poets of smaller gift, since the view is so much spoilt, and the garden or the meadow must replace the barren heath and the precipitous mountain-side, are now confined to little landscapes, to birds' nests, to acorns with every wrinkle drawn to life. The wider landscape is lost.

But to Chaucer the country was too large and too wild to be altogether agreeable. He turned instinctively, as if he had painful experience of their nature, from tempests and rocks to the bright May day and the jocund landscape, from the harsh and mysterious to the gay and definite. Without possessing a tithe of the virtuosity in word-painting which is the modern inheritance, he could give, in a few words, or even, when we come to look, without a single word of direct description, the sense of the open air.

. . . . . . Nature, uncompromising, untamed, was no looking-glass for happy faces, or confessor of unhappy souls. She was herself; sometimes, therefore, disagreeable enough and plain, but always in

Chaucer's pages with the hardness and freshness of an actual presence. Soon, however, we notice something of greater importance than the gay and picturesque appearance of the mediaeval world – the solidity which plumps it out, the conviction which animates the characters.

...... Once believe in Chaucer's young men and women and we have no need of preaching or protest. We know what he finds good, what evil; the less said the better. Let him get on with his story, paint knights and squires, good women and bad, cooks, shipmen, priests, and we will supply the landscape, give his society its belief, its standing towards life and death, and make of the journey to Canterbury a spiritual pilgrimage.

...... And so, when we shut Chaucer, we feel that without a word being said the criticism is complete; what we are saying, thinking, reading, doing, has been commented upon. Nor are we left merely with the sense, powerful though that is, of having been in good company and got used to the way of good society. For as we have jogged through the real, the unadorned country-side, with first one good fellow cracking his joke or singing his song and then another, we know that though this world resembles, it is not in fact our daily world. It is the world of poetry. Everything happens here more quickly and more intensely, and with better order than in life or prose; there is a formal elevated dullness which is part of the incantation of poetry; there are lines speaking half a second in advance what we were about to say, as if we read our thoughts before words cumbered them; and lines which we go back to read again with that heightened quality, that enchantment which keeps them glittering in the mind long afterwards. And the whole is held in its place, and its variety and divagations [wanderings] ordered by the power which is among the most impressive of all – the shaping power, the architect's power. It is the peculiarity of Chaucer, however, that though we feel at once this quickening, this enchantment, we cannot prove it by quotation. From most poets quotation is easy and obvious; some metaphor suddenly flowers; some passage breaks off from the rest. But Chaucer is very unequal, very even-paced, very unmetaphorical.[36] □

The diversity of Woolf's approach in the extract above, encompassing as it does the role of nature, Chaucer's morality ('we know what he finds good, what evil'), the 'solidity' of the Canterbury pilgrims and the pilgrimage motif, mirrors the very diversity of *The General Prologue* itself. Indeed, the poem's diversity has long been remarked upon by critics. In the 1930s, the topic was most comprehensively raised by John Livingstone Lowes in his lecture 'The Human Comedy' (1932). Drawing very heavily upon Kittredge's *Chaucer and his Poetry* (see above), Lowes observes of *The General Prologue*, the tales and their links, that '"Dialogue and action, gesture, costume and scenery, as in real life" – all are there'.[37] The sheer intricacy, both thematically and stylistically, of *The Canterbury Tales* was discussed in more depth by G.K. Chesterton in *Chaucer*, which also appeared in 1932. In chapter five of this book, Chesterton introduces his famous remarks on *The General Prologue* with an architectural analogy now much used by Chaucer critics. He then proceeds to evaluate the poem favourably against the work as a whole:

> ■ ... indeed *The Canterbury Tales* do remain rather like a huge, hollow, unfinished Gothic cathedral with some of the niches empty and some filled with statues, and some part of the large plan traced only in lines upon the ground.
>
> Just as in such a case, the arches would stand up more strongly than the statues, or the walls be made first and more firmly than the ornament, so in Chaucer's work the framework is finer than the stories which correspond to the statues. The prolonged comedy which we call the Prologue, though it includes many interludes and something like an epilogue, is made of much stronger material than the tales which it carries; the narrative is quite superior to the narratives. The Wife of Bath's Tale is not so good as the Wife of Bath; the Reeve's Tale is not so vivid as the Reeve; we are not so much interested in the Summoner's story as in the Summoner, and care less about Griselda than about the Clerk of Oxenford. The Miller does not prove even his own rather brutal energy, by telling a broad and rather brutal story, half so well as the poet conveys it in those curt and strong lines about his breaking a door by butting it with his red-bristled head. And the whole conception and cult of Chivalry is no better set forth, in all the seventy pages that unfold the Knight's Tale, than in the first few lines that describe the Knight. It is impossible to say for certain, of course, whether Chaucer realized how much more real and original were the passages which concern the Pilgrims than those which concern their imaginary heroes or martyrs. It is possible that, like many another original genius, he did not know which parts of his own work were really original, still less which were really great ... It may be that Chaucer really did regard the prologue as a mere frame, in the sense of a picture-frame. In that case, we can only say he invented a new kind of picture-gallery, in which the picture-frames are much better than the pictures. Still, a word must be said for the understanding of the pictures, even when he has stolen them out of other people's picture-frames. In other words, we must understand something about stories as stories, before we even open this medieval story-book.[38] □

Chesterton's opinion, that the characters of *The Canterbury Tales* are far more original than the tales they tell, is interesting in light of the fact that the bulk of criticism produced in the 1930s on *The General Prologue* was largely devoted to individual pilgrim portraits. A few articles also merit particular mention here: Benjamin B. Wainwright's 'Chaucer's Prioress Again: An Interpretative Note' (1933),[39] Carleton Brown's 'The Squire and the Number of the Canterbury Pilgrims' (1934),[40] B.J. Whiting's 'The Miller's Head' (1937)[41] and Joe Horrell's 'Chaucer's Symbolic Plowman' (1939).[42] The reader may wish to consult these articles at his or her leisure.

The final extracts to be considered in this chapter are taken from Muriel Bowden's *A Commentary on the General Prologue to the Canterbury Tales*. This work, published in 1948, is amongst the best and most exhaustive of the pre-1950 scholarship on *The General Prologue*. That it was reissued with additional material and a new preface in 1967 is a testament to its continuing value. Bowden begins with an historical introduction that places Chaucer within the 'immensely complicated political scene of the years 1380 to 1387', the years when 'the ideas for the *Canterbury Tales* took root in his mind and germinated'.[43] In this opening chapter Bowden also confirms what Virginia Woolf previously observed about the 'savagery' of nature in the Middle Ages. Bowden writes: 'The world of the late fourteenth century was wholly medieval in that it was still harassed by combat with monstrously powerful and inimical forces: the cold and the darkness, the storm and the sea, the unfriendly mysteries waiting beyond the horizon, disease and sudden death, and an avid Satan ever ready to lay hold of the soul.'[44] Identified here, then, are the natural, political and religious forces afoot at the time of *The General Prologue*'s composition. Bowden then turns to a familiar subject, the 'Spring opening' of the poem. In chapter two she gives an admiring close reading of these lines in which, once again, the question of possible sources is paramount:

■ Each time we read the opening lines of the *General Prologue* the familiar words conjure up April's sun-caressed and rain-washed skies, the bright and delicate green of young leaves, the joyous rediscovery of love and new life. Chaucer gives us the feeling, as we read, that he is the first poet ever to have put this picture into words, yet of course we are aware of the sober fact that all poets, from earliest antiquity to the present day, have celebrated the coming of the spring, and what is more, that the very phrases employed by medieval poets were often set in conventional patterns.[45] As Professor Tatlock remarks [Bowden's Note: [in] *Anglia*, 37, pp. 85f.]:

. . . Literature was currently conceived not as a sheer creation of the imagination, but rather as an adapting and re-telling of what had been told before. The medieval reader, and writer, felt vividly the impressiveness and charm of authority, precedent and associations, and in general did not find inventiveness and originality a thing to be striven for or claimed.

Chaucer uses an opening for the *Prologue* that, while it may have had charm for some of his contemporaries because of its zest and elusive freshness of style, had a special fourteenth-century appeal in "precedent and associations." What more natural than for Chaucer to use as a model a passage from Guido delle Colonne's *Historia Destructionis Troiae* [Book III]? For Guido was an author Chaucer much admired, and the *Historia* was one of the sources of Chaucer's recently completed *Troilus and Criseyde*; certainly Chaucer's lines show striking parallels with this passage, a translation of which follows:

> It was the season when the sun, hastening under the turning circle of the zodiac, had now entered its course under the sign of the Ram, in which the equinox is celebrated, when the days of the beginning of spring are equal in length to the nights; then when the season begins to soothe eager mortals in its clear air; then when as the snows melt, gently blowing zephyrs wrinkle up the waters; then when fountains gush out into slender jars; then when moistures breathing out from the earth's bosom are raised up within trees and branches to their tops, wherefore, seeds leap forth, crops grow, fields become green brightened by flowers of various colours; then when trees put on renewed foliage everywhere; then when the earth is decked with grass, and birds sing, sounding like the cithara in the euphony of sweet harmony.

Here are nearly all the actual expressions Chaucer uses; the time is in the Ram, when moisture ("licour") flows through every sap-vessel ("veyne") after the drought of March; the sweet zephyrs have quickened ("inspired") the tender tops of the branches ("croppes"); the young sun is now beyond the spring equinox and the second half of Aries; the birds sing in melody; even the very repetition of the word *when* seems to be borrowed from Guido. Chaucer adds one detail from Guido's conventional picture: the little birds, incited by nature in their desires ("so priketh hem nature in hir corages"), sleep all the night with open eye! The poet uses this same idea again, as we shall see, in describing his young Squire, who loved so hotly that he slept no more "than dooth a nyghtyngale." Medieval natural history taught that nightingales did not sleep in the mating season.

But the medieval Chaucer is also the timeless Chaucer, and realism comes as naturally to him as the acceptance of a literary convention: the traditional spring picture is not followed by the usual romantic or heroic events, but by a freshly matter-of-fact statement:

THE GENERAL PROLOGUE

> Thanne longen folk to goon on pilgrimages,
> And palmeres for to seken straunge strondes,
> To ferne halwes, kowthe in sondry londes; (ll. 12–4)

... Later on in the *Prologue* the poet names some of those shrines specifically [in the portrait of the Wife of Bath], but now he speaks only of England's most famous place of pilgrimage, the shrine of St. Thomas à Becket at Canterbury:

> ... from every shires ende
> Of Engelond to Caunterbury they wende,
> The hooly blisful martir for to seke,
> That hem hath holpen whan that they were seeke.[46] (ll. 15–8) □

The passage above brings together several of the topics dealt with in this chapter of this Guide: sources, the mediaeval poet's attitude towards originality, the pilgrimage frame and the 'Spring opening' of *The General Prologue*. The latter two subjects are also brought together in an interesting way in a more recent study, Edward I. Condren's *Chaucer and the Energy of Creation: The Design and Organization of the Canterbury Tales* (1999), and it is a worthwhile exercise for the student of Chaucer to compare Bowden's remarks above with the following extract from Condren's work:

■ ...... the frame that opens and closes the poem [*The Canterbury Tales*] presents two opposing halves, not only where its opening lines celebrating a new beginning of the natural world point to its closing lines, which prepare human beings for death, but also in the catalogue of pilgrims that follows the opening and the catalogue of sins that precedes the closing. The tales, too, divide evenly into two thematic halves. The twelve tales in the first five fragments seem driven by some desire to enhance the physical circumstances of life; the twelve tales in the second five concern the attempt to reshape the world for the purpose of gaining access to a higher order. The first half explores various kinds of management; the second, various kinds of creation. It matters little that the "enhanced physical life" in the first half and the "higher order" in the second are often fallaciously defined and doubtfully achieved, as for example the Wife of Bath's campaign for marital sovereignty in the first half and the Canon's Yeoman's fascination with converting lead into gold in the second. The desire itself is more important to the poem's overall design than the objective sought. Though the pilgrims and the characters they create in their tales may fall short of their own ideals in both halves of the poem, they do so for different reasons: a failure to balance competing forces of human nature in the first half, an inability to coordinate substance and form in the second.

One of the poem's subtler oppositions, highly instructive for understanding Chaucer's method, contrasts the Host and the Narrator. Harry Bailly and Chaucer-the-Pilgrim are complete opposites – the one gregarious, intolerant of values other than his own, yet unable to understand even his own; the other demure, fully able to understand the standards of others, though unable to discriminate among them, yet holding no criteria of his own. Because each of these two pilgrims represents an extreme example of a certain type, neither is a fully believable character, although touches of both reside in everyone. Similarly, no one would seriously argue, outside of literature, that the Wife of Bath's campaign for female sovereignty or that Griselda's [in *The Clerk's Tale*] unconditional subservience to her husband holds promise for a harmonious marriage or an ideal society, although one or the other strategy may be effective in a given situation. On the contrary, both of these pairs – the Host and the Narrator as well as the Wife of Bath and Griselda – define the limits of the spectrum within which may be found the poet himself in the first instance and a promising philosophy of marriage in the second. The same is true of the whole litany of opposing pairs with which Chaucer criticism has long been familiar.

. . . . . . No literary strategy, however canonized by its time, nor dynamic pattern, however universal, can ever be more than a preface to a literary work, a suggestion of one possible approach among many that the work may be asking its readers to follow. Let us turn, then, to [*The General Prologue* of] the Canterbury Tales, with the reminder that acceptance of the pattern discussed thus far must await "the awful business of facing [the] poem directly" [This and the following quotation are from E. T. Donaldson's study of 1970, *Speaking of Chaucer*, p. 153]. Moreover, the *Canterbury Tales* marks so great a departure, in both kind and quality, from other writings of its time that the only reliable instruction on how it is to be read must come from the poem itself, for nothing "should be permitted to replace an interpretation of the poem arising from the poem." As it happens, the most useful tutorial for the poem is also the poem's most famous sentence, its opening eighteen lines where Chaucer applies the apparently contradictory principles of opposition and synthesis to accomplish gently what the opening of Genesis accomplishes thunderously. Before our very eyes he creates the earth and everything on it:

> Whan that Aprill with his shoures soote
> The droghte of March hath perced to the roote,
> And bathed every veyne in swich licour

THE GENERAL PROLOGUE

> Of which vertu engendred is the flour;
> Whan Zephirus eek with his sweete breeth
> Inspired hath in every holt and heeth
> The tendre croppes, and the yonge sonne
> Hath in the Ram his half cours yronne,
> And smale foweles make melodye,
> That slepen al the nyght with open ye
> (So priketh hem nature in hir corages),
> Thanne longen folk to goon on pilgrimages,
> And palmeres for to seken straunge strondes,
> To ferne halwes, kowthe in sondry londes;
> And specially from every shires ende
> Of Engelond to Caunterbury they wende,
> The hooly blisful martyr for to seke,
> That hem hath holpen whan that they were seeke.

The ease of this lyric opening so bedazzles the ear and the eye that we may miss a yet-more-dazzling movement occurring as if incidentally. Earth, air, fire, and water play subordinate roles both semantically and syntactically, as the sweet showers of April and the equally sweet breath of the west wind freshen a mere temporal clause, while the progress of the sun and March's drought only remotely imply fire and earth. Yet, according to medieval science, these are the four basic elements of which all things are made, two pairs of opposites. Neither of the properties of fire – that is, hot and dry – may be found in cold, moist water. Cold, dry earth opposes hot, moist air. In short, all things result from an uncertain combination of opposites.

That these lines implicitly mark the process of creation is evident in the gentle ascent they make up what Theseus will call [in *The Knight's Tale*] the "faire cheyne of love" [l. 2988]. Add four elements in the right mix and plant life appears in the "flour" of line 4 and again in the "tendre croppes" of line 7. Yet life does not just happen when the right elements enrich the poetic tureen, unless they are stirred by the right metaphors. In lines 2–4 images of penetration and insemination underscore the masculine principle implied etymologically by "vertu" (L[atin] *vir*, man) and physiologically by "engendered," a verb of simple begetting. Lines 5 and 6 make the same point, although their ethereal metaphor of the west wind's gentle breath calls up the loftier "inspired" (L[atin] *inspirare*, to breathe [spirit] into). Having acquired simple corporeal existence by line 4, plant life receives an essence two lines later. In addition, Chaucer's version of creation incorporates the two contradictory accounts of the Creation in the opening chapters of Genesis: (1) that God's positive, external acts of division, culminating with His dividing man into male and female, individually created all things (Genesis 1:1–2; 4a). We may even add that by realizing the events of creation within lines of poetry Chaucer also includes Scripture's final account found in John 1:1: "In the beginning was the Word." Taking his initial impulse from the texture of language, and letting spirit be breathed into matter, Chaucer then permits everything else to evolve from the interaction of opposites.

At just this point an interesting paradox develops. While the metaphors that had turned from physical "engendering" to metaphysical "inspiring" now turn back again to the corporeal activity of the eighth line, where the young sun runs his course half way into the sign of the Ram, the created universe continues to ascend. Like a clock's pendulum, whose swing from one extreme to the opposite provides the energy to measure time's continuous advance, each change of direction in nature's energy lifts the poem to the next link in creation's chain. The eighth line's return to physical activity seems to beget the small fowls of line 9, who are nevertheless associated with melody, an aesthetic dimension more sophisticated than any kind of order yet mentioned. These same birds are next identified in the tenth line with explicit physical activity, a swing away from melody, prompting in turn the next higher level of creation, the human level of line 12.

A subtle shift in tense here effects an equally subtle transition from particular to universal. Since the present perfect tense appears four times in the first three clauses – "hath perced" (2), "[hath] bathed" (3), "Inspired hath" (6), and "Hath . . . yronne" (8) – we anticipate the same tense when another parallel clause begins in line 9. But the actual verb "maken" throws us off. It cannot be the past participle, which normally appears "maked." Nevertheless, "maken" suggests a slant-form past participle, while actually expressing the present tense, thus effecting a gentle transition to the unambiguous grammatical present of the next two lines and preparing us for the universal present-tense main verb of the whole eighteen-line sentence: people long to go on pilgrimages.

Ah, but do they? Do they long for the pilgrimage, or for the mere going? For it is just at this point that the whole, carefully controlled ascent tumbles. While wonderful images of harmony characterize most nature, a jarring image of disharmony characterizes human nature. The lines move quite logically through successively higher levels of creation – from simple matter to plant life, from plant life to animal life, and from animal life to human life. Words like "pilgrimages," "ferne halwes," and especially "the hooly blisful martir" prepare for a still higher level. Yet that ascent dramatically breaks off at the very moment when the poem anticipates communion with the saints and angels. Our expectation that these pilgrims are traveling to Canterbury for pious purposes suddenly shatters in the face of an opposing purpose, the desire to draw upon St. Thomas's power to cure bodily ill.

THE GENERAL PROLOGUE

Brought by the poem to the very threshold of spiritual perception, a threshold that other creatures could neither recognize nor cross, the pilgrims retreat to a concern they share with lesser creatures, a preoccupation with physical well-being. In the whole of these opening lines, then, only Man leaves doubt whether God's creation is actually advancing, or merely swinging back and forth.

Softly folded into this wonderful opening sentence, as if in symphonic overture, lies the structural pattern of the entire *Canterbury Tales*, the dynamic principle by which nature expresses itself in pairs of opposite extremes whose interaction brings reality into existence. This principle – one of the most fundamental patterns in nature, a constant shifting back and forth between opposite extremes, from "shoures soote" to the "droghte of March," from the warm daylight of the "yonge sonne" to the cold night-time of birds sleeping "with open ye" – provides the poem with its source of energy. Like the unvarying waves of a sine curve ['the length of a straight line drawn from one end of a circular arc parallel to the tangent at the other end, and terminated by the radius,' *OED*] which alternate between positive and negative values, Chaucer's lines appear to retreat from one kind of excess until they reach another in the opposite direction. Although these alterations normally make possible nature's miraculous stability, the energy they produce occasionally leads away from stability, either towards an increasingly disorganized state or toward a newer, more complex order of existence. The imaginative image of the "yonge sonne," conceived as both the celestial sun penetrating the house of the Ram early in its annual course and as some king's princely son flanked by "tendre croppes" on one side and small melody-makers on the other, emphasizes the stability of the yearly cycle and the universality of romance. But at the same time the ominous word "seeke" (l. 18) which ends the first sentence, alludes to a larger disorganization which ends life. Yet the fructifying combination of April's showers and the west wind, as well as the implied fruitfulness associated with romance, allude to the possibility of new life springing into existence.

Oppositions may be viewed in two ways: first as the friction that provides the energy in all dynamic activity, and second, as the extreme limits that enclose some entity in equilibrium . . . the opening lines of [*The*] *Canterbury Tales* call greater attention to the former of these . . . [47] ☐

Condren, in his detailed, grammatically based analysis of the opening lines of *The General Prologue* raises the issue of why, exactly, Chaucer's pilgrims embark upon their journey to Canterbury. A legitimate question to ask, then, as we conclude this section is: what were the historical reasons behind the popularity of the pilgrimage and the veneration of relics seen in Chaucer's poem? To answer this, a return to Muriel

## 'TALES OF BEST SENTENCE AND MOOST SOLAAS': 1892–1949

Bowden's *A Commentary on the General Prologue to The Canterbury Tales* is necessary:

> ■ . . . . . . Medieval man, searching always in desperate hope for assurance in his extraordinarily complicated and hazardous world, came to be even more deeply convinced than his ancestor of the Dark Ages that intercessory powers and miraculous manifestations were attached to the bodies of saints and their relics, and the number of pilgrimages to the graves of local martyrs, and of the treasures left there in propitiation, saw steady increase throughout the Middle Ages. Indeed, the honour paid to some of the venerated saints at times exceeded that paid to God. At Canterbury [during the reign of Henry II] "we find at the altar of God no oblation, at the Virgin's only 4*l*. 1*s*. 8*d*., at Becket's 954*l*. 6*s*. 3*d*.!" In the year 1220, when St. Thomas's body was translated from the crypt to Trinity Chapel, the receipts were immense, amounting to between one-fifth and one-quarter of a million dollars in modern currency; in the anniversary year of 1420, the monetary receipts were less (about half as much as in 1220), but other gifts – rings, brooches, jewels, gold, spices, tapers, cups, and statues – continued to be donated with unabated enthusiasm. And it was as much the relics as the tomb of the martyred archbishop which drew peasant and prince to Canterbury . . . . . . Chaucer's Pardoner [in light of the resulting 'mania' for the invention and sale of relics], with his pillow-case which he says is the veil of "Oure Lady," his fragment of St. Peter's "seyl," and his "pigges bones" that are to be sold as the hallowed remains of some saint, is no unusual figure.[48] □

In the almost sixty years covered in this chapter of this Guide, we have seen a variety of labels and images being attached to *The General Prologue*. It shifted, for example, from being talked about as a Human Comedy to a picture-gallery. Indeed, the sheer variety of scholarly responses to the text was itself not unlike a Gothic cathedral and the scene was now set for the new, ever expanding, readings of the text developed in the 1950s and 1960s.

# CHAPTER THREE

# 'So as it Semed me': The 1950s and 1960s

- honour corruption villainy holiness
  riding in a fragrance of sunlight (side by side
  all in a singing wonder of blossoming yes
  riding) to him who died that death should be dead

  humblest and proudest eagerly wandering
  (equally all alive in miraculous day)
  merrily moving through sweet forgiveness of spring
  (over the under the gift of the earth of the sky

  knight and ploughman pardoner and wife and nun
  merchant frere clerk sumnour miller and reve
  and geoffrey and all) come up from the never of when
  come into the now of forever come riding alive

  down while crylessly drifting through vast most
  nothing's own nothing children go of dust[1]  □

This poem of e.e. cummings, published in 1950 in his collection *XAIPE*, is an evocative example of how *The General Prologue* continued to inspire other works of art even as the mid-point of the twentieth century dawned. The Age of the Amateur Critic was long past, however, and the 1950s saw a genuine and sustained flourishing of professional Chaucer criticism. *The General Prologue*, as a result, came under a new type of scrutiny, though scholars still seemed drawn to many of the same topics with which their predecessors had grappled. This application of fresh approaches to time-honoured topics is found in J.S.P. Tatlock's *The Mind and Art of Chaucer*, which came out the same year as cummings's poem.

## 'SO AS IT SEMED ME': THE 1950s AND 1960s

In a brief section devoted to *The General Prologue*, Tatlock commences by going over familiar ground, painting a picture of nature not dissimilar to that of Virginia Woolf or Muriel Bowden. Thus, we find phrases such as 'Wild nature [in the Middle Ages] was full of beasts and bandits and thorns'.[2] After this preamble, he arrives at the heart of his thesis:

■ The people in the *Prologue* make us realize that we are near the beginnings of modern literature, for in general they are middle-class; none outranks the knight, or the Monk (who ranks as a prior), none is beneath the rather prosperous Plowman. The persons might appear as mere names; or as vague types; or as vivid types; or as individuals. As befits poetry, which deals with general truth, vivid types are what decidedly they are, though sometimes with individual and non-typical traits (as with the Cook and the Wife of Bath). The spirit is rationalistic; Chaucer is becoming fully his essential self, realistic, not romantic, which he actually is only superficially and at times. Accordingly the descriptions tend to be short and condensed, and also to be epigrammatic. That is why the ten-syllable couplet is fitting, and each element of form aids the other; and why the Ovidian closed and balanced couplet tends to recur.[3] □

The vocabulary of modernity is evident in this extract: words like 'rationalistic', 'middle-class', and, most tellingly, 'essential self' permeate Tatlock's analysis and aid him in his definition of Chaucer the modern, as opposed to the mediaeval, man. He also, in his remarks about the 'epi-grammatic' quality of the pilgrim portraits, makes a valuable connection between the style and content of *The General Prologue*. This interest in style is also seen in the next extract, which is taken from Kemp Malone's *Chapters on Chaucer* of 1951. Malone begins with a topic that the previous chapter of this Guide has already explored, the 'Spring opening' (lines 1–18). He then analyses the language Chaucer employs, as well as its stylistic function, in lines 19ff. of the poem. Readers new to Chaucer will find Malone's description of the specific divisions of *The General Prologue* particularly helpful:

■ We see . . . that Chaucer, in his capacity as a traditionalist, began his poem with an elaborate, conventional dating, done in high style. But by the end of the eighteen-line period the style has become familiar, and this without giving the reader any stylistic shocks. Having made an opening bow to traditional formality and artifice, Chaucer can now proceed in the informal style which he prefers.

Throughout the next passage, lines 19–42, the style is familiar. But in addition Chaucer makes it personal and even conversational by speaking of himself and by addressing his readers directly. I will

THE GENERAL PROLOGUE

dwell for a moment on the latter device. Once Chaucer has got everybody settled and comfortable at the inn, he says (lines 30–4),

> And shortly, whan the sonne was to reste,
> So hadde I spoken with hem everichon
> That I was of hir felawshipe anon,
> And made forward erly for to ryse
> To take our wey ther as I yow devyse.

The *shortly* of this passage tempts one to digression. It is a favorite stylistic trick of the poet to insist upon his own brevity. Others may string a story out, but he cuts it short. I must resist the temptation to go into this, however, and stick to my second person. The *yow* of line 34 obviously adds to the easy, chatty stylistic effect. But after all *ther as I yow devyse* is only a tag, one may say. So it is, but Chaucer makes of it a springboard from which he plunges into what amounts to a *tête-à-tête* with his readers. He takes time out, as it were, to talk to them about his plans:

> But natheles, whyl I have tyme and space,
> Er that I ferther in this tale pace,
> Me thinketh it acordaunt to resoun
> To telle yow al the condicioun
> Of ech of hem, so as it semed me,
> And whiche they weren, and of what degree,
> And eek in what array that they were inne;
> And at a knight than wol I first bigynne.

In this passage of eight lines Chaucer uses *I* three times, *me* twice, and *yow* once. By the end of the passage the readers not only know what to expect but they feel at home with the author. He has taken them into his confidence, and a certain intimacy has already been established between him and them. But for the poet's use of the first and second persons here, no such effect would have been possible; at any rate, it would have been much harder to achieve.

Next comes the descriptions of the pilgrims in lines 43–714. Here Chaucer has to use the third person, but he takes care to insert, from time to time, a construction with a pronoun of the first or second person. I have counted twenty-three of these constructions. Of the pronouns, *I* occurs fifteen times, *us* thrice, as follows:

| | | |
|---|---|---|
| I gesse 82, 117 | I seyde 183 | I undertake 288 |
| I trowe 155, 524, 691 | I telle 619 | as I was war 157 |
| I woot 389, 659 | telle I 330 | I durste swere 454 |
| I noot 284 | I seigh 193 | us 363, 566, 623 |

48

# 'SO AS IT SEMED ME': THE 1950s AND 1960s

The other pronouns of the first and second persons occur once each: *me* 385, *my* 544, *our* 62, *ye* 642, *yow* 73. The occurrences are well distributed:

| knight 2       | prioress 2    | clerk 1        |
| squire 1       | monk 2        | man of law 1   |
| yeoman 1       | merchant 1    | burgesses 1    |
|                |               |                |
| cook 1         | parson 1      | reeve 1        |
| shipman 1      | Chaucer 1     | summoner 3     |
| wife of Bath 1 | miller 1      | pardoner 1     |

It is the stylistic function of these pronouns to emphasize the informal, conversational effect of the passages in which they occur.

At this point let me make a digression on the cook of London. This pilgrim is introduced with line 379, which reads

A COOK they hadde with hem for the nones

Since Chaucer regularly refers to the body of pilgrims in the first person (beginning with line 34, immediately after he has made himself one of them), the pronoun *they* of line 379 cannot have reference to the pilgrims as a whole and must refer to the group of burgesses described in the lines immediately preceding. In other words, this group of would-be aldermen took a cook along with them on the pilgrimage as a servant.[4] The only other pilgrim said to have a servant is the squire, whose yeoman Chaucer presumably intended us to think of as serving father as well as son.[5] Chaucer lays great stress on the wealth, dignity, and importance (or self-importance) of the little group of burgesses. The fact that they have a servant with them emphasizes still more their high standing, or at any rate their pretensions, which our court poet evidently regards as amusing, burgess though he himself was in origin. Snobbishness did not fail to flourish even in Chaucer's day.

The long series of descriptions fall into two parts. The division is marked by the following passage (lines 542–4):

Ther was also a REVE, and a MILLERE,
A SOMNOUR, and a PARDONER also,
A MAUNCIPLE, and myself – ther were namo.

The passage serves as a special introduction to the five descriptions which end the series. By this simple and highly effective stylistic trick the reader is reassured. He has known from the start that the series would not be interminable: in line 24 the size of the group is specified as "wel nine and twenty." But by line 541 most readers have lost count, if they ever tried to keep count, and it is time for them to be told how much more of this kind of thing they may expect before the story proper is resumed.

Chaucer's division of the series of descriptions into two parts is decidedly unequal: Part One is about three times as long as Part Two. One might therefore expect to find more use made of subgrouping in Part One than in Part Two, and this is actually the case. We find five groups of pilgrims in the longer part, only one group in the shorter.[6] □

There can be no doubt that Malone's minute analysis of *The General Prologue* was a vital contribution to Chaucer studies in the 1950s. Perhaps the most influential commentary on the poem during this period, however, was E. Talbot Donaldson's 'Chaucer the Pilgrim' (1954). Donaldson, as the title of this article suggests, 'invented "Chaucer the Pilgrim"'[7] and, in the words of R.T. Lenaghan which will be considered further in chapter four of this Guide: ' . . . nicely described the narrative sympathies and ironies of the *General Prologue* in such a way as to clarify the fine combination of amiability and criticism that emanates from the narrator. The structure and descriptions of the *General Prologue* define the narrator's position; he is different but central'.[8] The following extract, taken from the opening of Donaldson's article, demonstrates the accuracy of Lenaghan's summary:

■ Verisimilitude in a work of fiction is not without its attendant dangers, the chief of which is that the responses it stimulates in the reader may be those appropriate not so much to an imaginative production as to an historical one or to a piece of reporting. History and reporting are, of course, honorable in themselves, but if we react to a poet as though he were an historian or a reporter, we do him somewhat less than justice. I am under the impression that many readers, too much influenced by Chaucer's brilliant verisimilitude, tend to regard his famous pilgrimage to Canterbury as significant not because it is a great fiction, but because it seems to be a remarkable record of a fourteenth-century pilgrimage. A remarkable record it may be, but if we treat it too narrowly as such there are going to be certain casualties among the elements that make up the fiction. Perhaps first among these elements is the fictional reporter, Chaucer the pilgrim, and the role he plays in the Prologue to the *Canterbury Tales* and in the links between them. I think it time that he was rescued from the comparatively dull record of history and put back into his poem. He is not really Chaucer the poet – nor, for that matter, is either the poet, or the poem's protagonist, that Geoffrey Chaucer frequently mentioned in contemporary historical records as a distinguished civil servant, but never as a poet. The fact that these are three separate entities does not, naturally, exclude the probability – or rather the certainty – that they bore a close resemblance to one another, and that, indeed, they frequently got together in the same body. But that does not excuse us from keeping them distinct from one another, difficult as their close resemblance makes our task.

The natural tendency to confuse one thing with its like is perhaps best represented by the school of Chaucerian criticism, now outmoded, that pictured a single Chaucer under the guise of a wide-eyed, jolly, rolypoly little man who, on fine Spring mornings, used to get up early, while the dew was still on the grass, and go look at daisies. A charming portrait, this, so charming, indeed, that it was sometimes able to maintain itself to the exclusion of any Chaucerian other side. It has every reason to be charming, since it was lifted almost *in toto* from the version Chaucer gives of himself in the prologue to the *Legend of Good Women*, though I imagine it owes some of its popularity to a rough analogy with Wordsworth – a sort of *Legend of Good Poets*. It was this version of Chaucer that Kittredge, in a page of great importance to Chaucer criticism, demolished with his assertion that "a naïf Collector of Customs would be a paradoxical monster." He might well have added that a naïve creator of old January [from *The Merchant's Tale*] would be even more monstrous.

Kittredge's pronouncement cleared the air, and most of us now accept the proposition that Chaucer was sophisticated as readily as we do the proposition that the whale is a mammal. But unhappily, now that we've got rid of the naïve fiction, it is easy to fall into the opposite sort of mistake. This is to envision, in the *Canterbury Tales*, a highly urbane, literal-historical Chaucer setting out from Southwark on a specific day of a specific year (we even argue somewhat acrimoniously about dates and routes), in company with a group of persons who existed in real life and whom Chaucer, his reporter's eye peeled for every idiosyncrasy, determined to get down on paper – down, that is, to the last wart – so that books might be written identifying them. Whenever this accurate reporter says something especially fatuous – which is not infrequently – it is either ascribed to an opinion peculiar to the Middle Ages (sometimes very peculiar), or else Chaucer's tongue is said to be in his cheek.

Now a Chaucer with tongue-in-cheek is a vast improvement over a simple-minded Chaucer when one is trying to define the whole man, but it must lead to a loss of critical perception, and in particular to a confused notion of Chaucerian irony, to see in the Prologue a reporter who is acutely aware of the significance of what he sees but who sometimes, for ironic emphasis, interprets the evidence presented by his observation in a fashion directly contrary to what we expect. The proposition ought to be expressed in reverse: the reporter is, usually, acutely aware of the significance of what he sees, no matter how sharply he sees it. He is, to be sure, permitted his lucid intervals, but in general he is the victim of the poet's persuasive – not merely sporadic – irony. And as such he is also the chief agent by which the poet achieves his wonderfully complex, ironic, comic, serious vision of a world which is but a devious and confused, infinitely various pilgrimage to a certain shrine. It is, as I hope to make clear, a good deal more than merely fitting that our guide on such a pilgrimage should be a man of such naïveté as the Chaucer who tells the tale of *Sir Thopas*. Let us accompany him a little distance.[9] ☐

Donaldson good-humouredly debunks earlier views of the Chaucerian narrator and paints, like Tatlock, an anti-romantic picture of the poet. This reading has generated a variety of critical responses, as Bernard F. Huppé shows in his book, *A Reading of the Canterbury Tales* (1964):

■ The structure of the *Prologue* is largely rhetorical; that is, it is framed on the narrator's descriptive catalogue and supported by contrastive and incremental repetition. Characterization is by contrastive use of descriptive detail: the ideal characters are poor in outward "array", but the Knight is rich in "deed", the Clerk in "thought", and the Parson in "deed" and "thought". The reverse is true of other pilgrims, in greater or less degree. Again, the speech of the pilgrims, contrastively described, reveals their true spiritual condition.

On the other hand, elements of dramatic structure also appear. First, the narrator . . . is dramatically conceived. The technique of presenting "Chaucer" as a reporter is dramatic irony; the narrative is reported by a "straight man" who leaves interpretation to the reader. The narrator's presence and personality provide an implicitly dramatic situation. This implicit drama is made explicit when control of the show is given to the master of ceremonies, Harry Bailley. His personality, his prejudices, his manner provide for a dramatic method of presenting the narrative of the pilgrimage proper. The management of the end of the *Prologue*, in fact, becomes entirely dramatic, as we observe the Host controlling his flock, and managing – by what we suspect to be sleight of hand – to have the Knight draw the straw, thus ensuring that the pilgrim of highest status – quite democratically – will begin the story-telling contest.[10] ☐

After establishing his own angle on the structure of *The General Prologue*, Huppé, in a footnote, points the reader in the direction of Donaldson's article and states:

■ Bertrand Bronson, *In Search of Chaucer* (Toronto, 1960), sharply dissents from the conception of a difference between Chaucer as author and as persona. Although my own view of this difference is independent of, and somewhat different from, the views of others it does fall under Professor Bronson's anathema, p.28: "The schizoid notion of two Chaucers, so named, presented simultaneously, one a puppet, the other the living, speaking poet with attitudes and intelligences radically different from each other's, could only have arisen in a time when authors would habitually think of themselves as completely separable from their books, and from their audiences, so that when they chose they could make the first personal pronoun stand for anything they pleased." This vigorous view seems contradicted by the medieval use of the *persona* and by the impossibility of Chaucer's expecting to be identified by his audience as a fool. The split personality, however, is not aware of his own madness, and I offer Professor Bronson's views by way of caution to the reader.[11] □

Another critic involved in the fashioning of 'schizoid Chaucer' is Rosemary Woolf. Her article 'Chaucer as Satirist in the *General Prologue to the Canterbury Tales*' (1959) re-examines the Chaucerian 'I' with an eye to initiating ' . . . a detailed and disciplined examination of Chaucer's style and methods of satire, which would include a careful consideration of Chaucer's work against the background of classical and Medieval satire'.[12] Woolf commences:

■ Many people nowadays acquire an early and excessive familiarity with the *General Prologue to the Canterbury Tales*, which later blunts their sharpness or perception. Since the *Prologue* is read at school, necessarily out of its literary-historical context, its methods of satire seem to have an inevitability and rightness which preclude either surprise or analysis. This natural tendency to remain uncritically appreciative of the *Prologue* has been partly confirmed by various works of criticism, which, though admirable in many ways, effusively reiterate that 'here is God's plenty': they thus awaken an enthusiastic response to the vitality and variety of the characterisation in the *Prologue*, at the cost of making the exact manner and tone of Chaucer's satire quite indistinct. Despite the bulk of Chaucerian criticism, there is still need for a detailed and disciplined examination of Chaucer's style and methods of satire, which would include a careful consideration of Chaucer's work against the background of classical and Medieval satire. Such a study would be of considerable scholarship and length: it is the purpose of this short article only to make a few general points about Chaucer's methods of satire.

It is sometimes taken for granted that the satirist speaks in his own voice, and that any reference to his opinions and feelings are a literal record of his experience. This assumption perhaps requires testing and reconsideration with reference to any satirist, but it is even more dangerous than when it is accepted without limitation about Chaucer. Chaucer was writing at a time when there was no tradition of personal poetry in a later Romantic sense: a poet never made his individual emotions the subject-matter of his poetry. Though the personal pronoun 'I' is used frequently in Medieval narrative and lyric poetry, it is usually a dramatic 'I', that is the 'I' is a character in the poem, bearing no different relation to the poet from that of the other characters, or it expresses moral judgments or proper emotions which belong, or should belong, to everybody. Chaucer's use of an 'I' character in his early poems belongs to the tradition of such characters in dream visions, but, with an ingenious variation that the character appears naive, well-meaning, and obtuse, and the joke thus depends on the discrepancy between this figure in the poetry and the poet of wit and intelligence who wrote the whole. Thus this treatment of the 'I' character is new in that it pre-supposes the poet in a way that the other characters do not.

It is well-known that this character re-appears strikingly in the links of the *Canterbury Tales*, when he is rebuked for telling a dull story, but his presence in the *Prologue* has not been particularly stressed, yet it is through this character that both the apparently vivid individuality of the pilgrims and the satiric aim are achieved. Though there are various departures from consistency (to be noticed later), it is through the eyes of Chaucer the poet, that the characters in the *Prologue* are chiefly presented. Obviously the choice of detail shows the sharp selectiveness of the satirist, but the friendly enthusiastic, unsophisticated, unjudging tone is that of Chaucer the pilgrim.

From this invention there result two important advantages. Firstly by his fiction of having been a close companion of his characters, Chaucer suggests their reality and individuality, an individuality which is largely an illusion brought about by poetic skill. Chaucer makes us feel that we know them as individuals, though often, apart from physical description, they are simply representative portraits of various groups in society – friars, monks, summoners, nuns, etc. The same details of their tastes and behaviour can be found in any Medieval moral denunciation [public condemnation] of these people. Secondly, in his satiric character-sketches, Chaucer achieves a twofold irony. He implies that most of the information which he gives us derives, not from a narrative-writer's omniscience, but from the characters' own conversation. In other words Chaucer unobtrusively uses a pointed satirical method, by which the characters are shown to have erred so far from the true moral order, that they are not ashamed to talk naturally and with self-satisfaction about their own inversion of a just and religiously-ordered way of life. At the same time Chaucer makes his response to this that of a man who accepts and repeats with enthusiasm, and without criticism, whatever he is told. It has been observed before how often Chaucer implies or states explicitly that each of his characters is an outstanding person (although a distinction should be made here between the statement when made of a virtuous character, such as the parson, when it comes as the climax of a well-ordered enumeration of his virtues, and when it appears as a random remark in the sketches of the satirised characters). This has been explained as part of Chaucer's genial enthusiastic appreciation of all kinds of people or, in a manner less wildly wrong, as part of a literary convention of magnifying each character (Kemp Malone, *Chapters on Chaucer*, p. 167). But it is surely Chaucer the easily-impressed pilgrim who so indiscriminately praises the characters, sharing with them through an obtuse innocence the immoral premises from which they speak.

Chaucer the poet, for instance, must have shared the common knowledge and opinion in the late 14th century, that the friars, instead of serving all classes of men differently, though with a special tenderness for the poor who reflected the poverty of Christ, instead chiefly sought out the rich and those from whom they could make profit, and took the opportunity given by the privacy of the personal interview and confession for exploitation and unchastity. All this Chaucer could not have failed to have known to be an abuse, evil and widespread, of what had originally been a holy and noble conception. But Chaucer the character relates these details of his fellow pilgrims as though they were both inoffensive and idiosyncratic, and in this way both the satiric point and the illusion of individuality are achieved. Similarly it was a common accusation that daughters of aristocratic households, who entered a convent, often did not discard their former manners and affectations. Genteel table-manners, careful attention to dress, and a narrowly sentimental affection for pet-animals, might possibly in a noble household appear signs of a refined sensibility, but in a convent their worldliness would be plain. But of the distinction between the lady of the house and a nun Chaucer the pilgrim is ignorant, so he records all the details sweetly, as though they were no matter here for blame.

The clearest example, however, of this method is the account of the monk. Just as in the description of the friar Chaucer shows clearly by a sudden change to colloquial rhythms that he is ostensibly repeating the friar's own arguments for not caring for the poor, 'It is nat honest; it may nat avaunce . . . ' [l. 246], so in the account of the monk Chaucer repeats the monk's arguments, and then even adds a reply, 'And I seyde his opinion was good' [l. 183], supporting this by two foolish rhetorical questions and a blustering retort 'Lat Austyn have his swynk to hym reserved' [l. 188]. That Chaucer the poet would reject

THE GENERAL PROLOGUE

the authority of St. Augustine is as manifestly untrue as that he had not the skill to tell an entertaining story. His protested sympathy with the monk is of the same kind as Juvenal's [the Roman poet famous for his *Satires*] stated agreement ('you have just cause for bitterness') with the utterly debased and contemptible Naevolus in the ninth satire. To suppose that Chaucer's attitude here is ambivalent is to be deceived by the sweet blandness of Chaucer's mask, just as to search for historical prototypes of the characters is to be deceived by the brilliant accuracy of Chaucer's sleight of hand, whereby he suggests an individuality which is not there.

Amongst many other examples of the simplicity of Chaucer the pilgrim may be noticed the frequent device of giving a false explanation of a statement – the physician loved gold because it was of use in medicine – and the making of absurd judgments: the remark that the wives of the guildsmen would be to blame if they did not support and approve their husbands in their smug prosperity, or the query of whether it was not 'by a full fair grace' that the maunciple was able to cheat and outwit his learned employers. It is in passages such as the latter that the ironic tone of Chaucer the satirist can be most clearly heard behind the blank wall of obtuseness of Chaucer the pilgrim. Illustrations of the naivete of Chaucer the character could be multiplied to the point of tediousness, and so too there could be laboured at length the demonstration that the substance of the description of each character consists solely of common Medieval observation about the group to which he belongs. It should be added, however, that the appearance of individuality is not achieved by the intimate tone of Chaucer the character alone: at least equally important is the style. The neat grace of Chaucer's lines often deceptively suggests that he has made a sharp and lucid observation, when in fact it is but a commonplace, and the precision lies, not in its thought, but in the style. Thus his method of pretending that the generalisation about a group is the idiosyncracy of an individual is given persuasive force by his exact use of words and the shapeliness of his couplets . . .

The question to what extent we are aware of Chaucer the poet in the *Prologue* is not easy to determine. Sometimes an example of obtrusive poetic skill draws attention to him: it is Chaucer the pilgrim who observes mildly of the unhealthy sore on the cook's leg that it was a pity, but the placing of this one line in the middle of the account of the fine dishes made by the cook exceeds the licence of poetic cleverness which may by convention be allowed to a dull character in poetry. Similarly the image which implies censure or ridicule is self-evidently the satirist's: the monk's bridle jingling like a chapel bell, the squire's coat so embroidered with flowers that it was like a meadow, the snow-storm of food and drink in the franklin's house, the fiery-red cherubym's face of the summoner, all undisguisedly spring from the imagination of a satiric poet. Occasionally Chaucer even speaks outright in his own voice, making a pointed exposure of affection or self-deception, which is in a quite different style of satire, and provides an exception to the general truth that the characters are not the result of actual observation. A well-known example is the comment about the lawyer:

> Nowhere so bisy a man as he ther nas,
> And yet he semed bisier than he was. [ll. 321–2]

... At first sight Chaucer seems to be an exception to the general rule of the classical period and 18th century that the satirist is to be feared. His disguise of Chaucer the pilgrim and elsewhere a sustained friendliness and moderation of tone imply that no man could be less alarming to those who knew him. But, whilst undoubtedly he was less to be feared in that he did not make individual contemporaries the objects of his satire ... yet only people free from all excesses of emotion and affectation could be sure that they would not be the source of some detail shrewdly observed in Chaucer's work.

Chaucer also speaks in his own voice in his occasional denunciation of evil in the descriptions of the Miller and the pardoner, and, most effectively in his descriptions of the virtuous characters, one drawn from each order of society with the addition of the Clerk. In these Chaucer establishes the true moral standard by which the topsy-turvyness of the rest may be measured. It was a tradition of satire to provide an ideal standard: some earlier Medieval Latin satirists made use of the classical fable of the Golden Age, identifying it uneasily with the Garden of Eden: an example is the famous *de Contemptu Mundi* of Bernard of Cluny; Langland in a more complex and magnificent scheme [in *Piers Plowman*] makes his standard the pure charity of the redemption of man by Christ. But Chaucer, lacking Langland's sublimity of imagination, but with a shrewd, clear thoughtfulness, gives a positive analysis of representative types of a well-ordered society, religious and secular. The detailed justice of these descriptions prevents the actual satire from seeming too mild or perhaps too pessimistic. Without them Chaucer's satire might seem to have too much detachment, too much ironic acquiescence. In Langland's angry denunciatory satire there is by implication a hope of reform; but in Chaucer's one feels the tone of a man, who, aware of the incongruity between the gravity of the abuse and his own inability to help, is moved to an ironic and superficially good-humoured laughter. The virtuous characters, however, by their very presence imply a censure of the rest, which dispels any impression of over-sophisticated aloofness. The idea that

Chaucer loved his satirised characters despite or including their faults is of course false, and springs from an imprecise consideration of Chaucer's methods of satire.

...... The fact that it is relevant to ask the question, was Chaucer influenced by classical satirists, is in itself interesting, and throws light on Chaucer's distinctiveness. Though it cannot be answered definitely, his indebtedness to classical writers in general is indisputable, and is most interestingly noticeable in the fact that he thought of himself as a poet in a way that earlier Medieval writers seem not to have done. He is the first English medieval poet explicitly to accept the permanent value of his work, and hence to care about the unsettled state of the language and its dialectal variety, the first to see himself as of the same kind as the classical poets. The writers of medieval lyrics, romances, plays, etc., almost certainly had a workaday conception of themselves, and did not think of a poet as a man of particular perception and judgment, but as a man who wrote verse in a craftsmanlike way for specific use. But Chaucer sees himself as a poet in the classical tradition, and it is for this reason that, despite the fact that the substance of his satiric portraits are medieval commonplaces, and despite his usual disguise of Chaucer the pilgrim, behind this disguise, and sometimes heard openly, is the truly personal tone of the satirist, which is quite un-medieval.[13] □

Woolf's reading of 'the disguise of Chaucer the pilgrim' and how it disarms 'the objects of his [Chaucer's] satire' discards older notions of a thoroughly benign Chaucerian narrator and is, therefore, a good example of the way approaches to *The General Prologue* had begun to change in the 1950s. The causes of the continuing shift in critical tone which occurred in the 1960s were, in turn, expertly diagnosed by Charles A. Owen, Jr. in his *Discussions of the Canterbury Tales* of 1961. Owen also acknowledges here the debt contemporary Chaucer critics owed to the scholars of the past:

■ Though the poet speaks to us directly of his own experience, his directness and the general ease of his manner are the opposite of simple artlessness. Chaucer attained to them fully only in his old age and in the maturity of his art. But the simplicity with which he speaks in the *Canterbury Tales* helps to explain the many generations who misconceived what they read, who thought of Chaucer as an untutored genius speaking to an uncouth age. We know now, thanks to the efforts of scholars over the past hundred years, how false an image that was. We know the extent of his borrowing, of his dependence on other books, in what seemed most direct. We have a reasonably accurate text to read and some knowledge of fourteenth-century pronunciation; hence we are more aware of his skill as a metrist. We have a firmer knowledge of the chronology of his works and can see the extent to which the simplicity and directness rest on a long training in his art as well as on native genius. But we are only beginning to carry on the kind of critical discussion of the *Canterbury Tales* that since Dryden we have conducted of *Hamlet*.[14] ☐

This accumulative awareness of Chaucer's 'long training in his art' began to play a part in the criticism of the 1960s and was evidenced, for example, in the keen interest displayed in uncovering the structural and aesthetic principles underlying *The General Prologue*. The work of two critics, J. V. Cunningham and Robert M. Jordan, is of particular relevance here. Cunningham, in *Tradition and Poetic Structure: Essays in Literary History and Criticism* (1960), posited the theory that the scheme of *The General Prologue* was not unlike that of a dream vision, a type of court poetry extremely popular in Chaucer's day. Here is how Cunningham tries to advance his theory:

■ But if we describe the Canterbury Prologue in terms of the scheme of experience which orders it, in terms of its elements and their succession, we will find a striking similarity to – in fact, an identity with – the scheme of the dream vision. The Prologue can be described accurately enough in this fashion: as a certain time of the year – and the season is then described – the author comes to a place, to the "Tabard" in Southwark. He then meets a company, who are then depicted, one after the other in panel fashion. After a brief digression, one of the company, not described so far (our Host, Harry Bailly), is singled out as a master of ceremonies and proposes the device that orders the remainder of the poem, the telling of tales on the journey.

I shall now describe in the same fashion the opening of the *Romance of the Rose* [a mediaeval French dream vision and major influence on all poetry of this type] . . . The *Romance* begins with some expository remarks on the truth of dreams, illustrated by the dream related in this book whose name is the *Romance of the Rose* and whose subject is an autobiographical account – for everything fell out just as this dream relates – containing the art of love. After a brief prayer and praise of the lady, the dream begins. It is May, and there is an extended description of the season. The author walks out into the fields, crosses a stream, and comes to a garden inclosed by a wall. He then describes, one after the other, a series of allegorical portraits painted on the wall, ten in number. He wants to enter the garden but can find no way in. Walking around the wall, he comes finally to a wicket gate and pounds on it. The porter Idleness opens the door, "whose hair was as yellow of hue as any basin newly scoured," and leads him into the garden, which is described at length. He finds Sir Mirth dancing and singing there in company and depicts the company in a series of set portraits, fifteen in number. He then walks in the garden, followed by the God of Love with his arrows ready. The garden is leisurely described, including the well where Narcissus died, which leads to the interpolated tale of Narcissus. In the well he sees a rose bush full of roses; there is one bud in especial which he has a great longing to pluck. At this point the God of Love, who has been stalking him, looses an arrow, and the author is committed to the sentimental enterprise which directs the remainder of the poem.

These are the elements and their order: after the preliminary matter and the dream, at a given time of year – and there is a description of the season – the author comes to a place where he sees a number of allegorical characters painted on the wall and describes them; a guide then appears and leads him into another place, where he sees a company in action, though the characters are personifications, and describes them in the same manner. There follows a framed tale, and then one of the characters initiates the action which leads to the remainder of the poem. This character is not strictly a master of ceremonies, but he might in another poem and in other hands develop into one. The form is clearly not too unlike the form of the Canterbury Prologue, particularly if we collapse into one movement the two instances of an author's coming to a place and substitute for allegorical characters and personifications realistic portraits of representative members of society.[15] □

Cunningham's thesis is plausible not only on a structural level, but also on a literary-historical one as well. After all, Chaucer himself wrote four dream-poems (*The Book of the Duchess*, *The Parliament of Fowls*, *The House of Fame* and *The Prologue to The Legend of Good Women*), and he and his contemporaries acknowledged a general indebtedness to the *Romance of the Rose*. As a result, criticism of Chaucer's dream-poems often mentions the French poem as a possible source. It was possibly only a matter of time, then, before a critic embarked upon a comparative analysis of the *Romance of the Rose* and *The General Prologue*.

A less pointed and more wide-ranging discussion of the structural scheme of *The General Prologue* is, as alluded to above, that of Robert M. Jordan. In *Chaucer and the Shape of Creation: The Aesthetic Possibilities of Inorganic Structure* (1967), Jordan sets out to explore 'the principles of medieval aesthetic theory and Gothic structure' in *The Canterbury Tales* and argues 'that the basis for a valid unified view of the *Canterbury Tales* is to be found not in the idea of "fusion" but in that of "accommodation"'.[16] In the extract which follows, Jordan explains his theory in more detail and begins by contrasting Chaucer's aesthetics to that of the novelist Henry James (1843–1916). Through this specific comparison he also attempts to identify the difference between mediaeval and modern aesthetic theory:

■ ... From a Gothic viewpoint the *Tales* can be understood both as a pilgrimage (literal and spiritual) *and* a compound of tales. The mode of relationship between whole and parts can be one which does not at any time rob the parts of integrity and completeness within their own formal outlines. Nor need the part, in its wholeness and complexity, detract from the integrity of the whole. In order thus to have it both ways, Chaucer's art must pay a price, or so it may seem to the modern reader; the price is hard outlines, imperfect resolutions, exposed seams, contradictory viewpoints – in short, conspicuous absence of the primary attributes of post-Jamesian fiction.

I think the most fundamental of these distinctions between Chaucerian and Jamesian canons of literary art concerns attitude towards fictional allusion. There is ample evidence to indicate that Chaucer was thoroughly indifferent toward a quality which modern theory has conditioned us to regard as indispensable to good fiction, namely, consistent, unbroken illusion. In fact ... illusion-breaking is as essential to Chaucer's artistry as illusion-making. It is in this context that I wish to re-examine the "roadside drama" theory.[17] Since that concept of the *Tales* posits a consistent dramatic illusion, it provides a convenient measure of Chaucer's departures from his assumed practice.

Efforts to show how consistently "in character" are the actions, expostulations, and narrations of the pilgrims are based upon the assumption that Chaucer is projecting an illusion unified in fictionalized time and space. The fact that some of the pilgrims, notably the Pardoner and the Wife of Bath, talk a good deal about themselves and are therefore "characterized" by what they say adds support to the "dramatic" view. The logic of this concept has created an attractive image of the poem as 'an organic whole, and that whole ... essentially dramatic.' [J.L. Lowes, *Geoffrey Chaucer*, p. 164] To the focal point of the Canterbury road on an April evening all persons and events are supposed to be referable; and, more important, incidents and speeches are supposed to characterize the pilgrims and thereby substantiate meaningful dramatic action. The General Prologue in many ways encourages these assumptions, but a close look at what goes on in some prominent passages ... will indicate that Chaucer's sense of illusion is more flexible – not to say inconsistent – than the dramatic theory would allow.

The realistic allusion of the Canterbury road in April is supported by a passage near the end of the General Prologue in which Chaucer appears to be moving out of fiction altogether and into journalism:

> But first I pray yow, of youre curteisye,
> That ye n'arette it nat my vileynye,
> Thogh that I pleynly speke in this mateere,
> To telle yow hir wordes and hir cheere,
> Ne thogh I speke hir wordes proprely.
> For this ye knowen al so wel as I:
> Whoso shal telle a tale after a man,
> He moot reherce as ny as evere he kan
> Everich a word, if it be in his charge,
> Al speke he never so rudeliche and large,
> Or ellis he moot telle his tale untrewe,
> Or feyne thyng, or fynde wordes newe. (ll. 725–36)

It has been evident from the very beginning of the narrative that the role of objective witness is being assumed by the poet, and therefore, strictly speaking, the present passage is totally superfluous according to the requirements of illusion. Here Chaucer deliberately raises the issue of "truth" by insisting so strongly and so unnecessarily upon the authenticity of his report. The effect is, of course, calculated, and here as in innumerable other instances we recognize the presence of the poet behind the reporter. The humor of the passage arises from the play of these two viewpoints, since the excess of the reporter's earnestness in expounding the obvious is apparent only from the more knowing viewpoint of the poet, the latter, "superior" viewpoint being the one which governs the passage. The reader's imaginative experience is complicated and active, almost violent, for it consists not only of being absorbed in the immediate surface that is the reporter's perspective, but also an abrupt disillusionment and ultimate transference of imaginative focus to the poet's perspective, that of better sense, finer discrimination, and fuller awareness of propriety. At places like this the poem in a sense divides.[18] ☐

Jordan's account once again promotes the image of doubleness in *The General Prologue*. A divided poem, two Chaucers. This view of the narrator(s) is, of course, indebted to E.T. Donaldson's 'Chaucer the Pilgrim' of 1954 (see above). Indeed, Jordan himself speaks a little later of how Donaldson had 'differentiated between the undramatized "invisible" poet, standing outside the fiction, and the concrete pilgrim-reporter projected into it'.[19] Jordan also provides an overview of critical responses to this issue, responses which have, in the main, already been presented in this Guide.

By way of introduction to the final extract to be given in this chapter, we must turn the clock back to 1963, the year in which D.W. Robertson's acclaimed *A Preface to Chaucer: Studies in Medieval Perspectives* was

## 'SO AS IT SEMED ME': THE 1950s AND 1960s

published. Like Jordan four years after him, Robertson was interested in advancing the understanding of mediaeval aesthetic principles, but he concentrated largely on the influence of iconography, the study of representative art, on Chaucer's poetry. In his absorbing examination of the visual inspirations of the poet's work, Robertson argues that 'iconographic descriptions made up of elements to which conventionally established areas of meaning were attached are frequent not only in [Chaucer's] formal allegories but also in *The Canterbury Tales*'.[20] He provides a copious supply of illustrations to substantiate his claims. In the extract that follows, he posits that a social critique lurks behind the iconography of the Miller:

■ ... ... In *The Canterbury Tales* it will suffice to mention the temples of Mars, Venus, and Diana in the Knight's Tale, and the garden of the Merchant's Tale, which is clearly a variant of the Garden of Deduit in the *Roman de la rose*. But even more significant than the appearance of these formally iconographic descriptions ... is Chaucer's tendency to mingle details of an iconographic nature with other details which produce an effect of considerable verisimilitude. We may compare this technique stylistically with that of the marginalia in fourteenth-century manuscripts, where conventional themes from earlier Gothic art are included in representations which seem on the surface to be more than reflections, sometimes a little fantastic, of "daily life." At the same time, new iconographic motifs appear which are either elaborations of old ones, or details whose meanings are supplied by the contexts in which they appear.

This technique is especially evident in the General Prologue to *The Canterbury Tales*. A few examples will suffice to demonstrate its importance. The miller, who leads the pilgrims out of town, is the very picture of *discordia* [discord]:

> Ful byg he was of brawn, and eek of bones.
> That proved wel, for over al ther he cam,
> At wrastlynge he wolde have alwey the ram. [ll. 546–8]

The wrestlers who appear on roof bosses, medallions, in the margins of manuscripts and elsewhere ... were sufficiently commonplace so that few in Chaucer's audience would have been likely to miss the suggestion. Alone it might mean very little, but it is reinforced by the exaggerated coarseness of the miller's features, which, as others have pointed out, suggest gluttony and lechery as well as contentiousness ... The miller proudly carries a "swerd and a bokeler," [l. 558] and is a "janglere" [l. 560] and a thief. As if these things were not enough, "A baggepipe koude he blowe and sowne," [l. 565] the instrument so frequently set in contrast with the *concordia* of the New Song in marginal illustration.[21] It is appropriate that this character should thrust himself forward out of order at the conclusion of the Knight's Tale, offer to "quit" the knight, stir up a quarrel with the reeve, and tell a tale whose high point is the "revel and the melodye" of the flesh. If the pilgrimage to Canterbury is a reflection of the manner in which the pilgrimage of life was generally carried out in Chaucer's England, the fact that it follows a drunken wrestler out of town to the tune of a bagpipe is an amusing if slightly bitter comment on contemporary society – a society which, Chaucer must have felt, was far from the amiable concord it should have developed in imitation of "Jerusalem celestial." The reality which underlies the description of the miller is not the reality of an individual, nor even that of a type; it is the harsh reality of discord nourished on gluttony, vainglory, and avarice as seen in one segment of fourteenth-century life. That the manifestation is convincing on the surface is a tribute to Chaucer's artistry, but the fact that the picture as a whole is a combination of convincing detail and conventional iconographic motifs is an indication that Chaucer was above all an artist of his own place and time.[22] □

Robertson next treats us to an iconographic analysis of the Prioress (*GP*, ll. 118–62), seeing in this figure, as with that of the Miller, much potential for irony and social critique. 'Are her manners "seemly" for a prioress?' Robertson queries before going on to answer his own question: 'They are taken directly from the cynical, worldly-wise instructions of La Vieille in the *Roman de la rose*. Far from being the manners of a great lady, who would doubtless have shown small concern for such trivial matters, or the manners of a prioress, who should have had her heart on the food of the spirit rather than on the ostentatiously "correct" consumption of the food of the flesh, they are the manners of the social climber who wishes to form a reputation for being ladylike.'[23] Robertson's work, like much of that discussed in this chapter of this Guide, demonstrates that in the diverse world of *The General Prologue* things are seldom as they seem. Similarly innovative approaches to the poem continued to appear in the 1970s, as the next chapter will demonstrate.

# CHAPTER FOUR

# 'Th'estaat, th'array, the Nombre, and eek the Cause': The 1970s

CRITICS CONTINUED to brush through *The General Prologue* with fine-tooth combs during the 1970s. If anything, the teeth got even finer as the criticism became more diverse, and more hairs were consequently split. As a reflection of the *zeitgeist* (or 'spirit of the times') of the Age of Aquarius, we find the appearance of such titles as William Spencer's 'Are Chaucer's Pilgrims Keyed to the Zodiac?' (1970).[1] Equally characteristic of the decade is the interest in sociology, a subject which came into its own at this time, demonstrated in R.T. Lenaghan's article 'Chaucer's *General Prologue* as History and Literature', again from 1970.[2] Lenaghan begins with the question 'Is Chaucer's fictional society sufficiently coherent to warrant taking it seriously as fourteenth-century sociology?' and gives an immediate, if only partial, answer: 'To put it rather grandly, Chaucer's imitation has the same general ontological status as the sociologist's model; both are representative fictions.'[3] The article then focuses on the role labour and money play in forging the social identities of the pilgrims:

■ . . . The basic fact of life in the society of the *General Prologue* is economic struggle. The pilgrims' occupational labels are obvious keys to their individual struggles or exemption from struggle and thus to their social position . . . Pilgrims are what they do, and what most of them primarily do is work. They work competitively within the rules like the Man of Law or outside them like the Pardoner. This stress on hustle and competition creates a society quite different from that implicit in the pattern of the three estates with its stress on complementary self-subordination in a system of cooperation.

 . . . . . . Chaucer seems to hold with Fitzgerald against Hemingway; the rich, at least the landed rich, are different from the rest.[4] □

## THE GENERAL PROLOGUE

Lenaghan's essentially Marxist critique leads him to observe that 'social conservatism [is] evident in Chaucer's narrative' and that this can ' . . . be referred to the poet' and his own social status as a 'civil servant'.[5] Attention is also drawn to the significant fact that 'Chaucer the pilgrim failed to provide for himself what he gave for all the other pilgrims – an occupational designation'.[6] Lenaghan's overall conclusions are, however, as already partially seen in chapter three of this Guide, influenced by E. T. Donaldson's seminal 'Chaucer the Pilgrim' (see chapter two of this Guide):

■ [*The General Prologue*] is a credible fourteenth-century model of the middle range of English society; it sets questions for historical verification.
  The major literary use of this model is to fill out or elaborate a connection between Chaucer the man and Chaucer the pilgrim-narrator . . .
  . . . Chaucer has been well served by Professor Donaldson, who has nicely described the narrative sympathies and ironies of the *General Prologue* in such a way as to clarify the fine combination of amiability and criticism that emanates from the narrator. The structure and descriptions of the *General Prologue* define the narrator's position; he is different but central.[7] □

Whilst Lenaghan refers back to the earlier criticism of Donaldson he also, in his consideration of the three estates, provides a neat bridge to one of the most important pieces of Chaucer criticism of the 1970s – Jill Mann's *Chaucer and Medieval Estates Satire: The Literature of Social Classes and the General Prologue to the Canterbury Tales* of 1973. Just as generations of post-1954 scholars acknowledged the importance of Donaldson's article, so those writing after 1973 claimed Mann's book as a major influence. There were also those like H. Marshall Leicester, Jr., who simultaneously expressed a debt to both: in the conclusion to his *The Disenchanted Self: Representing the Subject in the Canterbury Tales* (1990) he writes:

■ What seem to me the two best treatments of the *General Prologue*, E. Talbot Donaldson's "Chaucer the Pilgrim" and Jill Mann's *Chaucer and Medieval Estates Satire*, between them outline the general structure of Chaucerian practice in the Canterbury Tales, the telling of tales as the interaction between a subject and an institution. Donaldson, of course, concentrated on the subject side of the interaction in his influential characterization of the naive narrator of the *General Prologue* and the links, who so often misses the point of the complex phenomena he describes in order that Chaucer the satirist or the poet or the man can make sure that we see how complex they are. Donaldson was the first to call attention to the issue of voicing in the prologue and the first to

## 'TH'ESTAAT, TH'ARRAY, THE NOMBRE, AND EEK THE CAUSE': THE 1970s

apply to the poem the dramatic method that had previously been used only on the tales.

By contrast, Mann firmly established for the first time the genre of the *General Prologue* by demonstrating that the poem is an estates satire, one of a class of medieval treatments of the orders, or estates, of society. These works generally list the various members of society according to the traditional scheme of the estates and comment on their abuses – themselves stereotyped. Though she notes that Chaucer shows a freedom typical of him in the selection of the particular estates he presents, Mann proves that he "does cover the elements of social anatomisation made familiar by estates literature" as a means "to suggest society as a whole by way of [a] representative company of individuals" (*Medieval Estates Satire*, 4, 5). The traditional classification provides Chaucer with a conceptual framework shared with his audience (what I . . . [call] an institution) for organizing his observations of individuals in society, an underlying structure of common assumptions about what society is and the way it is put together.[8] ▫

As Leicester establishes, Mann argues for viewing *The General Prologue* as 'an example of a neglected medieval genre – that both its form and its content proclaim it to be part of the literature dealing with the "estates" of society'.[9] She then provides further elaboration of this point:

■ . . . . . . This claim needs special justification, since it is usually assumed that the Prologue has no source and only shadowy analogues, an assumption which probably arises from an over-limited conception of its basic form as 'a collection of portraits'. This aspect of the *Prologue* clearly cannot be ignored . . . But the *Prologue*'s form can equally well be defined as 'a satiric representation of all classes of society' – the form of an estates satire. This aspect of the *Prologue* has not escaped notice, but its recognition has never instigated close and thorough investigation of estates satire in relation to Chaucer's work. When estates satire has been used, it has been as supplementary evidence in a historically-oriented examination of fourteenth-century society. That is, the relationship between Chaucer and other estates satirists has most often been taken to be their common source of material in life itself.[10] ▫

In Mann's judgement, 'the real-life basis of the *Prologue* was propounded most strongly in J.M. Manly's influential book, *Some New Light on Chaucer* [1926]'.[11] After providing a summary of Manly's approach, Mann continues:

■ The meanings of the word 'estate' which concern us are thus defined by the *Middle English Dictionary*: 'A class or persons, especially a social or political class or group; also a member of a particular class or rank', and 'A person's position in society . . . [Mann's ellipsis] social class'. To these definitions I think it necessary to add a particular reference to the role played by a person's work in determining the estate to which he belongs. It is true that the estates included in estates literature are not classified only in terms of what we would now recognise as their occupation; they can, for example, be distinguished according to clerical or marital status. But clerical and marital status inevitably include some notion of the particular duties and temptations of the work that accompanies them.

Estates literature has been defined by Ruth Mohl, who has written the only book entirely devoted to the genre, in terms of four characteristics. First, an enumeration of the 'estates' or social and occupational classes, whose aim seems to be completeness. Secondly, a lament over the shortcomings of the estates; each fails in its duty to the rest. Thirdly, the philosophy of the divine ordination of the three principal estates, the dependence of the state on all three, and the necessity of being content with one's station. And last, an attempt to find remedies, religious or political, for the defects of the estates. However, these characteristics are by no means to be found in every piece of estates writing, and estates material is clearly recognisable in works not strictly belonging to the genre, such as *Piers Plowman*. My working definition of estates satire is therefore less rigid; it comprises any literary treatments of social classes which allow or encourage a generalised application.[12] □

Mann next focuses her attention squarely on *The General Prologue*:

■ . . . For one important purpose, however, it is necessary to distinguish works which have an estates form from those which simply contain estates material. For the form of the estates genre and the form of the Prologue are one and the same. The framework of the *Prologue* is a list of estates. Chaucer specifically says at the end of the *Prologue* that he has described the 'estaat' of all the pilgrims [l. 716]. The *Prologue* is also a collection of portraits, but this is a secondary consideration: if we had been presented with portraits of the Seven Deadly Sins, for example, we should quickly have recognised that the portrait series was merely a vehicle, while the conceptual framework belonged to the Sins tradition.

It is important to stress this relationship between the form of the *Prologue* and estates literature because of the assumption . . . that society itself, rather than a literary genre, would have been Chaucer's model. This assumption applies both to the question of the comprehensiveness of the *Prologue*, and to the order in which the characters

## 'TH'ESTAAT, TH'ARRAY, THE NOMBRE, AND EEK THE CAUSE': THE 1970s

are placed. On the first point, Manly, for example, questioned 'whether Chaucer really intended to present an exhaustive survey of fourteenth century society', because of his apparently arbitrary inclusion or omission of certain social classes (*New Light*, pp. 71–2). The assumption that the *Prologue* must be matched with fourteenth-century society if the pilgrims are to be taken as representative figures has characterised both the critics who think they are representative, and those who think they are not. Thus J. R. Hulbert, who thought that they were, commented, 'No one ever supposed it chance that there are *one* knight, *one* monk, etc.', but concluded from this that the *Prologue* was a 'conspectus of medieval English society'.[13] Manly's criticism of this kind of comment was surely right, for there are many aspects of fourteenth-century society which the *Prologue* does not cover. But it does cover the elements of social anatomisation made familiar by estates literature. Thus Bronson remarked on the 'relative scarcity of women in the company', and attributed this to the fact that their presence on the pilgrimage was 'realistically' unlikely.[14] It can equally well be attributed to the fact that estates literature rarely listed more than two estates of women – religious and secular.

 . . . . . . It can only have been with the aim of providing a full version of an estates list that Chaucer chose to introduce as many as thirty pilgrims in the *Prologue*. Thirty is an unwieldy number for description (and Chaucer evades describing all of them), for dramatic interplay, or for tale-telling – is there any other collection of tales with so large a number of narrators? Chaucer was concerned to impose an estates form on the *Prologue* in order to suggest society as a whole by way of his representative company of individuals – rather than to use estates material in the same incidental fashion as that which he may have culled from physiognomies, allegorisations of the sins, romances and so on. To adapt a phrase of [Charles] Muscatine's to a different purpose, the estates framework provides a 'formal, *a priori* ideal ordering of experience, without which the naturalistic detail would have only the barest sociological significance'.[15]

On the second question, that of the order in which the estates are presented, two misconceptions seem to prevail. The first is that estates literature always proceeds, in an orderly way, from the top to the bottom of the social scale, in contrast to the fairly haphazard method of the *Prologue*. Support for this view has been found in Chaucer's apparent admission, at the end of the *Prologue*, that he is unusual in ignoring social ranking:

> Also I prey yow to foryeve it me,
> Al have I nat set folk in hir degree
> Heere in this tale, as that they sholde stonde. [ll. 743–5]

THE GENERAL PROLOGUE

This may indeed mean that he is thinking of the more tightly-organised works of estates literature, and pointing out the vagaries of his own scheme. But tight organisation is not a *sine qua non* of an estates work . . . and Chaucer's apology cannot therefore be read as a statement that he is writing something else.

The second misconception is about the exact nature of the order which is being neglected in the *Prologue*. Modern writers have tended to assume that medieval perceptions of the class-hierarchy were the same as our own. [J.S.P.] Tatlock, for example, found the characters mostly middle-class: 'none is beneath the rather prosperous Plowman.'[16] On these grounds it is usually assumed, for example, that it is correct for Chaucer to begin with the Knight, that the Prioress is of high status, and that the Wife of Bath is middle-class. The estates lists show that it would be more 'correct' for the clerical figures to precede the Knight, and that despite the high rank achieved by some women, their estate is placed lower in the list than *all* those of men. The estates framework is more concerned to distinguish 'qualitatively', to separate clergy from laity, men from women, than to arrange an exact hierarchy of rank cutting across these divisions. The estates habit of distinguishing by function rather than by rank determines, for example, the treatment of women according to their material, rather than their social status, the undifferentiated treatment of *burgenses*, and the presentation of the lowest ranks of the clergy before the secular emperor. Clearly this literary order did not reflect the actual status of each class in society, and it is possible that social actualities affected the order which Chaucer developed for the *Prologue*. But if we say that the *Prologue* neglects a proper order, we must make clear whether we mean a literary order, or actual social ranking. And we must provide empirical evidence for the way in which both were perceived in the fourteenth century.

As for Chaucer's apology for not setting his figures 'in hir degree' [l. 744], it may just as well refer to a literary as to a social order, since it occurs at the end of a discussion of literary propriety. He apologises for the apparent lack of literary decorum that he is about to demonstrate in reporting the ribald tales of some pilgrims, and defends himself with a literary principle: 'The wordes moote be cosyn to the dede' [l. 742]. He continues this line of thought – '*Also* I prey yow to foryeve it me' [l. 743] – with an apology for another apparent violation of literary decorum; he has not proceeded in the 'right' order. The literary context of this apology strongly encourages the belief that the standard of correctness to which Chaucer is referring is provided by estates literature. Chaucer is consciously producing an example of this genre, and just as consciously refusing to adhere to the one principle of order that usually characterises it, the separate treatment of the clergy and the laity.

## 'TH'ESTAAT, TH'ARRAY, THE NOMBRE, AND EEK THE CAUSE': THE 1970s

Chaucer's reasons for imitating the least regular, rather than the most regular estates pieces are not immediately obvious; the attempts that have been made to find conceptual schemes in the order of the portraits are forced, and depend on the development of external concepts as the 'key' to each portrait. The likelihood that an order which is haphazard and casual as far as significance is concerned is operating, is surely strengthened by the fact that exactly this casualness of procedure operates within the portraits. They have indeed been praised for the 'lack of regular order' which was 'deliberately planned to produce the effect of spontaneity that creates a sense of intimate acquaintance with each pilgrim'.[17] Just as the haphazard order *within* the portraits does not prevent us from recognising the form of the *descriptio*, so the vagaries on a larger scale are not sufficient to destroy the recognisable estates form of the *Prologue*.

However, if we cannot find an abstract significance determining a particular order in the *Prologue* portraits, perhaps there is an abstract significance in their disorder. The strict order of estates literature is governed by the notion of function, of hierarchy in a model whose working is divinely established. It is precisely this notion of function that . . . Chaucer discards. He shows us a world in which our view of hierarchy depends on our own position in the world, not on an absolute standpoint. For some the Knight is at the apex of 'respectability' (in both its modern and etymological sense), for some the Ploughman, for others the 'gentil' Pardoner. More than once, Chaucer uses the estates concept against itself: the notion of specialised duties, when taken to its limit, destroys the idea of a total society in which all have their allotted place and relation to each other. Chaucer's use of the estates form, that is to say, is not the traditional one of criticising (even in a less heavy-handed, more amusing way) the failures of social classes in the light of a social ideal. What exactly happens to the estates form in the *Prologue* is a subject that will occupy us to the end of the book.[18] □

Aside from exploring what 'happens to the estates form' once Chaucer has got hold of it, Mann also pauses to consider the uses to which estates literature might be put. She identifies three possibilities in relation to *The General Prologue*:

■ 1. As a possible source of a direct kind for the form, the content, and the satiric techniques of the *Prologue*. Chaucer's use of such sources can be detected through similarities in language and technique.

2. As evidence for the medieval tradition of stereotypes for those estates that are featured in the *Prologue*. Because these stereotypes could have been conveyed to Chaucer by informal means such as

conversation and anecdote as well as through literature, we can, and should, extend our own knowledge of them by using works of which Chaucer was ignorant, but which illustrate commonplace notions. And on the same principle, we can also glean evidence of commonplaces from literary sources other than estates works.

3. As evidence of the kind of conceptual frameworks within which Chaucer would have organised his observation of individuals he knew, if or when he was drawing a portrait from life. The third approach is less important here, since it seems clear that the 'estates' features of the Canterbury pilgrims are not just the result of frameworks within which Chaucer observed individuals belonging to certain social groups, but were deliberately used by Chaucer for the basis of his portraits.

The reason for thinking this is the large proportion of the *Prologue* devoted to the details of the pilgrims' occupations, which can have no other function than to ensure our sense of the estate.[19] ☐

The true importance of this last point is made clear in Mann's concluding comments to her work:

■ The *Prologue* presents the world in terms of worldly values, which are largely concerned with an assessment of façades, made in the light of half-knowledge, and on the basis of subjective criteria. Subjectivity characterises both the pilgrims' attitude to the world, and the world's (or the reader's) attitude to the pilgrims. But at least in their case, it must be repeated that their views on the world are not individual ones, but are attached to their callings – in medieval terms, their estates. The *Prologue* proves to be a poem about work. The society it evokes is not a collection of individuals or types with an eternal or universal significance, but particularly a society in which work as a social experience conditions personality and the standpoint from which an individual views the world. In the *Prologue*, as in history, it is specialised work which ushers in a world where relativised values and the individual consciousness are dominant.[20] ☐

In her final remarks, Mann presents an implicit challenge to those critics who, mesmerised by the so-called individuality of the Canterbury pilgrims and their narrator, have set out to uproot Chaucer from his contemporary context. As previous chapters have shown, such critics make impassioned arguments for his modernity. Mann, conversely, in identifying the possible wellspring of this 'individuality', traces it to decidedly mediaeval perceptions of community and work. Her comments about subjectivity are also interesting in light of the fact that subjectivity was to become another favourite topic of Chaucer scholars.

## 'TH'ESTAAT, TH'ARRAY, THE NOMBRE, AND EEK THE CAUSE': THE 1970s

A good illustration of this is found in John Norton-Smith's book *Geoffrey Chaucer*, which appeared in 1974, the year after *Chaucer and Medieval Estates Satire*. In his chapter on *The Canterbury Tales*, Norton-Smith discourses on the narrative structure of the poem and the nature of its narrator ('[he] is not an authoritative guide'[21]) before offering his thoughts on the continuing experience versus authority debate which runs through it: 'The subjectivization of "authority" is obvious from the initial satiric technique of the *General Prologue*. Every man becomes his own authority, "experience" appears to have become the queen of the proofs of truth.'[22]

It is necessary to wait until 1991 and the publication of Lee Patterson's *Chaucer and the Subject of History*, however, for the most comprehensive treatment of this issue. Though this work will be discussed in chapter six of this Guide, one comment by Patterson is of particular relevance here. In his Introduction, he states that 'part of the argument of [his] book' involves 'trying to understand Chaucer's relation to the subject of history – to history as a topic for poetry, as a material and social world of representation, and (to shift the meaning of the word "subject") as the individual person forged in the dialectic between the subjective and the social'.[23] Like Mann before him, Patterson expresses an interest in the 'material and social world'. Writing almost twenty years after her, however, he has access to a theoretical vocabulary only in its infant stages in the 1970s. This shall be explored more fully in the final chapter of this Guide.

In light of previous remarks about Chaucer's modernity, it is not surprising that the 1970s saw an increasing interest in the idea of 'Renaissance Chaucer'. This is exemplified by the publication of such studies as Alice Miskimin's *The Renaissance Chaucer* in 1975, and, three years later, Ann Thompson's *Shakespeare's Chaucer: A Study in Literary Origins* (already discussed in chapter one of this Guide). Miskimin provides 'a broad historical survey of Renaissance readings of Chaucer' and attempts 'to reopen the larger, more philosophical questions of the status of the poet and of his fiction which I think Chaucer himself was the first English poet to raise'.[24] She also makes an intriguing observation about audience reception/perception of *The General Prologue* during the Renaissance:

■ . . . Both Chaucer and, to a lesser extent, Gower, underwent a process of reverse projection and simplification in the course of the evolution of their *Works* in the fifteenth and sixteenth centuries . . . The satire of the *General Prologue* was easily understood, but the *Monk's Tale* was read, not as a further evaluation of the Monk, but as 'Chaucer's' kind of tragedy.[25] □

The very whirligig of time itself, as Miskimin also shows, did much to alter Chaucer's work and its comprehensibility:

■ . . . after 1400, Chaucer's late fourteenth-century world became immediately, then even more distantly, a shadowed past. The deposition of Richard II, virtually coincident with Chaucer's death, was to contemporaries truly an end, and the Lancastrian accession a new order . . . The blur of change – in language as in the image of events – occurs in a single generation.[26] □

Then, after revealing that the 'medieval canon of Chaucer's works' was 34,000 lines while Renaissance Chaucer comprised some 55,000 lines, Miskimin concludes that:

■ . . . the Renaissance re-editing of Chaucer involved two kinds of conflation [fusion]: the evolution of the language and the amplification of the text.[27] □

The work of both Alice Miskimin and Ann Thompson is invaluable to any study of 'Renaissance Chaucer' or, more specifically, 'Shakespeare's Chaucer'. Nevertheless, E. Talbot Donaldson still saw the need for more 'quality' criticism in this area and produced a contribution of his own, *The Swan at the Well: Shakespeare Reading Chaucer*, in 1985. Donaldson, in somewhat disgruntled fashion, declares: 'My essays are the result of my discontent with the shallowness of the majority – though, to be sure, not all – of the comparisons that have been made [between Chaucer and Shakespeare]. Shakespeare himself provides the final indication of the way Shakespeare read Chaucer, and that way is with full appreciation of his complexity.'[28] There is, however, no direct mention of *The General Prologue* in this book, so we must allow Donaldson the last word here.

One of the best treatments of Chaucer's poetic artistry also saw the light of day in the 1970s – Charles A. Owen, Jr.'s *Pilgrimage and Storytelling in the Canterbury Tales* of 1977. In this book, Owen explores many of the themes which have now become familiar in our study of *The General Prologue*: the nature of the pilgrim portraits (Owen's emphasis being 'on character as the ground for action'[29]); the underlying structural principles of the *Prologue* (' . . . the storytelling will supersede pilgrimage in projecting the deepest levels of insight in the poem, just as the enjoyment of fiction will replace didacticism'[30]); and evidence of Chaucerian morality ('He [Chaucer] gives us no easy definition of his own moral position'[31]). The following extract, from chapter three, 'The Meaning of Chaucer's Prologue and its Art', presents Owen's more extended thoughts on the poem. His ultimate argument is that the real meaning of *The Canterbury Tales* is to be found in the pilgrim portraits of *The General Prologue*:

## 'TH'ESTAAT, TH'ARRAY, THE NOMBRE, AND EEK THE CAUSE': THE 1970s

■ The Prologue to the *Canterbury Tales* opens with a description of nature; it proceeds with the perfectly casual concurrence of pilgrims at the Tabard – "Bifil that in that seson on a day" [l. 19] – and then, while the pilgrims sleep and Chaucer has, as he so reasonably puts it, time and space, it plunges into a series of twenty-four portraits. The casual and reasonable quality of the introduction should not conceal from us the presumption of the poet, the challenge he was setting to his skill, and the significance of these portraits for the stories that were to follow. He will tell us, he says,

> al the condicioun
> Of ech of hem, so as it semed me,
> And whiche they weren, and of what degree,
> And eek in what array that they were inne. [ll. 38–41]

This exhaustive program for each of the portraits makes by implication a considerable claim for the poet's observation and insight, relieved by the modesty of the limitation, "so as it semed me," but only superficially. For the phrase keeps before us the fiction of the narrator's presence at the inn and on the pilgrimage. He is telling us what he experienced, what he has learned of the pilgrims by observation and contact. Furthermore, this program implies the detailed and systematic description of each pilgrim . . . . . . Within the portraits themselves, we discover that the modest "so as it semed me" takes precedence over the promise of a complete description for each pilgrim. The poet is at once more ingenious and more skillful than to depend on system to imitate life. What he does finally, in the fiction he has set up, is to rely on his own impressions to determine what he will teach us of each of the pilgrims. The presumption of such a decision is mitigated for us by the mildness and apparent simplicity of Chaucer the pilgrim as he complies, for instance, with the Monk's and the Friar's self-justification, and by the withdrawal from overt criticism of Chaucer the narrator. It is justified by the sharpness of his observation and by the constantly varied strategies he employs to project the observation. The shifting interplay in the portraits between detail and generalization, between the fact and its implications, between the explicit and the omitted, between the naive and the witty, between the ordered and the random, keeps the reader's expectations constantly alert. The several scales of value by which the pilgrims reveal their worth suggest the complex standards of a living society. They include not only the moral, the social, the financial, but also the extent to which each pilgrim emerges as an individual.

The time and space relationships are also complicated. We are simultaneously at the Tabard as Chaucer talks to the Pardoner, on the road to Canterbury as he observes the pilgrims' horses and the relative positions of the Miller and the Reeve in the caravan, and omnipresent as he tells us what only the Merchant knew of his net worth: "Ther wiste no wight that he was in dette" [l. 280]. The final effect of the portraits is paradoxically one of movement, movement not only of the pilgrims but of the observer. Chaucer seems to have realized, in meeting the challenge he had set himself, that life cannot be caught standing still. The fiction that he created of himself as one of the pilgrims, and the fact that it was a fiction, gave him opportunities to move about as he observed now this facet, now that, of the life he was imitating; as he noted down at once the sudden insight rather than wait for its logical place in the portrait and risk losing it entirely.

The long series of portraits provides the key to the meaning of the *Canterbury Tales*. The fact that, coming at the beginning, they are so numerous and loom so large compels attention from the reader. Their impact is given direction, when the series is finished, by what seems another example of the poet's simplicity, his apology for plain speaking:

> But first I pray yow, of youre curteisye,
> That ye n'arette it nat my vileynye,
> Thogh that I pleynly speke in this mateere,
> To telle yow hir wordes and her cheere,
> Ne thogh I speke hir wordes proprely.
> For this ye knowen al so well as I:
> Whoso shal telle a tale after a man,
> He moot reherce as ny as evere he kan
> Everich a word, if it be in his charge,
> Al speke he never so rudeliche and large,
> Or ellis he moot telle his tale untrewe,
> Or feyne thyng, or fynde wordes newe. [ll. 725–36]

While seeming to apologize for the vulgarity of some of his pilgrims, Chaucer is really asserting the autonomy of all of them. They are the basic reality. What the poet is about to write he has simply heard them say. By dissociating himself from any responsibility except to the truth, Chaucer implies an identity for each of his pilgrims capable of being misrepresented; he alerts us to the importance of the smallest details ("everich a word"); he prepares us to accept the stories as utterances of the pilgrims, as further revelations of their characters.

The sense of simultaneous realities – of a poet telling us his experiences, of a group of miscellaneous people on pilgrimage, of the extension of actuality through the inner world of each pilgrim's imagination – does not wait for the stories to impress itself on our awareness. We get it from the portraits. Each of the pilgrims carries

## 'TH'ESTAAT, TH'ARRAY, THE NOMBRE, AND EEK THE CAUSE': THE 1970s

with him his previous experience, his habits, his learning, his knowledge of the world, as well as his clothes and his physical appearance. Chaucer does not hesitate to define his characters in terms of their past, as well as what he could see and hear in the moments of his contact with them. Three things result. First of all, there is a far wider range of possibilities in each portrait and at each moment of each portrait. Secondly, the opportunities of presenting character through specific detail are greatly extended. And finally, the quality of the detail becomes a sign of the direction and a measure of the extent of the pilgrim's vision. What we see is occasionally not the pilgrim at all, but what it has meant most to him to do in his life.[32] ☐

Some forty pages later, Owen continues with his thoughts on Chaucer's grand design for *The General Prologue*:

■ The art of the Prologue makes possible all that follows. It establishes the groundwork of character, the sense of community, the impression of a literal actuality, and the potential of polysemous meaning that the game of storytelling may release. The autonomy of the pilgrims, confirmed by Chaucer's denial of his own responsibility for what they say, was already subtly suggested by their refusal to stand still under his scrutiny. Their movement and his compel an avoidance of system; they stimulate alertness in both the narrator and the reader; they contribute to the lifelikeness of the imitation. That the judgments of the narrator are sometimes outrageous, that at other times the meanings are to be ferreted out from ambiguity or apparent nonsense, draw the reader into the game of evaluation. The pilgrims will tell stories. The Host will judge them. As in the Prologue, this overt judgment will have validity only if it is confirmed by the literal details, the patterns they form, and the meanings the patterns imply. The ultimate values will not be verbally imposed. They will emerge from the interplay and the development of the elements that the Prologue sets in motion. The enjoyment that the narrator so clearly takes in his companions will extend to the stories they tell, and will communicate itself to us as one of the most important implicit values in the story he tells.[33] ☐

In the above extract, we find Owen laying emphasis on 'the game of storytelling' taking place within *The General Prologue* and the narrator's 'enjoyment' of this process. It is useful to pause a moment from our retrospective of seventies' criticism and compare Owen's treatment of these subjects with that produced by Laura Kendrick in 1988. Kendrick, in her book *Chaucerian Play: Comedy and Control in the Canterbury Tales*, offers a commentary steeped in the recognisable language of literary theory. Kendrick announces, in her meta-fictional reading of the poem, that she would 'like to lay bare some of the techniques Chaucer uses in the "General Prologue" to set up his interpretative game to place us at the crossroads of intentions (or associations)'.[34] As can be discerned from the brief extract below, one heavily influenced by anthropological and psycho-analytical thought, much had changed in the world of literary criticism in the eleven years separating Owen's and Kendrick's work:

■ . . . Why does Chaucer's writing move in the direction it does, toward the "comedy" of the *Canterbury Tales*, toward laughter? Is he just being devilish or "elvish" – or are we to perceive humour where we should not – or is it more complicated than that? What are the mechanisms and meanings of medieval mirth, and, more especially, of Chaucer's literary play?

 . . . . . . [Johan] Huizinga in *Homo Ludens* [a study of the play-element in culture]; Clifford Geertz in his study of cockfighting in Bali [*Kinship in Bali*]; Freud in his analysis of little Hans's game of "fort/da", as well as in *Civilization and its Discontents* and other writings; Melanie Klein, Jean Piaget, and other analysts of children's play; Boccaccio, and . . . Chaucer, in the metacommentaries with which they framed their fictions – all understood, albeit in different terms, something of the meaningful *depths* of play and how man's creation and identification with unreal, fictional worlds helps him, not only to cope with the real world, but also to change himself and thereby, to some extent, the world. Play enables man to sublimate and channel his dangerous desires and to master his anxieties as he expresses these or sees them expressed in the safe, ordered "other world" of the game via transforming, controlling fictions comparable to Freud's idea of the dream-work or joke-work or, we might add, to art-work. Virtually all types of play turn life temporarily into art. It is, indeed, not too much to claim, as Huizinga did, that culture arises from play, or that civilization rests on fiction.[35] □

Returning to the 1970s, it can be seen that structural analyses of *The General Prologue* were coming into vogue during this decade: one of the better examples of this approach is found in Loy D. Martin's highly philosophical article 'History and Form in the General Prologue to the *Canterbury Tales*' of 1978. Adding another explanatory piece to the puzzle that is this poem, Martin brings us back to the perennial question of sources through his suggestion that the 'rhetorical catalogue of types . . . [is] the main organizing principle of the General Prologue'.[36] His critique, as our next extract will show, begins with an overview and an interrogation of a piece of criticism already discussed in the previous chapter of this Guide. He then embarks upon a comparative analysis of the organising principles of *The General Prologue* and of one of Chaucer's early dream visions, *The Parlement of Foules*. Martin's key point is that Chaucer, in 'imagining a mode of knowledge or experience which transcends the strict Augustinian dualism of time and eternity',[37] projects a similar, ambiguous vision of time and space in both of these poems:

■ Is the form of the General Prologue to the *Canterbury Tales* new or old? Critical sentiment seems on the whole to favor newness; yet there has always remained a sense of craftsmanship and conventionality about the poem which continually reinvigorates the search for a strong antecedent genre. In recent years, a few attempts have been persuasive, notably J. V. Cunningham's structural analysis of the Prologue as a dream vision [see chapter three of this Guide]. Cunningham begins with the assumption that there *must be* an available generic "tradition" which functions intact to shape a poet's experience into poetry, but even his most convinced reader must wonder why Chaucer's use of that tradition escaped notice until the twentieth century. I think this suggests that Cunningham's ideal notions of tradition and genre cause him to overstate his case, but I also think that there are very good reasons why he perceived such a strong affinity between the Prologue and the form of the dream vision. In order to save his valuable intuition, then, while offering an alternative set of assumptions about genre formation, I should like to turn briefly to an idea offered by Alastair Fowler in an essay called "The Life and Death of Literary Forms" [*New Literary History*, 2 (1971): pp. 199–215].

Fowler notices that genres, after complex developments in time, often do not simply disappear. Rather they break up into what he calls "modes," methods of writing, like satiric language, which are still recognizable but which can no longer account for the formal properties of entire works. This is a very simple and useful observation; it is undoubtedly true. The question that Fowler does not address is whether genres can appear as well as disappear in this way, whether new genres can sometimes be recognized as expansions of previous "modes" as modes can be recognized as diminutions of previous genres. This seems to me likely and provides a framework in which to identify an historical relationship between the form of the General Prologue and a rhetorical device which appears in, but does not generically constitute, the dream vision poems.

The particular stylistic framework I have in mind is the rhetorical catalogue of types, which appears frequently in Chaucer's earlier dream vision poems. It not only appears there, it develops, and my very simple argument here will be that it develops finally into the main organizing principle of the General Prologue. I would begin, therefore, by submitting a catalogue from the *Parlement of Foules*, one which seems merely to list the species of trees that the dreamer sees:

> The byldere ok, and ek the hardy asshe;
> The piler elm, the cofre unto carayne;
> The boxtre pipere, holm to whippes lashe;
> The saylynge fyr; the cipresse, deth to playne;
> The shetere ew; the asp for shaftes pleyne;
> The olyve of pes, and eke the dronke vyne;
> The victor palm, the laurer to devyne [ll. 176-82]

Cataloguing, as Cunningham implies, is central to the dream vision, and even in a simple case like this one, analysis will show us why. Each tree is named by a practical use or a practical problem it presents in the familiar world; they appear in a dream, and what is most important, they appear in a garden which is immediately represented as timeless. Birds sing the eternal harmony of angelic music, there are no fluctuations of hot and cold, men may not "waxe sek ne old" [l. 207], and day never changes into night. Change, in other words, is explicitly excluded as a normal condition of existence in this garden. Therefore, the temporal functions of the trees are, for the most part, inapplicable. They will not be cut down for their uses because those uses have meaning only in a world in which time rules with implications that are irrelevant here. In the garden, there is no need for shelter and no need to build, no need for coffins because there is no "carayne" [l. 177], no need for pipes because the perfect music of heaven emanates from nature; birdsong and the wind in the living arboreal "instruments." There is no need to sail, no reason to cut and plane boards, and "the shetere ew; the asp for shaftes pleyne" [l. 180] are not useful because there is no war or strife. Thus, there is no need to make peace or celebrate victory, and there is no need to "devyne" the future, because time does not imply change. What seems a simple list of observed trees, then, on second glance, displays a most peculiar structure of irrelevance. Why is this so?

I would argue that through the dream vision, Chaucher [sic] is trying to project a realm of experience or knowledge which transcends some of the obvious limitations of life in time without aspiring to the perfect timelessness of eternity. The trees ornament a timeless realm, and yet their differentiation into species and mundane uses links them irrevocably to the sublunary world. We cannot dismiss the contradiction; we can only say that Chaucer has conceived of his garden as something ambiguously *medium aeternitatem et tempus* [between eternity and time].[38] □

Some paragraphs later, Martin returns to *The General Prologue* and Cunningham's theory about the structural significance of the dream vision. He also launches into an intriguing linguistic reading of the depiction of the Knight; this, in turn, becomes a template for many of the other pilgrim portraits:

■ . . . . . . In the *Parlement*, the dream vision validates the idea of a garden which seems timeless in some details yet earth-bound in others. I wish to propose that the Canterbury pilgrimage displays a similar ambiguity and that Chaucer, in the General Prologue, abandons the dream and expands the catalogue technique to signify a profound if brief and partial departure from ordinary life. This view will help explain the Prologue's affinity with the dream visions without identifying it with them generically. Thus, in order to see why I wish to assert the Prologue's lineal descent from the simpler catalogue, let us turn to the Canterbury pilgrimage in detail.

The Prologue begins, as we all know, by describing the pilgrimage as a typical event recurring each year in spring, the time of natural and spiritual regeneration[39] – much as the fowls' ritual of mate-choosing recurs annually on St. Valentine's Day in the *Parlement*. People who go on pilgrimages seek "straunge strondes" [1.13]; they travel to shrines far away from home "in sondry londes" [1.14]. The concept, in other words, which orders Chaucer's account of the custom of the time is that of persons leaving their homes, the locations of their daily lives, to meet in a place which is "straunge," somehow apart from their accustomed environments.

The poet reports that "in that seson on a day" [1.19] he joined such a group of pilgrims at the Tabard, and he proceeds to describe them in his famous series of portraits. Immediately, in the portrait of the Knight, we can begin to see why we must understand this series in terms of a contrast between pilgrimage and daily life. We first learn of the Knight's personal history. He is a great and honorable soldier and a gracious courtier, and he has fought for his lord in many great battles. Those conflicts, moreover, are specifically named; his fifteen mortal battles Chaucer dwells upon at length. Before relating a single detail of his appearance on the occasion of the pilgrimage, the narrator insistently engages our attention with a life of danger and strife, toil and death. And when description finally follows, it relates that life to the present occasion:

> But for to tellen yow of his array,
> His hors were good, but he was nat gay.
> Of fustian he wered a gypon
> Al bismotered with his habergeon,
> For he was late ycome from his viage,
> And wente for to doon his pilgrymage. [ll. 73–8]

We have been apprised of that active, worldly life in order that we might know the nature of what the Knight has *left behind* in joining the travelers. His garments show the wear and debris of battle, but he has moved away from his accustomed occupation to share another kind of experience with men and women of the widest possible variety of vocations, social ranks and conditions. The relation of the person to his complex of physical attributes in the Knight's portrait is identical to the relation of noun to modifying phrase or adjective for each tree in the catalogue I discussed earlier. The person (noun) is located in an unaccustomed place (semantic context), and his (its) attributes (modifiers) denote a normal function which is irrelevant to that place or context. The difference is that, in the General Prologue, this rudimentary grammar has been expanded and enriched to become a principle of narrative structure.

I would suggest that the entire series of portraits represents an astonishing realization of the potential of the Chaucerian catalogue as we find it incidentally in the earlier poems. Chaucer introduces all of the pilgrims, as he does the Knight, by relating the nature of their lives and professions. As in the catalogue of birds in the *Parlement*, most are given moral as well as physical attributes, and several, like the Squire, the Merchant, the Clerk, the Shipman, the Wife of Bath, the Reeve and the Pardoner, are associated with specific locations in keeping with the initial assertion that persons from all over England come together for pilgrimages. Furthermore, the detail which Chaucer devotes to his accounts of the normal life of each pilgrim serves, by implication, to emphasize the departure from those lives represented by the pilgrimage itself. For a fair number of pilgrims, this sense of separation between what they usually do and what they are doing now remains implicit; such is the case with the Squire, the Friar, the Man of Law, the Merchant, the Franklin, and several others.[40] □

The middle section of Martin's article is given over to discussions of the portraits of the Monk, the Yeoman, the Parson and the Pardoner and how they lend a 'kind of structural principle to the *Canterbury Tales*'.[41] Martin then moves into estates satire territory and the influence of Jill Mann is apparent, as the following extract shows. Martin also returns here to the symbolic significance of time in *The General Prologue*:

■ The Canterbury pilgrims come from various points of origin to share in cyclic, ritualized time through pilgrimage. Furthermore, they represent not only regions but a variety of different classes or social types. The interaction of these types provides the central dramatic principle of the journey, and, if I am correct, it also locates Chaucer's source of anxiety. In short, the relative accessibility of different social groups to one another was changing in fourteenth century England, and the Canterbury pilgrimage posits an access which was, as yet, outside the realm of ordinary experience but which reflected some of the currents of contemporary change.

...... Changes in social structure, of course, take time, and while they are in progress, they can be simultaneously frightening and fascinating to those who are involuntarily subject to their implications. Moreover, in periods of relatively rapid change, conservative customs and taboos tend to retain their strongest hold on individual behavior in the most familiar (and usually least urban) circumstances. I think, therefore, that we must see Chaucer's insistence on displacement from home, the introduction of pilgrimage as a special (though predictable) event, and the breadth of social representation among the pilgrims as formally related in a conceptual structure which reflects concrete social ambiguities and tensions. The pilgrimage is an occasion on which a kind of experimentation in social interaction is possible which is perhaps still less comfortable among peasants, craftsmen, monks, friars, pardoners, seamen, land holding widows, franklins and nobles when all are part of the same small community.[42] □

Martin's article, as has been seen, provides a good overview of, and interaction with, some of the most important approaches to *The General Prologue* developed in the 1960s and 1970s. Statements like 'Thus, in a large number of cases, the details with which Chaucer chooses to locate his pilgrims in the actual world involve the ways they use or otherwise relate to money or wealth'[43] also reflect a familiarity with Ruth Nevo's article 'Chaucer: Motive and Mask in the *General Prologue*' (1963) and, perhaps, that of R.T. Lenaghan (see above). Before we end our reprise of the scholarship of the 1970s, however, we must take a detailed look at Donald R. Howard's book *The Idea of the Canterbury Tales* of 1976. H. Marshall Leicester, Jr. has referred in his own work to Howard's 'much praised book', testimony enough to the fact that it ranks up there with *Chaucer and Medieval Estates Satire* as one of the most important illuminations of *The General Prologue* produced during this decade.[44]

Howard's thesis was broad and his interest in the reader's response to the text was truly cutting edge for its time, as the following *New York Review of Books* summary, quoted on the back cover of the book, indicates:

■ Howard wants us to start by taking seriously the possibility that what we have here [in *The Canterbury Tales*] is neither a random collection nor a small fragment of some mighty work we can only guess at, but a precisely planned work of art with only one or two minor elements missing or still to be worked out. He asks us to try to understand *what happens to us* as we read the book, and he realizes that this means using all of the available means of scholarship to try to understand *how it came to be* . . . His book is a vindication of the alliance between criticism and scholarship, and the work of Chaucer . . . ▫

And here is Howard's own description of his initial thoughts on, and his ultimate radical design for, the book (notice the emphasis here on the poem's structure and its author's intent):

▪ . . . . . . I conceived of this book first as a history of a literary idea, then as an anatomy. I wanted first to know how the poem came to be, in its own time and milieu, to understand its creation as a unique event. If we could understand that we would understand a lot, but not everything. We might understand what the poet wrote for his contemporaries, but not necessarily what he wrote for himself or for posterity. And we would not understand why we still read his works or how it is that many of them retain the power to interest us and move us. Chaucer was not unaware of posterity: he showed an interest in Fame's house early on [fittingly in *The House of Fame*], addressed the *Troilus* to a literary tradition, worried about the accurate preservation of his text [in *Troilus and Criseyde* as well as in his short poem *Chaucers Wordes unto Adam, His Owne Scriveyn*], and joked (in the Man of Law's Prologue) about his reputation. It is fair to say he wrote for us as well as for his contemporaries. So we want to know what the work *is*, not merely what it *was*. I set out *not* to write a linear "reading" which would proceed in the conventional way from tale to tale. I wanted somehow to see the whole "idea" of the work in a historical perspective, but a diachronic treatment would have had little to say about the fifteen years during which Chaucer was writing it. So I have written instead an anatomy.

When you write an anatomy it is an inconvenience that an arm has so many things in common with a leg. The form promotes repetition and discourages structure. But I believe such an approach will further an understanding of *The Canterbury Tales* better than historical or biographical approaches have done.[45] ▫

As may be imagined, the very nature of Howard's 'anatomical' approach makes it somewhat difficult to extract passages from the larger body of the work for comment here. But though discussions of *The General Prologue* (the head, one assumes, of *The Canterbury Tales*?) are continually interwoven with other related strands, chapter four of Howard's book does contain a section devoted exclusively to it. As this chapter is called 'Memory and Form', it is easy to see why the following extract begins as it does. It may also be helpful to know that it is prefaced by a more general discussion of the importance of memory to story-telling: 'Memory is

## 'TH'ESTAAT, TH'ARRAY, THE NOMBRE, AND EEK THE CAUSE': THE 1970s

endemic to all story-telling and all literary composition: Mnemosyne [the muse of memory] . . . was the mother of the Muses.'[46]

■ . . . . . . Memory is . . . central to the reading experience which *The Canterbury Tales* affords: as we come to each new tale we must call to mind from the General Prologue the description of the pilgrim telling it; if we do not, a whole level of meaning drops away. This is, everyone knows, one of the notably original elements of *The Canterbury Tales*: the tales themselves characterize the tellers and so contribute to the narrative of the pilgrimage itself. If it is true that Chaucer read the work aloud at court, his audience could not have kept the left index finger stuck in the General Prologue, as we do, at the beginning of each tale. They would have had to recall "the condicioun/Of ech of hem . . . And whiche they weren, and of what degree,/And eek in what array that they were inne" [ll. 38–41]. If they could not do this, their memories would have had to be refreshed from time to time, or they would have had to miss an exciting feature of the work. Sometimes the headlinks, prologues, and tales themselves remind us of the pilgrim's traits as set forth in the General Prologue, but this is not always so. True, the tales fascinate in themselves. But the unity of conception which distinguishes *The Canterbury Tales* in its fullest complexity relies on memory or the refreshing of the memory: it presupposes a listener who can remember the pilgrims or a reader who can turn over the leaves.

The narrator claims to be remembering the pilgrims, and seems to be describing them as he first encountered them at the inn; that is the setting, at the moment when he launches into the description – "Er that I ferther in this tale pace" [l. 36]. Yet as he describes them he includes details about their appearance on the road and even details about their private lives at home. Though he claims to be an objective reporter, he turns out strangely omniscient – a fact sometimes put forth as evidence against the "realism" of the General Prologue, which it is. If we ask "where we are" as we read the General Prologue, the answer must be neither on the road nor in the inn, but in the realm of mental images, of memory, of hearsay and surmise, of empathy, even of fantasy. And Chaucer draws attention to himself fictionalized as observer and recorder; we relate to him, and his participation in the pilgrimage becomes part of the fictional reality. We pass through the looking-glass of the narrator's mind into the remembered world of the pilgrimage; from it into the remembered worlds of the various pilgrims; and from these sometimes even into the remembered worlds of their characters.

The controlled lapse from one remembered world to another, this regression by successive steps into the past and the unreal, is the essential principle of form in *The Canterbury Tales*. The General

Prologue which introduces it is structured upon principles of memory as memory was then experienced; and it introduces principles of form and structure which are to operate in the work as a whole. Its memory structure is comprised of several components superimposed, and these we shall see best by separating them into the features of association and order which they owe to the habit of artificial memory.

The characters are arranged in associations easiest to remember, associations of class, alliance, and dependency endemic to medieval society.[47] □

Howard amplifies this last point for several pages, then goes on to offer, like Cunningham, his thoughts on *The General Prologue*'s relationship to the dream vision:

■ The General Prologue is . . . a natural evolution from the dream-vision with memory replacing the dream. It is like a *vade mecum* which we must carry with us as we proceed into the tales. It informs the whole; it centers attention upon the artist-narrator's consciousness as essential to the conception of the whole, and makes us aware that in consciousness things remembered are by nature things of this world. The General Prologue is therefore above all what gives unity to the whole. In constructing his work this way Chaucer followed Geoffrey of Vinsauf's advice [in *Poetria nova* I: pp. 55–6] perfectly: "Let the mind's inner compass," said Geoffrey, "first circumscribe the entire area of the subject matter." The General Prologue in a number of ways reveals and imposes principles of unity upon the tales that follow:

The General Prologue *seems* to have a random lack of organization, but is artfully structured to reveal a typifying group. The tales seem to follow spontaneously, but many are artfully ordered into thematic or dramatic clusters.

The General Prologue includes ideal figures at fixed though seemingly random intervals. The tales include ideal narratives – the tale of Constance, Griselda, Virginia, Cecilia – dispersed among the tales or clusters of tales.

In the General Prologue, the Host dominates the group and is the leader. In the tales he directs their order when he can.

In the General Prologue we get elements of class conflict, conflict of interest, and temperamental differences. In the tales these produce moments of competition and aggression which account for the order of most other tales.

In the General Prologue, the very first thing mentioned after the season is the pilgrimage to Jerusalem (in the allusion to "palmers" and "straunge strondes" [l. 13]). In the Parson's Prologue we are reminded of the glorious pilgrimage to Jerusalem celestial.

## 'TH'ESTAAT, TH'ARRAY, THE NOMBRE, AND EEK THE CAUSE': THE 1970s

In the General Prologue the narrator's feat of memory is announced and begun. In the tales it opens to us a world of remembered fictions, the irrepressible world of story, passed by books or traditions to the pilgrims, by them to the author-narrator, and by him to us.

In the General Prologue the narrator thus brings the pilgrims into the present through memory, and the Host invites them to tell "Of aventures that whilom han bifalle" [l. 795]; in their tales each, recaptured from the past, recaptures some part of the past. Literary tradition, notable to the point of exaggeration in the opening lines of the General Prologue, becomes the substance of the work: things remembered, known to the mind and spirit, and preserved in language, are the world of *The Canterbury Tales* – a world more real, more articulate, and more per-durable than the day-to-day world, the pilgrimage of human life, which purports to be its subject. At the end we get a prose meditation about how to deal with that day-to-day world, and after it a terse statement in which the author rejects that world, and with it his books about that world, and "many another book, if they were in my remembrance" [*CT*, l. 1087], to embrace the world he believed existed beyond memory.

...... Chaucer used the medieval conceptions of memory as a faculty which stores images and intentions and as an artificial skill by which one stores intelligible ideas; and so he centered remembrance on the structure of a game played along a road and called upon the memories of others, upon tradition . . . In Chaucer memory is voluntary: the narrator will do his best to recall "Everich a word" [l.733] and will set out the cast of characters not as they spring from his own inner experience but as they exist in the social world which he shares with his audience. And in the end that memory of a pilgrimage must be allowed to pass out of mind, to take its place among all past things and all forgotten books in the ordered rightness of a transcendent realm.[48] □

We would have to look very hard to find a more rigorous or impassioned defence of the vital role *The General Prologue* plays in relation to its 'body', *The Canterbury Tales*. Howard presents it as the wellspring, both structurally and thematically, of the poem as a whole: the *aide-mémoire* for its audience and its poet alike. Howard's reading also promotes Chaucer as a '"personal" poet in that his works point to the man in a personal way'.[49] And this is, most of all, a man steeped in 'medieval conceptions of memory'. Howard's masterly synthesis of so many of the Big Issues surrounding *The General Prologue* guaranteed his work (not unlike *The Canterbury Tales* themselves) a certain fame and longevity. That does not mean, of course, that his theories about either the absolute inter-relatedness of the various fragments of *The Canterbury Tales* or about Chaucer the poet were unanimously accepted. Voices of critical dissent began to clamour in the 1980s, as the next chapter of this Guide will show.

CHAPTER FIVE

# 'What Nedeth Wordes Mo?': The 1980s

'DO WE drown in the impending "new wave" of Chaucer criticism [?]' This was the pressing question asked by Alastair J. Minnis in 1981 in 'Chaucer and Comparative Literary Theory',[1] an essay that explores Morton W. Bloomfield's remark that 'medieval literary theory of the later Middle Ages does have some bearing on our understanding of modern literary theory'.[2] Indeed, Minnis's work on 'late-medieval literary theory, the theory contemporaneous with Chaucer'[3] was a vital contribution to the brave new world of Chaucer criticism being created in the 1980s. This world was fostered on both sides of the Atlantic by an emergent interest in literary theory, an interest reflected in Minnis's declaration that 'Knowledge of late-medieval literary theory will help us understand how Chaucer's writings "entered into the culture" of their own time and will provide criteria for the definition and adaptation of those modern literary concepts and terms that are relevant to Chaucer's writings'.[4] Whilst Minnis speaks in a general way about Chaucer's writings, H. Marshall Leicester, Jr. applied these 'modern literary concepts and terms' specifically to *The General Prologue* as early as 1980 in 'The Art of Impersonation: A General Prologue to the *Canterbury Tales*'. This article begins with an interrogation of Donald R. Howard's *The Idea of the Canterbury Tale*. Leicester's particular interest lies in Howard's analysis of *The Knight's Tale* and his coining of the phrase *'unimpersonated artistry'*. According to Howard:

■ ... we read the tale as a dramatic monologue spoken by its teller but understand that some of Chaucer's attitudes spill into it. This feature gives the tale an artistry which we cannot realistically attribute to the teller: I am going to call this *unimpersonated artistry*. In its simplest form it is the contingency that a tale not memorized but told impromptu is in verse. The artistry is the author's, though selected features of the pilgrim's dialect, argot or manner may still be impersonated.[5] □

And here is Leicester's response:

> ◼ ... ... "Unimpersonated artistry" implies a technique, or perhaps an experience, of reading something like this: we assume that the Canterbury tales are, as they say, "fitted to their tellers," that they are potentially dramatic monologues or, to adopt what I hope is a less loaded term, that they are instances of *impersonated* artistry, the utterances of particular pilgrims. After all, we like to read Chaucer this way, to point out the suitability of the tales to their fictional tellers, and most of us ... would agree that at least some of the tales, and certainly the Canterbury frame, encourage this sort of interpretation.[6] ☐

Howard is far from Leicester's sole interest, however. As Leicester's article advances, it becomes, in effect, an A–Z of twentieth-century criticism on *The General Prologue*. The theories of G. L. Kittredge, E. T. Donaldson, Charles Muscatine and Paul Ruggiers (among a host of others) are engaged with here, and R. M. Lumiansky's insistent belief in the 'dramatic illusion of real people taking part in real and present interaction with one another'[7] is used as a springboard to Leicester's own argument:

> ◼ ... ... The objection to this "dramatic" model that I would particularly like to single out is its disregard for the poem's insistent, though perhaps intermittent, *textuality*, for the way the work repeatedly breaks the fiction of the spoken discourse and the illusion of the frame to call attention to itself as a written thing ... ... It seems to me that the "roadside-drama" approach, the critiques of this approach, *and* compromise positions (whether explicitly worked out like Howard's or more intuitive) have in common a central confusion: the confusion of *voice* with *presence*. All these views demand that the voice in the text be traceable to a person, a subject, *behind* the language, an individual controlling and limiting, and thereby guaranteeing, the meaning of what is expressed. The language of a given tale, or indeed of a given moment in a tale, is thus the end point of the speaker's activity, the point at which the speaker delivers a self that existed prior to the text. For this reason all these approaches keep circling back to the ambiguous traces of such an external object – in the frame, in the poet, in the facts of history, or in the "medieval mind." But what I mean by "impersonated artistry" does not involve an external subject.
>
> In maintaining that the *Canterbury Tales* is a collection of individually voiced texts, I want rather to *begin* with the fact of their textuality, insist that there is nobody there, that there is only the text.[8] ☐

The spirit of the French philosopher-critic Jacques Derrida lurks behind Leicester's thesis here, and is seen most vividly in the comments on voice

## THE GENERAL PROLOGUE

v. presence and textuality. Leicester himself speaks of his debt to Derrida in a footnote where a useful bibliographical reference is also provided:

■ In what follows I ought to acknowledge a general obligation to the work of Jacques Derrida, perhaps more to its spirit than to any specific essay or formulation. For a representative discussion of the problem of presence and a typical critique of "logocentric metaphysics" see "Writing before the Letter," Pt. I of *Of Grammatology,* trans. Gayatri Chakravorty Spivak [(]Baltimore: Johns Hopkins Press, 1976)[9] . . . □

In his application of this new (for 1980) theory of textuality to *The General Prologue,* however, Leicester simultaneously rejects Howard *et al.* and the cosier, more traditional image of Chaucer as a highly 'personal' poet. Leicester's view has also been remarked upon by Judith Ferster in her book *Chaucer on Interpretation* (1985):

■ In his provocative article . . . H. Marshall Leicester, Jr. turns [Howard's notion of Chaucer as a 'personal' poet] **upside down**. Leicester says that rather than search for the ways in which the poet creates the persona in the poem, we should study the ways in which the poem creates the poet. Chaucer impersonates himself in the text, creating the self appropriate to the task of narration; as Harry Bailley might say, he shapes himself for telling. The virtue of this formulation is that it takes into account the cotextuality of identity . . . Its difficulty is that, by saying that all we can know about the poet is in the poem, it denies the turn of the hermeneutical circle [cycle of interpretations] that encompasses the author and his life. I agree with Leicester insofar as he expresses the frustrations we experience if we try to identify Chaucer the man. But it is my position . . . that this is a frustration we are invited to feel: that we are constantly directed toward Chaucer the man, and constantly unable to find him, because of the distance imposed by death, writing, and the separation of minds. His work stimulates awareness of the necessity and the insufficiency of interpretation of people (including writers) as well as of texts. As Donald Howard points out, the question Harry Bailley asks the pilgrim narrator, "What man artow" (VII [B2] l.695), is just what we need to know. It is also what we will never know definitively, both because he is an absent author and because the mind of the other is never fully available to us.[10] □

Ferster's own views about *The General Prologue* are, in turn, influenced by 'modern phenomenological [to do with phenomena rather than being] hermeneutics'.[11]

In our final extract from Leicester's article, we see him considering

## 'WHAT NEDETH WORDES MO?': THE 1980s

Donaldson's 'notion of Chaucer the pilgrim' and further formulating his own complex ideas about the speaker of *The General Prologue* and the speaker's beguiling mystique:

> ......... it seems clear on the face of it that issues of the sort I have been discussing are raised by the notion of Chaucer the pilgrim, the naïve narrator of the General Prologue and the links, who so often misses the point of the complex phenomena he describes in order that Chaucer the satirist or the poet or the man can make sure we see how very complex they are. The idea leads to a multiplication of speakers of the same text, not serially (though some critics have considered this possibility too),[12] but simultaneously. It requires that in any given passage we decide what Chaucer the pilgrim means by what he says and then what Chaucer the poet means by what the pilgrim means. Here, too, there is often confusion about the distinction between the voice of the text and a presence behind and beyond it who somehow guarantees the meaning we find there. Descriptions of Chaucer the poet sometimes take on a distinctly metaphysical cast, as in this passage from [E.T.] Donaldson's *Speaking of Chaucer* [1970]:
>
> ["]Undoubtedly Chaucer the man would, like his fictional representative, have found [the Prioress] charming and looked on her with affection. To have got on so well in so changeable a world Chaucer must have got on well with the people in it, and it is doubtful that one may get on with people merely by pretending to like them: one's heart has to be in it. But the third entity, Chaucer the poet, operates in a realm which is above and subsumes those in which Chaucer the man and Chaucer the pilgrim have their being. In this realm prioresses may be simultaneously evaluated as marvellously amiable ladies and as prioresses.["] (p. 11)
>
> But the "higher realm" Donaldson is talking about is and can only be the *poem*, the text – as he himself knows perfectly well – and Chaucer the poet can only be what I have been calling the voice of the text. Donaldson is, as always, attentive to what the text says here, in particular to the tensions among social, human, and moral elements that the General Prologue undeniably displays. The division of the speaker into pilgrim, man, and poet is a way of registering these tensions and their complexity, of suggesting "a vision of the social world imposed on one of the moral world" (p. 9), and I can have no objection to this aim. I do not see the need, however, to reify these tensions into separate personalities of the same speaker, and I think this way of talking about the narrator of the General Prologue is misleading because it encourages us to treat him *as if we knew who he was* apart from his utterances. The general personality traits of Chaucer the pilgrim have themselves become reified in the Chaucer criticism of the last

twenty years, and this frozen concept of the character has fostered a carelessness in reading that Donaldson himself rarely commits.

If I were going to try to characterize the speaker of the General Prologue myself, I would follow the lead of John M. Major [in 'The Personality of Chaucer the Pilgrim', *PMLA*, 75 (1960), pp. 160–2] in calling him, not naïve, but extraordinarily sophisticated. I doubt, however, that this characterization, even if accepted, would go very far towards solving the problems of the poem, because it still does not tell us much about who the speaker is, and that is what we want to know. The notion of Chaucer the pilgrim at least offers us an *homme moyen sensuel* with whom we can feel we know where we are, but I think that it is just this sense of knowing where we are, with whom we are dealing, that the General Prologue deliberately and calculatedly denies us. For a brief suggestion of this intention – which is all I can offer here – consider these lines from the Monk's portrait, a notorious locus for the naïveté of the narrator:

> He yaf nat of that text a pulled hen,
> That seith that hunters ben nat hooly men,
> Ne that a monk, whan he is recchelees,
> Is likned til a fissh that is waterlees –
> This is to seyn, a monk out of his cloystre.
> But thilke text heeld he nat worth an oystre;
> And I seyde his opinion was good.
> What sholde he studie and make hymselven wood,
> Upon a book in cloystre alwey to poure,
> Or swynken with his handes, and laboure,
> As Austyn bit? How shal the world be served?
> Lat Austyn have his swynk to hym reserved!
> Therfore he was a prikasour aright: ([ll.] 177–89)

The Monk's own bluff manner is present in these lines. I agree with most commentators that he is being half-quoted, that we hear his style, for example, in a turn of phrase like "nat worth an oystre!" Present too are the standards of his calling, against which, if we will, he may be measured. The social and moral worlds do indeed display their tension here, but who brought these issues up? Who is responsible for the slightly suspended enjambment that turns "As Austyn bit" into a small firecracker? For the wicked specificity with which, at the beginning of the portrait, the Monk's bridle is said to jingle "as dooth the *chapel* belle"? Who goes to such pains to explain the precise application of the proverb about the fish, "This is to seyn . . . "? Who if not the speaker? But these observations do not permit us to say that he is *only* making a moral judgment or only making fun of the Monk (the two are not quite the same, and both are going on). A sense of the positive claims made by the pilgrim's vitality, his "manliness," is also registered by the portrait. The speaker's amused enjoyment of the Monk's forthright humanity is too patent to let us see him as just a moralist. The way his voice evokes complex possibilities of attitude is neatly caught by "And I seyde his opinion was good": that's what he said when he and the Monk had their conversation, but is he saying the same thing now in this portrait? Did he really mean it at the time? Does he now? In what sense?

The point of this exercise is not merely to show that the speaker's attitude is complex and sophisticated but also to stress how obliquely expressed it is, all in ironic juxtapositions and loaded words whose precise heft is hard to weigh. What we have, in fact, is a speaker who is not telling us, any more than he told the Monk, his whole mind in plain terms. The tensions among social, moral, and existential worlds are embodied in a single voice here, and they are embodied precisely *as tensions*, not as a resolution or a synthesis, for we cannot tell exactly what the speaker thinks either of the Monk or of conventional morality. What we *can* tell is that we are dealing with a speaker who withholds himself from us, with the traces of a presence that asserts its simultaneous absence. The speaker is present as uncomprehended, as not to be seized all at once in his totality. He *displays his difference* from his externalizations, his speaking, in the very act of externalizing himself. It is this effect, I think, that creates the feeling of "reality" in the text, the sense that there is somebody there. In literature (as in life) the reality of characters is a function of their mystery, of the extent to which we are made to feel that there is more going on in regard to them than we know or can predict. Criseyde [in *Troilus and Criseyde*] is a well-known and well-analyzed example in Chaucer, and I suggest that the general narrator of the *Canterbury Tales* is another. His lack of definition may also explain why he can be taken for Chaucer the pilgrim. Because his identity is a function of what he leaves unspoken – because it is derived from implication, irony, innuendo, the potentialities of meaning and intention that occur in the gaps between observations drawn from radically different realms of discourse – there is a temptation to reduce his uncomfortable indeterminacy by forcing the gaps shut, by spelling out the connections. But suppressing the indeterminacy in this way involves reducing complex meanings to simpler ones. One infers "Chaucer the pilgrim" by ignoring these things the speaker "does not say" (since, after all, he does not *say* them – only suggests) and by insisting that he "means" his statements in only the plainest, most literal sense. Such an interpretation does not fail to recognize that the complexities of meaning are there; it simply assigns them to "the poem" or to "Chaucer the poet," thus producing what I am arguing is a contradiction: the simple and naïve narrator of a complex and sophisticated narration.

In fact, however, not only the General Prologue but the whole of the *Canterbury Tales* works against a quick or easy comprehension of the speaker.

... ... I have tried to evoke, however briefly, the incompleteness – the indeterminacy and the resistance to classification – of the voice that speaks in the General Prologue. One corollary of this quality is the cognate incompleteness of the Prologue itself, one of whose principal themes is the insufficiency of traditional social and moral classifying schemes – estates, hierarchies, and the like – to deal with the complexity of the individuals and their relations. The speaker not only embodies this insufficiency, he recognizes it and feels it: "Also I prey yow to foryeve it me,/Al have I nat set folk in hir degree/Heere in this tale, as that they sholde stonde" ([ll.] 743–5). From this insufficiency he turns to the pilgrims. He sets them free to speak in part to free himself from the constraints and uncertainties generated by his own attempt to classify them – an attempt that, however universal and impersonal it may look at the beginning of the Prologue, is always only his view and one too complex for him to speak by himself. The Prologue does not do justice to the pilgrims. By the same token and for the same reasons it does not do justice to the narrator and his understanding of his world. In the tales, therefore, he slows us down, keeps us from grasping him too quickly and easily, by directing our attention to the variety and complexity of the roles he plays, the voices he assumes. He is, we know, each of the pilgrims and all of them, but he seems to insist that we can only discover him by discovering for ourselves who the Knight is, who the Parson is, who the Pardoner and the Wife of Bath.

We may be impatient to know the speaker of the General Prologue, but as the voice of the poem as a whole, he is the last of the pilgrims we may hope to comprehend, and then only by grasping each of the others individually and in turn and in all the complexity of their relationships to one another. The relation of the voice that speaks in the General Prologue to the personality of the poet is like that of an individual portrait to its tale and that of the Prologue itself to all the tales. It is a prologal voice, a voice that is only beginning to speak.[13] □

Once Leicester concluded that the voice of *The General Prologue* was 'only beginning to speak', other critics of the 1980s commenced speaking in their own unique voices on this subject. Indeed, some of these articulations were partial echoes of Leicester. A good example of this is Barbara Nolan's '"A Poet Ther Was": Chaucer's Voices in the General Prologue to *The Canterbury Tales*' (1986), where she writes that 'All the voices are finally Chaucer's, of course, all of them impersonations'.[14] As can be seen in the following extract, taken from the opening of her article, Nolan arrives at this conclusion after first examining the structure of *The General Prologue* in relation to an established vernacular literary tradition:

> ... ... the entire Prologue, like so many vernacular invitations to narrative from the twelfth century on, is designed to introduce the poet, describe his task, and gain the goodwill of the audience ... ... In fact, the parts of the General Prologue seem to function as several attacks on a beginning, each of them probing from a different angle a problem that traditionally belonged to prologues, "How shall I begin and to what purpose?"
>
> ... The General Prologue, I suggest, contains not one voice of the poet but three major attempts at authorial voicing.[15]

These three voices are identified as the 'voice of the April opening', the 'devout "I" of Chaucer the pilgrim, intent on giving systematic order to his experience', and that of the tavern keeper, Harry Bailley.[16] This leads on to an astute observation about genre: 'To be sure, in Chaucer the art of playing voice against voice assumes a decisive new direction predictive of the novel's complexities.'[17] *Troilus and Criseyde*, with its psychologically complex characters, has also been compared to a novel by some critics. Thus, we have two instances in Chaucer's poetic corpus where a new genre is being anticipated. This speaks volumes for those who wish to argue for Chaucer's modernity.

Nolan next considers a more general issue, the 'main theoretical basis for multiple voicing in the Middle Ages'.[18] She finds the source to be the rhetorical handbooks of the period. The issue of multiple voicing in *The General Prologue* is then returned to, and its true purpose is revealed:

> The real question is not autobiographical but rhetorical and dialectical. For what rhetorical purpose does the poet assume the pilgrim's voice? How and why is this voice juxtaposed with others in the Prologue and in the tales?
>
> In the General Prologue, we must listen closely to all the voices – the impersonal voice of the opening lines, the pilgrim's, the Host's – as aspects of an argument in which the poet himself participates through his juxtaposition of tonally and stylistically different voices. The poet's presence and his self-definition inhere in his acts of manipulation and his multiple impersonation. Seen in this light, Chaucer emerges from the Prologue, as from the tales, as a quick-change artist, a shape shifter, a prestidigitator, a player with voices.[19]

Curiously, the image of Chaucer conjured up here is of a cross between two of his own, female, creations – Criseyde, the emotional 'quick change artist', and Fame, the archetypal shape shifter and possessor of multiple tongues. The latter is described by the narrator of the poem which bears her name as:

> Me thoughte that she was so lyte
> That the lengthe of a cubite
> Was lengere than she semed be.
> But thus sone in a whyle she
> Hir tho so wonderliche streighte
> That with hir fet erthe reighte,
> And with hir hed she touched hevene . . .
> . . . also she
> Had fele upstondyng eres
> And tonges, as on bestes heres . . .
> [*The House of Fame*, ll. 1369–75, 1388–90]

It is certainly something to think about. ☐

As stated above, Nolan begins her article by discussing *The General Prologue* as a vernacular text. She finishes by contemplating it as a secular one:

■ . . . . . . The Knight's remarkable achievements in battle, the Pardoner's fashionable cape, the Friar's girlfriends, the Wife of Bath's old and young husbands – all distract the pilgrims more or less from their single proper concern, the destiny of their souls. In rhetorical terms, the lives and speeches of most of the pilgrims are "troped," turned in one way or another away from transcendent truth in the direction of Harry Bailley's kind of worldly fiction making . . . . . . The fictions themselves, together with Harry's framing commentary, become the pilgrims' "pleasure garden" for the duration of the Canterbury journey. At the same time, however, the inescapable fact of the pilgrimage serves as an ever-present critique of the game, reminding us that there is another "right" course.
. . . . . . Transcendent truth remains largely absent from the Chaucerian narratives, and it must. In Chaucer's argument, this is just the kind of truth that makes all secular fiction untenable. Nonetheless, Chaucer the poet in his several voices points directions, marks boundaries, poses questions and puzzles that bear heavily on the truths beyond his fictions.[20] ☐

Here, Nolan brings us back to some of our earlier discussions about game and story-telling and her delineation of the tales as 'pleasure garden(s)' distracting the pilgrims from the 'transcendent truth' of the spiritual pilgrimage is striking for its mediaeval quality. I say mediaeval because it brings to mind the struggle related by St. Augustine in *The City of God* between the earthly and the heavenly city: the former was seen as a place of temptation and distraction, the latter of salvation and redemption. Chaucer, of course, would have been familiar with these images.

The next article we shall consider was published in 1982, four years before that of Barbara Nolan. It is Elton D. Higgs's 'The Old Order and the "Newe World" in the General Prologue to the *Canterbury Tales*', and it has been chosen for inclusion here partly because of its engagement with Chaucer's social conscience. Though the poet was 'a life-long Royalist',[21] it was, has been and even continues to be common currency amongst a certain group of scholars that Chaucer is an apolitical poet; that in his work he is not striving to address the pressing issues of his day. And yet, by the 1980s, attempts 'to interpret Chaucer in the "context of his age"' were increasingly acknowledging that there were ' . . . as many historical approaches as there are histories – personal, social, spiritual, intellectual, economic'.[22] Through close engagement with historical and literary debates, Higgs sets out to persuade us that the major social and economic changes of Chaucer's day are addressed in *The General Prologue*. These changes are most keenly reflected, he argues, in the structure of the poem and the grouping of the pilgrim portraits. Thus, the characters are discussed in detail, something the student should find particularly useful. The article itself, presented here in full, has a tight structure of its own, divided as it is into six distinct sections. As an extra bonus, the reader's bibliography for *The General Prologue* will be greatly expanded once s/he has got to the end of this extract:

## ■ 1. Background

It is a common observation that Geoffrey Chaucer showed a relative unconcern in the *Canterbury Tales* for the great upheavals of his time. As Nevill Coghill puts it: "Plague, schism, the Peasant's Revolt, and the clashes between Richard II and his Nobility, that were to end in deposition and regicide, have no place in his poem of England. Jack Straw's massacre of the Flemings in 1381 was poetically no more to Chaucer than the flurry in the farmyard roused by the rape of Chanticleer" [*The Poet Chaucer*, p.124]. Though it is true that Chaucer did not reflect the contemporary scene so explicitly as did William Langland, he nevertheless was very aware that his age was one of profound change. Even the portraits in the General Prologue to the *Canterbury Tales*, genial and detached as they seem, show a sensitivity to the tensions in the late fourteenth century between the Old Order – feudalism, a static rural economy, and the united and unchallenged Church – and the forces of plague, urbanization, and entrepreneurship which were pushing toward fragmentation of the society and a greater degree of individualism.

Alfred David [in *The Strumpet Muse*, 1976] puts his finger on these tensions in the General Prologue when he observes that "the *ideal* represented by the Knight, the Parson, and the Plowman [corresponding to the Three Estates of mediaeval society] was still potent in Chaucer's time," and although "Chaucer himself belongs very much to an emerging new order . . . he still loves and believes in the ideal order" [p. 62] represented in a timeless way by the idealized pilgrims. David outlines succinctly the social situation he sees reflected in the General Prologue:

> We learn in the Prologue that the body is sick. Chaucer could not know that the disease was mortal and that the old feudal order was slowly dying through the civil wars, the corruption in Church and State, and the beginning of capitalism in the waning Middle Ages, but he was able to portray the symptoms as they appeared in everyday life. Ideally, the Christian community is structured so that each man performs the task to which God has assigned him to assure the physical or spiritual welfare of the whole. The order is being gradually eroded by the desire of most of its members to promote not the common profit but their own welfare and status. The Church has been infected by the commercialism of the Commons. Both Church and Commons try to emulate the pride and ostentation of the Nobles. As a result, the society is in ferment and offers a rich field for ironic observation of the gap between ideal and reality. [p. 56]

Donald Howard [in *The Idea of the Canterbury Tales*, 1976] also underlines this "gap between ideal and reality" in the General Prologue by observing that: "*The Canterbury Tales* gives us a picture of a disordered Christian society in a state of obsolescence, decline and uncertainty; we do not know where it is headed" [p. 115]. He points out that in contrast to the very current and concrete activities spawned by the ambitions and avarice of the pilgrims, "The true ideals of the 'ideal' pilgrims – the Knight's crusading spirit, the brotherhood of the Parson and the Plowman, perhaps the Clerk's selfless dedication – seem obsolescent" [p. 113]. He thus sees an element of nostalgia in Chaucer's establishment of these four pilgrims as ideals, for "Nothing can be obsolescent until it has been institutionalized, has enjoyed some measure of stability in the life of a society" [p. 91]. Howard is surely right in saying that Chaucer was not merely being conservative in idealizing the Old Order; rather, he "presented social-class distinctions in such a way as to point up the disparity between what people thought and what they did – between the obsolescent idea of social class which his society held and the more complicated actuality of its gradations" [p. 94].

Both David and Howard mention a set of idealized pilgrims in the General Prologue as being at the center of Chaucer's depiction of an Old Order that was dying. Howard goes on to show how this select group – the Knight, the Clerk (not included by David), the Parson, and the Plowman – can be seen as the major points of reference for the portraits in the General Prologue. After reminding us of Kemp Malone's observations [in *Chapters on Chaucer,* 1951] of the grouping of some of the pilgrims according to their natural or expected relationships (such as the Knight and his son and their Yeoman, or the Prioress and her retinue), Howard notes another, more nearly schematic principle governing the order in which the pilgrims are presented:

> The well-known "idealized" portraits seem to be thrown into this order at random. Three of them (Knight, Parson, and Plowman) correspond to the Three Estates. The portrait of the Clerk is idealized, too, and perhaps he represents a style of life (that of the universities, or of humanism) which Chaucer considered separate from the usual three. But the Clerk comes for no apparent reason between the Merchant and the Man of Law, the Parson and the Plowman for no apparent reason between the Wife and Miller. I should like to offer a possible explanation for this seemingly haphazard arrangement. If we take the description of the Prioress and her followers and that of the Guildsmen and their cook as single descriptions (which they are), and if we count the description of the Host, the portraits of the General Prologue can then be seen symmetrically into three groups of seven, each headed by an ideal portrait:
>
> Knight: Squire, Yeoman, Prioress, Monk, Friar, Merchant
>
> Clerk: Man of Law, Franklin, Guildsmen, Shipman, Physician, Wife
>
> Parson/Plowman: Miller, Manciple, Reeve, Summoner, Pardoner, Host
>
> . . . The kinds of order we perceive in this complex arrangement leave some loose ends, but each detail has a rightness of its own. The Parson and the Plowman are put together because they are "brothers" – which suggests an ideal relationship between clergy and commons. The idealized Clerk represents an estate other than the traditional three, but by Chaucer's time the universities *were* a world unto themselves [pp. 150–2].

## THE GENERAL PROLOGUE

Howard's point is that the order of the pilgrims in the General Prologue is neither conventional nor haphazard: it has a "rightness of its own" which, he suggests, is connected with a medieval habit of mind which created emblematic signposts as an aid to memory and in this instance provides "convenient mnemonic groups which correspond to actualities and probabilities of fourteenth-century life." I would like to expand on the social implications of Howard's tripartite division of the pilgrims, and to show how each of these sections presents a particular aspect of the struggle between an idealized Old Order (represented by the Knight, the Clerk, the Parson, and the Plowman) and the representatives of the "newe world" (a phrase applied to the Monk in describing his contempt for monasticism) [Howard, pp. 151–4].

Although many of my observations on the groupings of the pilgrims and the social rationale behind it may be gleaned from Howard and other previous interpreters of The General Prologue, I have several major points of my own which I wish to develop as a detailed exposition of the structural integrity of the tripartite division of the pilgrims introduced by Howard. They are: (1) Each of the idealized pilgrims as the head of a section has a particular kind of virtue which is set against a corresponding type of vice in the pilgrims who follow in that section; (2) There are several kinds of incremental development of themes and characters in the three sections; (3) Chaucer's idealization of the Old Order is based not so much on a desire to preserve or even to comment on the traditional "Three Estates" of medieval society as on his admiration for a degree of dedication by the "commune profit," which he considered more vital to an ordered society than the keeping of social distinctions.

To help in following the exposition, a schematic outline of the grouping of the pilgrims is given below. To Howard's listing of the pilgrims I have added the particular clash of values which I believe to be the focus of each group.

I. *Knight*
Squire
Yeoman        Feudal Fealty
Prioress
                   *vs.*
Monk
Friar           New Mobility,
Merchant     Appearances

II. *Clerk*
Man of Law
Franklin            Old Learning
Guildsmen
                          vs.
Cook
Shipman
Physician           Professions & Crafts for Personal Gain
Wife of Bath

III. *Parson & Plowman*
Miller              Old Rural Service
Manciple
                          vs.
Reeve               Unprincipled Manipulation
Summoner            of People
Pardoner

In presenting my argument, I shall first make some general observations by way of overview, and then present an exposition of each of these three sets of pilgrims.

## 2. An Overview

There are several kinds of developmental movement in the three central sections of the General Prologue. The portraits of the three idealized pilgrims who head these units (counting the Parson and the Plowman as a coordinated pair) are progressively more remote from the center of society, moving from the secular, though virtuous, Knight, to the more scholarly Clerk of Oxford, to the rural and socially obscure Parson and Plowman. Correspondingly, the portraits which conclude the units present figures who are incrementally more frank and obvious about their being disruptive of the Old Order: the Merchant represents the subtle undermining of feudalism by increased trade and the accompanying rise in the influence of towns [see Harry A. Miskimin, *Money, Prices, and Foreign Exchange in 14th Century France*, 1963]; the Wife of Bath in her Prologue openly challenges the quiet authoritarianism and traditional learning of the Clerk; and the Pardoner, the most egregiously self-serving of all the pilgrims, traffics in sacrilege and deliberately makes shipwreck of the Faith.

The three sections, as a whole, show a shift of focus; from the concern with noble behavior and reputation (both true and false) in the first section, to the uses of learning and knowledge in the second section, to the attitudes toward being a servant in the third section. Not every pilgrim fits neatly with the emphasis in his or her section, but the overall pattern seems clear: each section of the portraits in the General Prologue is developed on a theme which is an appropriate counterpoise to the ideals represented by the virtuous person whose description begins the group. The pilgrims of the first section are overwhelmingly concerned with their appearance and their importance, as the Knight is not. Most of the pilgrims of the second section are notable for their distinctive knowledge or skills, but unlike the Clerk they see what they have learned primarily as a means of gaining advantage and precedence over others and enriching themselves. The unprincipled scoundrels in their group manage businesses and manipulate people, in contrast to the Parson, and scorn simple rural service, in contrast to the Plowman.

These sets of opposed values do not focus narrowly on accepted social categories, even though, as has often been pointed out, the Knight, the Parson, and the Plowman represent idealizations of the "Three Estates" of medieval society: the nobility (warriors), the Church (priests), and the commons (tillers of the soil) [see H. Hilton, *Bond Men Made Free*, 1973]. By adding the Clerk as the fourth ideal figure and merging the portraits of the Parson and the Plowman, Chaucer chose not to emphasize the Three Estates (nor any other arbitrary system of stratification) as the core of the Old Order. The themes of the three sections of pilgrims suggest that he saw the key to the order of society in the willingness of its citizens to subordinate individual ambition to service for the good of all, according to one's calling and talents. Accordingly, in the General Prologue Chaucer emphasizes *noblesse oblige* in the Knight, the responsibilities of learning in the Clerk, the care of souls in the Parson, and the dignity of common toil in the Plowman; for together they represent faithful service – with body, mind, and soul – for the good of their society. Those who have inherited secular power must wield it without bullying; those who are responsible for the preservation, development, good use, and transmission of knowledge (whether theoretical or practical) must not be arrogant or irresponsible in the status or influence they enjoy; those who have been given spiritual charges must serve with a humility that inspires confidence.

Although there is no evidence that Chaucer relied specifically on the following words of Paul in the Epistle of First Corinthians, the passage expresses the viewpoint implicit in the General Prologue.

> Now there are varieties of gifts but the same Spirit; and there are varieties of service, but the same Lord; and there are varieties of working but it is the same God who inspires them all in every one. To each is given the manifestation of the Spirit for the common good. [I. Corinthians 12: 4–7]

The key words in this passage, "for the common good," are of course echoed several times in Chaucer's own term, "commune profit." It is for their dedication to this ideal that the Knight, the Clerk, the Parson, and the Plowman are set forth as models by Chaucer, rather than for their membership in a particular class. Indeed, their bond of common virtue transcends any divisive barriers of class, and the gap between them and the pilgrims who reject the "commune profit" is much larger than any separation in social status.[23] The conflicts which develop among the pilgrims are based much more on lapses in personal charity than on class rivalries.

Jill Mann [in *Chaucer and Medieval Estates Satire*, 1973] holds to the contrary, arguing that the "sense of common profit" cannot be taken as the "the social ethic implicit in the Prologue" [p. 55]. She says further that "Chaucer has no systematic platform for moral values, not even an implicit one, in the *Prologue*" [p. 192]. Although Mann is certainly correct in observing that the point of view of the *narrator* is rather relativistic and all-accepting, she makes too little of the moral backdrop which Chaucer *the author* creates for the Prologue with the portraits of his four idealized pilgrims. Chaucer is no thundering moralist like Langland, but he does indicate what kind of behavior he finds admirable and socially constructive. His geniality and his wide sympathies – either in his own person or that of his narrator – should not be mistaken for lack of concern with the moral order of society. Mann does admit that Chaucer allows the Parson to present a counter-view to the "worldly values" of the General Prologue, but she does not give due weight to Chaucer's bias toward presenting the obligation of every person to fulfill his calling to the best of his ability [p. 201].

It is quite remarkable that Chaucer was able to create a common context in which to describe so diverse a group of people, and that we accept the verisimilitude of their being brought together in this way [in a footnote, Higgs draws our attention to Loy D. Martin's 'History and Form in the General Prologue to the *Canterbury Tales*' which was discussed in the previous chapter of this Guide]. A great part of our willingness to give credence to such a fiction springs from the narrator's apparent serendipity [an accidental, happy discovery] in choosing the order of the pilgrims. A detailed look at the three groups in the General Prologue demonstrates that Chaucer has managed to have it both ways: he has preserved a feeling of spontaneity by avoiding any stated plan of organization; and at the same time he has provided a subtle structure by which the reader can assess each pilgrim's attitude towards his or her place in society by comparing each one with the others in the same group, and especially with the idealized pilgrim of the group. This tolerance toward individual personalities, while maintaining an inconspicuous but firm presentation

THE GENERAL PROLOGUE

of moral and social norms, is the mark of a mature and accomplished poet.

## 3. Group One

The first group presents seven people, all of whom, except the Knight, are very conscious of their appearance and reputation. The Squire is "embrouded" [l. 89], reminds one of a meadow full of flowers, and hopes by his exploits "to stonden in his lady grace" [l. 88]; the Yeoman carries three weapons and is dressed in forest green; the "lady" Prioress wishes "to ben holden digne of reverence" (141); the Monk, with his ostentatious horse and rich clothing, wants to be seen as a "fair prelaat" (204); the Friar will associate only "with riche and selleres of vitaille" (248); and the Merchant is "Sownynge alwey th'encrees of his wynnyng" (275). In contrast, the Knight wears a "gypon/Al bismotered with his habergeon" and "of his port as meeke is as a mayde," even though he has more "worthynesse" than all the rest (75–6; 69; 50; 67–8).

The Squire and the Yeoman are somewhat eclipsed by the Knight. Although nothing openly negative is said about their characters, they appear rather vain. The promising young Squire, it may be hoped, will grow out of his interest in superficial "noble" behavior – the clothes, the horsemanship, the artistic refinements – and acquire some of his father's depth of character. The Yeoman represents, as the Knight's servant, an important instrument of the English military successes in the middle of the fourteenth century. But his longbow is not an unambiguous support to the Knight's way of life, for it is also the weapon that made a shambles of the flower of the French knighthood on the battlefield. The Yeoman cannot be unaware of the prestige he gains by displaying such a weapon, and the rest of his attire suggests a full military parade. Thus, as much as they seem on the surface to support the Knight and the Old Order he represents, the Squire and the yeoman show characteristics which are not entirely subordinated to the spirit of humble service embodied in the Knight.

Of the four pilgrims in the first group who are outside the Knight's party, three are members of the regular clergy and are flawed by an aspiration to upper-class status which is destructive to their vows. The fourth is a merchant who ignores any rules that will not add to his profits. All four offer a contrast to the integrity with which the Knight pursues his calling and all four represent elements in late medieval society which seriously threatened that which was best in the Old Order.

The Prioress is the least offensive of the four as her major fault is her greatest attention to trivial things: courtly etiquette, lap-dogs, and elaborate religious jewelry. In aspiring to an unattainable courtly way of life, she has sacrificed the contribution she might have made to the "commune profit" and has instead adopted only the appearance of the Knight's mode of conduct. Although her charm masks the disorder of her life, she too contributes to the erosion of the order which it is the purpose of religious houses to establish and maintain. Ironically, all three reject the opportunity to participate in the order to which they are called because they are intent on a more "genteel" standard of behavior.

The high-living Monk explicitly rejects the Old Order: he "leet olde thynges pace/And heeld after the newe world the space" (175–6). The time is past, he says, for adherence to the standards of such ancient authorities as St. Benedict and St. Augustine. There is a special irony in the question, "How shal the world be served?" [l. 187] – that is, if the Monk and his fellow cloisterers do not contribute their secular talents to the orderings of worldly affairs. The question ignores the disorder that the Monk has brought about by his pursuit of the hounds and the hare. These "gentlemanly" activities are for him, as is the "cheere of court" for the Prioress, the baubles which obscure the essence of *noblesse oblige*.

The movement of laborers from country estates to towns after the depopulating ravages of the Black Death provided the greatest threat to the feudal system upheld by the Knight [see Christopher Brooke, *The Structure of Medieval Society*, 1971, pp. 82ff.]. Higher wages, due to the scarcity of labor, tempted many people to leave an estate on which they had grown up and search for a better way of life in town. This upheaval, which was accompanied by an increase in the sale of land and a wider circulation of money [see M. M. Postan, *Essays on Medieval Agriculture and General Problems of the Medieval Economy*, 1973], provided an excellent opportunity for those tricksters and sharp dealers who depended on an unstable population and abundant flow of money for the success of their schemes. The Friar, the Merchant, and, later in the Prologue, the Sergeant of Law, the Physician, and the Pardoner are all examples of such scoundrels. In the first section, the Friar is the most mobile and the most corrupt of the regular clergy. Chaucer reflects the common complaints against friars, in general, when he depicts the self-serving wanderings of Huberd in the Prologue. Although the Friar's most destructive blow to the Old Order of the church was his interfering with the confessional function of parish priests by giving easy penance for money, he fits into the major scheme of the first section because of his concern with appearances, especially the trappings of nobility. The Friar especially cultivates the "worthy wommen of the toun" (217) and concludes that it does not befit "swich a worthy man as he" to mix with lepers and the poor (243–5). All of this emphasis on the "worthy lymytour" [l. 269] is an ironic echo of the truly worthy Knight. For all his consorting with the "right" people, Huberd has corrupted his calling and grossly violated the spirit of faithful service exemplified by the Knight. Profit alone can motivate the Friar even to pretend to be "curteis" and "lowely of servyse" [l. 250].

The Merchant seems an unlikely choice with which to end this section since his main concern appears to be earning money. His bragging about his ability to make money could be taken as a willingness to admit that he did not inherit wealth and is not a nobleman. But once again we have the ironic emphasis on the word "worthy":

> Wel koude he in eschaunge sheeldes selle.
> This worthy man ful wel his wit bisette:
> Ther wiste no wight that he was in dette,
> So estatly was he of his governaunce
> With his bargaynes and with his chevyssaunce.
> For sothe he was a worthy man with alle. [ll. 278–83]

The Merchant is not intent, as are the other pilgrims in the first section, on imitating the style of nobility, for he has begun to establish his own order, one where money is the basis of social standing, rather than vice versa [see Sylvia Thrupp, *The Merchant Class of Medieval London*, 1948]. He achieves status through unscrupulous international trade, and the pomp with which he conducts his affairs conceals the uncertainty of his enterprises. He is, then, very much concerned with appearances, not in order to be seen as one of the nobility, but to justify the acquisition of wealth through large-scale entrepreneurial trade – trade that was to develop into capitalism [see Robert E. Lerner, *The Age of Adversity: the 14th Century*, 1968]. The competitive and unprincipled "bargaynes and chevyssaunce" of the Merchant brings us a world and an age away from the Knight's Old Order of feudal honor and stability, for the Merchant's dealings represent the fluid transactions of a money economy, in contrast to the simpler, narrower economy of goods in the older, agrarian society [see Harry A. Miskimin, *Money, Prices, and Foreign Exchange in 14th Century France*, 1963]. We sense Chaucer's hope that the best of the Old Order will be able to curb the unbridled exploitation of the New.

## 4. Group Two

There is some debate as to whether the single-minded Clerk is idealized, or mildly satirized. His unworldliness and intense concentration on his studies invite the suspicion that Chaucer intends us to see him as rather narrow and ingenuous, although he is a dedicated student.

Certainly the lean horse and threadbare overcoat evoke the conventional image of a learned but dull scholar, preoccupied with books and content with an obscure and impecuniary life. There is more than that to the Clerk, however. We infer that he could have gotten a benefice, if he had wanted it; that he has friends who will support him, even after he has spent a number of years in school; and that he is willing to share his learning unostentatiously, which implies that there are those who are willing to listen to him. In short, he is highly respected, and his speech ("Sownynge in moral vertu" [l.307]) marks him as one who honestly and gracefully makes his contribution to society by using his particular gift of intellect: "gladly wolde he lerne and gladly teche" (308).

Chaucer chose the Clerk, a devout and humble Oxford scholar, to be the exemplar of this group of pilgrims because the social order that he upholds falls between those represented by the Knight and the Parson. The Knight's domain is the physical world, where he defends the earthly political powers and the economy that supports them; the Parson ministers to the spiritual order, seeing first of all to the welfare of people's souls and also showing compassion for their material problems; the Clerk's domain is the intellect, which enables mankind to apply the divine gift of reason to earthly experience in order to organize this experience toward the most constructive ends. All but one of the pilgrims in the second section have some specialized knowledge used in a craft or profession. The theme of the section is thus the misuse of intellect and learning for personal aggrandizement, rather than for the "commune profit."

The Sergeant of Law (called the Man of Law later) is a very effective practitioner of his profession, largely because his "purchasyng" of land was reinforced by his ability to recite from memory "every statut" [l. 327] that bore on the plot in question, so that "Ther koude no wight pynche at his writyng" (326). The break-up of many great estates because of the shortage of labor was a boon for such clever dealers as the Man of Law, who must have made a fine profit from his ability to obtain property and free it from the complicated entailments of feudal landholding ("Of fees and robes hadde he many oon" [p. 317]). He cares nothing for either the honorable stability upheld by the Knight or the unselfish use of learning exemplified from the Clerk; though he seems to be a sterling member of society, he is contributing to the dissolution of the Old Order, entirely to his own advantage.

The Franklin has also properly profited from the recent availability of land, and now he wants respectability to go with his newly acquired property. The theme of misused knowledge applies less obviously to him than to the others in the group, but he ostentatiously uses his expertise in *haute cuisine* to impress people with his wealth and taste. Like those in the first group, he has a superficial grasp of gentility, and (as is disclosed later, in the prologue to his tale) he does not realize that mere association with the "proper" crowd cannot endow him or his son with the aura of nobility. He is one of the *nouveaux riches* who will displace many of the upper-class notables in the Old Order. Although he presides at local court sessions and serves as sheriff and member of parliament from time to time, his preoccupation with the surface of life cannot impart an ethical sense to his service to match that of the Clerk or the Knight.

The five Guildsmen, accompanied by their own Cook, are also self-conscious about their newly attained status. Since they are all of different crafts, it is obvious that their Guild is a social "fraternitee" [see Thomas Garbaty, 'Chaucer's Guildsmen and their Fraternity', *JEGP* 59 (1960), pp. 691–709], and that the specialized knowledge they have of their individual trades has been subordinated to the social aspirations cultivated by the Guild. Their "wisdom" (371) is not directed primarily – or perhaps even at all – toward the "commune profit," but rather toward political influence and personal gain. It is not good character, nor good craftsmanship, nor a spirit of public service that will advance them "to been an alderman" (372), but the possession of "catel . . . ynogh and rente" (373). As if to make clear that the desire "to sitten in a yeldehalle on a deys" (370) is to satisfy vanity rather than a sense of duty, Chaucer has the wives of the Guildsmen revel in the pomp of being called "madame" [l. 376] and in leading the processions of Guild affairs (374–8). Once again, these rising members of a new middle class are using their money to establish a semblance of order, but one which is shallow and lacking in the moral foundation. In particular, they have forsaken the whole-hearted pursuit of their "mysteries," or crafts. It is through these crafts that they might have shared with the Clerk the important task of acquiring and transmitting the knowledge by which a society may prosper.

The Guildsmen's Cook also knows his craft well, but the running sore on his shin puts into question the value of that skill. Both the sore and his drunkenness, seen later, may be indications of a dissolute life. In a similar way, his accompaniment of the Guildsmen may be a symbolic undercutting of their pose of civil dignity; Roger (as he is called by the Host later) represents the open sore of their ambition, which they have money enough to indulge, but not sophistication enough to try to hide.

The last three pilgrims of the second group are more demonstrably flawed than the others. Although it is the Shipman who is said not to be bothered by "nyce conscience" [l. 398], the statement might be applied in different degrees to the Doctor of Physic and the Wife of Bath. All three have used their knowledge to take advantage of others, and none manifest any tendency to work for the "commune profit."

Later in the *Canterbury Tales* the Wife of Bath openly challenges the Clerk by using Scripture and learned treatises to support her heresies of sexual hedonism and female sovereignty in marriage. She is thus the most fitting character to conclude the section.

The Shipman is the first character in Chaucer's Prologue who does not pretend to some refinement or aspire to be "gentil," and in this respect he anticipates the group of five rascals in the last section. The Shipman and the Cook are the first of the pilgrims (except the Knight and the Clerk) who seem not to care how they look. But if anyone were disposed to laugh at the sight of the Shipman riding a horse "as he kouthe" [l. 390], the sight of the dagger hanging around his weathered neck would no doubt serve to keep that mirth concealed. From what Chaucer tells us, he recognizes no law and takes without compunction whatever he can get by his cleverness and strength. He makes no pretense to uphold any social order or strive for any kind of social approval. His one skill which might be a social asset is his proficiency in navigating the English Channel and its coastline; but he uses that skill only to be a more effective pirate and smuggler. He apparently lacks all conscience, let alone a "nyce" one.

The same might be said of the Physician, although he is a learned and practical man, and appears respectable. But with all his learning, "His studie was but litel on the Bible" (438) – nor, can we surmise, on moral treatises of any kind. He has no scruples against conspiring with the apothecary at the expense of his patients, nor against enriching himself through the unfortunate victims of the Plague. His skill, like the skills of others in this section, is turned to the acquisition of gold, which "he lovede . . . in special" (444). In spite of his reputation of being a "verray, parfit praktisour" (422) of medicine, healing is not a great service to him, but only a way of gain.

Although there is much personal rebellion and disorderliness in the Wife of Bath, we tend, as with Shakespeare's Falstaff, to take her liveliness, wit, and energy as self-validating characteristics, especially as Chaucer reveals them in her great confessional prologue to her tale. Dame Alice's unabashed boast of having had five husbands, and her admission that she would welcome the sixth, however, are quite enough to elicit a response from the sober and conservative Clerk. By sharing her knowledge of the practice of sexual love ("For she koude of that art the olde daunce" [476]) and usurping the traditional place of men (not only in domestic matters, but in teaching as well), she throws into question the basic assumption of the Clerk's life: that learning and skills are most appropriately exercised with modesty and humility, in service to both God and man. The Wife of Bath is not loath to use her skills, nor to learn and to teach; but the order she supports will serve her own purposes in both affairs of the purse and affairs of the body. Delightful though she may be in some ways, she has not learned to be subordinate to anyone, not even, one suspects, to God.

The pilgrims who end the three sections of character descriptions in the General Prologue are, taken together, the most "confessional" of all the pilgrims, as the prologues to their tales show.[24] The Merchant tells us of his woes with his new wife; the Wife of Bath details her experience with five husbands; and the Pardoner describes his techniques for deceiving gullible people into giving him their money. The circumstances confessed are (in the order of the confessor's appearance in the General Prologue) each progressively more threatening to social order, culminating in the predatory coldness of the Pardoner's exploits.

## 5. Group Three

At a time when many country priests had taken advantage of the "market" for chantry appointment in London, brought about by deaths from the Plague, the poor Parson stayed with his parishioners, even though his learning and conscientiousness would no doubt have qualified him for a more distinguished position. It is hard to imagine a more humble and truly serviceable man than this rural priest. He is keenly aware that the welfare of his parishioners depends on his instruction, but he does not become "despitous,/Ne of his speche daungerous ne digne" (516–7). On the other hand, if any person is deserving of rebuke, "What so he were, of heigh or lough estat,/Hym wolde he snybben sharply for the nonys" (522–3). The Parson is not only socially and economically unambitious, but he is also free of class-consciousness. He thus avoids the source of most of the moral weaknesses of the other pilgrims: that is, a willingness to prostitute oneself for social and economic gain, and to settle for surface glitter rather than true nobility. Quite to the contrary, the Parson is willing to accept the real disadvantages of a post in a poor parish, where the economy of the Old Order was breaking up, for he "was a shepherde and noght a mercenarie" (514). Similarly, his brother the Plowman represents the willingness to do his best wherever God has placed him, a quality as necessary to a new order as to an old one. The two brothers, in their piety and their concern for the "commune profit," stand in stark contrast to the five self-serving rascals whose portraits fill the rest of the third section, and who are, as a group, the worst of all the pilgrims.

The exaggerated animality of the Miller, his need to be loud and physically intimidating, and his unvarnished cheating at his mill indicate the extreme distance which separates these last five pilgrims from the spiritual center of order embodied in the Parson and the Plowman.

It is ironic that the supposedly religious procession leaving the Tabard Inn should be led by the loud-mouthed Miller playing his bagpipes. Perhaps it is Chaucer's way of acknowledging that here in the song and dance, rather than in the idealized pilgrims – or even those who pretend to respectability – lies the fundamental motivation of this (or any) group of people. Most of the pilgrims have a kinship, admitted or not, with the spirit of the Saturnalian holiday in which the Miller leaves behind the restrictions of ordinary, everyday life. It should come as no surprise that he is the first to disrupt the orderliness of Harry Bailley's game of tale-telling, for his drunkenness merely makes more palpable the inherent disorderliness of his personality.

The last four pilgrims – the Manciple, the Reeve, the Summoner, and the Pardoner – are categorized together by Ruth Nevo as having "gravitated from the ranks of the labourers to those of salaried officials, or upper servants, of an estate or institution" [see 'Motive and Mask in the "General Prologue"', *Modern Language Review* 58 (1963), p.6]. Both Nevo and [John] Reidy [in *PMASAL* 47 (1962): pp.595–603] characterize them as "parasites"; one could say "bureaucratic parasites" or "managerial parasites." They produce nothing, and they use their positions of responsibility not to make the machinery of society run more smoothly, but to line their purses. The enormity of their violation of the "commune profit" lies in their abuse of trust [see Harold F. Brooks, *Chaucer's Pilgrims: The Artistic Order of the Portraits in the Prologue*, 1962, p.49]; they claim to serve their masters while in the very process of deceiving them. The opportunities for such manipulations and betrayals arose in the fourteenth century from the mobility of the population and the growth of a money economy. The lawyers for whom the Manciple works are perhaps too busy and land-grabbing, like the Sergeant of Law, to keep tabs on him; the Reeve's master evidently found the management of his estate too complicated under the new conditions; the Summoner and the Pardoner no doubt found a mobile population easier to deceive than a stable one, and in any case their success depended on the easy flow of money. It should also be noted that all four of these pilgrims are associated with towns and that they make their money dealing in falsified commodities or documents. Their cool cleverness only makes their crimes seem the more perverse. Their portraits are a fitting climax to the increasing alienation from the Old Order which has been building throughout the General Prologue.

There is rich irony in the Manciple's being able to "sette hir aller cappe" [l.586] in working as a food buyer for the lawyers; with a chuckle, Chaucer the Narrator considers it "a ful fair grace/That swich a lewed mannes wit shal pace/The wisdom of an heep of lerned men" (573–5). The chicanery of the Manciple and the other scoundrels at the end of the Prologue could not be carried on without some culpable

## THE GENERAL PROLOGUE

laxness on the part of their masters. The breakdown in order is thus traceable to all levels of society, and often those at the higher levels, Chaucer implies, are undermined before they realize the direct results of their own disorderly actions.

The Reeve, like the Manciple, has found it too easy to defraud his lord, and has built a power base that the other servants of the estate are afraid to challenge. The reeve has turned the proper order upside down, so that "He koude bettre than his lord purchace" (608); he is able even to lend the lord's own money to him. Clearly, neither servant nor master has adhered to the concept of being faithful to one's calling.

The Summoner and the Pardoner obviously reinforce one another in their evil-doing. Both are physically deformed and morally depraved, and both make their living from the sins and guilt of others. The song they sing together as they ride along betokens the most tragic substitution yet of superficial satisfaction for the substance of order; "Com hider, love, to me!" [l.672], whatever it means precisely to them, is at the farthest extreme from the love of God and man that brings order to the lives of the Parson and the Plowman.

The Summoner would seem an ordinary man gone wrong. None of his exploits mark him as exceptionally intelligent or talented. The comparison of his pseudo-learned snatches of Latin to the empty words of a trained jay-bird indicate that even his villainy is not particularly subtle. But even if the Summoner lacks complexity and depth, his surface is terrifying enough. He is a formidable foe when aroused, as the Friar finds out, and he thrives on the fear he inspires. His chief sacrilege lies in his evoking fear of himself rather than of the "ercedekenes curs" [l.655] and the judgment of God. In thus corrupting the process of church discipline, the Summoner commits, with the Pardoner, the grievous sin of bringing disorder to the care of souls, thereby compounding their own damnation with that of others.

The Pardoner, like that other sharer of secrets, the Wife of Bath, is one of Chaucer's perpetual puzzles. As the Summoner's companion, he appears first as merely another bizarre, degenerate con-man; but as details are added to his portrait (both here and in the prologue to his tale), a complex personality emerges. The Pardoner's deceits are so egregious and his conscience so seared that we are awestruck at his wickedness. His alienation from the Old Order, and from all order, is further intensified by his being a eunuch. Some modern readers question whether the Pardoner is to be held entirely responsible for his villainy, since from birth (according to Walter C. Curry [in *Chaucer and the Medieval Sciences*, rev. ed., 1960]) he was defective and was excluded from a normal life. But if Curry's analysis is right, this kind of eunuch would, in Chaucer's day, have been assumed to be an evil monster, "an outcast from human society, isolated both physically and morally, [one who] satisfies his depraved instinct by preying upon it" [pp. 59–70]. Even if a more sympathetic attitude is taken toward the Pardoner (as in the recent article by Monica E. McAlpine [see 'The Pardoner's Homosexuality and How It Matters', *Publications of the Modern Language Association* 95 (1980): pp. 8–22]), his pursuit of his way of life is so wholehearted that he has lost all inner moral controls, and can find satisfaction only in his ability to overcome others by his rhetoric and to enrich himself at their expense. It can be inferred that he has such contempt for himself as a man that he perceives no possibility of his functioning as part of an ordered society.

Thus the Pardoner is a negative summation of the theme of disorder in the General Prologue. More than any other pilgrim he manifests detachment from the Old Order. He is committed solely to himself, and, having no hope of being integrated into the normal activities of mankind, he takes joy in being slyly disruptive. He admits no order in the world except that of his own cleverness and exults in the irony of preaching against avarice while at the same time making more money in a day "Than that the person gat in monthes tweye" (704). This statement of his financial success underscores the contrast between him and the poor, virtuous Parson with whom Chaucer began the third section of pilgrims, but he contrasts equally as much with the strong, quiet Knight and the noble learned Clerk. His greatest spiritual disability is the bitter pride which will not let him submit to being a servant: "I wol do no labour with myne handes" he says in the prologue to his tale (VI, 444). The Pardoner has become almost a symbol of the Prince of Disorder himself, refusing to serve God and substituting his own gospel for the true one.

## 6. Conclusion

With the Pardoner's offertory song ringing in our ears, we might feel that Chaucer has stacked the deck in the General Prologue in favor of the Rogues of Disorder. The noble representatives of the Old Order are severely outnumbered, and the prognosis for an orderly pilgrimage is not made any more favorable by Harry Bailley's custodianship of the trip to Canterbury. In fact, his lack of success in controlling the disorderly pilgrims indicates the need for the positive influence of such servants of the "commune profit" as the Knight, the Clerk, the Parson, and the Plowman. They will never be the majority in any society, and Chaucer realized that they could not – and perhaps should not – stem all of the tide of change that was flowing around him [see pages 15–16 of Loy D. Martin, 'History and Form in the *General Prologue* to *The Canterbury Tales*' which is discussed in the previous chapter of this

Guide]. But his setting them at key spots in his descriptions of the pilgrims indicates that they are to remind people of the touchstones of good order, even in the midst of those sometimes fascinating rogues who were willing to take advantage of change for their own profit.

Thus, within a seemingly arbitrary sequence of portraits, Chaucer has provided in the General Prologue a subtle principle for grouping the pilgrims. The worthy Knight, the dedicated scholarly Clerk, and the truly pious Parson and his brother (whose positions in the sequence of the Prologue divide the portraits approximately into thirds) bring us by degrees from the virtues of the body, to the virtues of the mind, to the virtues of the soul. Their disruptive counterparts at the end of each section – the Merchant, the Wife of Bath, and the Pardoner – constitute the major gradations in a concomitant crescendo of vice in the General Prologue. The representatives of disorder are given progressively more attention in each of the three sections, until, in the last, we are presented with five unprincipled and consummate rascals, in sharp contrast to those virtuous and community-serving brethren, the Parson and the Plowman. Throughout the Prologue, the measure of each pilgrim can be taken by contrasting him or her to the standard set by the model pilgrim of the respective groups.

These patterns reflect Chaucer's concern with the possible consequences of the emerging economic and social individualism of his day. He was too much a Boethian [a follower of the Roman philosopher Boethius, who lived from c. 480–524] to think anything in this world immutable, and he took great pleasure in painting the great variety of human beings around him; but he also keenly sensed the need we have for norms that let us know how far we have strayed. One of his verities is that no social order can be maintained without a moral commitment from most of its members. No system is perfect, and the Old Order in his day was on shaky ground; but, he seems to say, whatever takes its place will have to manifest the strength of character seen in the Knight, the Clerk, the Parson, and the Plowman in order to subordinate personal ambition to "commune profit."[25] ☐

To agree fully with Higgs's thesis about 'commune profit' in *The General Prologue* it is necessary to accept his belief that the Knight, Clerk and Parson are 'ideal' character types. With regard to the Knight, for example, it is true that many scholars have seen him as something of an ideal. In *Chaucer's Knight: The Portrait of a Medieval Mercenary* (1980), Terry Jones summarises this popular stance as follows:

■ Chaucer's Knight stands out as a key figure in one of the great landmarks of the English language: *The Canterbury Tales*. He is usually presented to the modern reader as the perfect Christian warrior. In

## 'WHAT NEDETH WORDES MO?': THE 1980s

1907, J.M. Manly called Chaucer's Knight 'a figure at once realistic and typical of the noble and adventurous idealists of his day'. This opinion has become generally accepted among academics. The most eminent of present-day editors, F.N. Robinson, commented in 1957: 'It is worthy of note that Chaucer presents in the Knight a completely ideal figure. Although chivalry in the fourteenth century was in its decline and had a very sordid side, Chaucer has wholly refrained from satirizing the institution.' In 1969, Muriel Bowden – perhaps the best-known commentator on the *General Prologue* – still saw the Knight as the personification of the ideals of knighthood: 'The champion of the Church, the righteous and implacable enemy of the infidel, the compassionate protector of the weak and oppressed, the defender of all Right and Justice.'[26] ☐

Jones, however (as may be discerned from the subtitle of his book), argues as an historian against this received opinion and comes up with some startling observations:

■ And yet, as 'the quintessence of chivalry' the Knight leaves much to be desired: he is not endowed with any physical beauty or grace; there is no mention of any family background, no coat-of-arms, no shield, no belt (crucial to the truly 'gentil' or noble knight), no manorial estates. He shows no interest in the courtly pastimes of hunting, hawking or courtly love. His dress is shabby, his retinue small, and his life-long career on the battlefield has been exclusively abroad and has apparently missed out on all the great English victories of the period – such as Crécy, Poitiers and Nájera – on which the reputation of English chivalry in the fourteenth century rested. On the contrary, throughout a period when England was constantly at war with her neighbours and repeatedly threatened with invasion from the French, Scots, Spaniards and even Danes, the Knight has not once fought for his own king and country.

Moreover, the assertion that all the Knight's campaigns were idealistic crusades against the infidel is inaccurate and ignores the fact that there was, in Chaucer's day, a lively debate as to whether such 'crusades' were justifiable at all. In any case, is it credible that Chaucer – the humanist who chooses a polemical pacifist tract as his own tale – could really have believed that killing heathens was the best way of converting them to the religion of love and peace?[27] ☐

In his final chapter, Jones explores the reasons for the Knight's interruption of the Monk. He then concludes his work with a composite assessment of the Knight's character and behaviour:

THE GENERAL PROLOGUE

■ Far from finding *The Monk's Tale* boring, the other pilgrims on that road to Canterbury must have been enjoying themselves hugely at the Knight's expense. The Monk 'quits' the Knight's eulogy of the proud conqueror Theseus [in *The Knight's Tale*] by a compendious exposition of the folly of those who, like the Knight, put their trust in Fortune and in worldly glory, for

> . . . Fortune alwey wole assaille
> With unwar strook the regnes that been proude;
> [*The Monk's Tale*, 11.2763–4]

> (Fortune will always bring low with an unexpected blow, the rulers that are proud [Jones's translation].)

With *The Monk's Tale* and the Knight's irritable interruption, Chaucer completes a cycle within the overall structure of his great work. In the *Prologue* he describes a typical mercenary of his day, whose career has been one of bloodshed and oppression and yet who pretends to the dignity of the old-style feudal retainer. In *The Knight's Tale*, he presents a chivalric romance, seen through the eyes of a mercenary captain, which consequently turns into a hymn to tyranny – just as the mercenaries themselves had become the mainstay of the modern tyrant. In *The Monk's Tale*, he 'quits' the Knight's authoritarian and materialistic vision of the world by illustrating the debasement of modern chivalry and by asserting the right of the people to bring down tyrants. At the same time the Monk asserts the Boethian view of the folly of seeking human happiness in worldly power and glory [see Douglas L. Lepley's 'The Monk's Boethian Tale' in *The Chaucer Review*, XII 3 (1978): pp.162–70].

The whole cycle is vibrant with the political realities that Chaucer saw around him – the established tyrannies abroad and the nascent tyranny at home. It shows Chaucer as a concerned, committed writer, very much involved in and remarkably outspoken about the problems that most concerned the government and the ordinary people of his day.[28] □

Higgs's and Jones's reading of the Knight could not be more different, yet, when all is said and done, these two critics share the belief that the creator of *The General Prologue* was 'concerned' and socially aware. Both also paint Chaucer as a poet who was interested in exploring the dynamics of power in this poem. In this they are not alone, for Judith Ferster promotes a similar vision in the already mentioned *Chaucer on Interpretation* (1985). Our final extracts from the 1980s show Ferster exploring 'the themes of literary and political authority' via the figure of the narrator and, at more length, that of the Host. Ferster suggests that the Host is a signifier of, well, a whole host of things:

■ The narrative frame of the *Canterbury Tales* is the tale about the tales. The relationships among Harry Bailly, the narrator, and the pilgrims demonstrate the themes of literary and political authority . . . The political questions about who will lead and how decisions will be made bear upon the literary questions because at stake are the terms of the storytelling game and the order of the stories. All the negotiations and arguments concern the shape and meaning of the text (although only the narrator refers to the literary text explicitly).

As Alan T. Gaylord has pointed out [in '*Sentence and Solaas* in Fragment VII of the *Canterbury Tales*: Harry Bailley as Horseback Editor', *Proceedings of the Modern Language Association*, 82 (1967): pp. 226–35], when the Host becomes master of ceremonies of the pilgrimage, he tries to commission certain kinds of tales in a certain order, and judges and interprets some of them. He is part editor, part patron, part literary critic. He is both a producer and a consumer of the text. As he stands before the pilgrims, nominating himself as leader and requesting election by acclamation, he stands for authors, especially those who perform their works orally. Like poet-performers, he must have the consent of the group in order to entertain them. But since he tells no tale of his own, he is also consumer as producer, representing the audience's power over the shape and meaning of the text. In contrast, the narrator is producer as consumer, or rather he pretends to be. He claims to be merely a reporter of the events and stories of the trip. Only at the beginning of Fragment II is "Chaucer" identified as a poet, more prolific than talented (by the Man of Law, ll. 45–76). It is significant that Chaucer lets one of his characters announce him as a poet. This is not merely a joke, although it has all the fun of Don Quixote's discovery of a book about his own adventures or Mozart's self-quotation in *Don Giovanni*. The issue is how much the author is willing to claim for himself.

Both Harry Bailly and the narrator are wrong in how much they claim. The Host claims too much authority for himself, as the intransigence of his 'material' shows; the narrator claims too little, as we can see by careful examination of what he says about his role. The narrative frame articulates the paradox that I [have] . . . called the too-powerful powerlessness of the author. If we compare the two figures and "correct" their inaccurate statements about their roles, we can see another version of the paradoxes of interpretation: Identity, meaning, and political power are independent and yet created in and for specific social contexts . . . [The] Host . . . embodies the paradox of combining partial self-revelation with selective imitation of the pilgrims as he becomes their leader.[29] ■

Ferster goes on to acknowledge that 'Others have noted that Harry Bailly is a tyrant' (see David R. Pichaske and Laura Sweetland, 'Chaucer on the Medieval Monarchy: Harry Bailley in the *Canterbury Tales*', *The Chaucer Review*, 11 (1976–7), pp. 179–200).[30] She herself elaborates upon this in relation to the Host's agreement to be the 'governour,/And of oure tales juge and reportour' (ll. 813–14) of the tale-telling contest. We are asked to be mindful that it was, after all, his idea in the first place:

■ In becoming their ruler, he is . . . shaping himself to their desires.

    In the morning the pilgrims begin to reap the rewards of their pact with the Host. Whereas the night before he referred to the possibility that someone would "withseye" his judgment (l. 805), now anyone who disagrees does not merely "seye" something, but mutinies, becoming "rebel to my juggement" (l. 833). The Host adopts language consonant with his new role. He addresses some people with the familiar form of the second-person pronoun, issues commands, and, in an authoritarian move that defies both logic and courtesy, orders the Knight to draw lots because "that is myn accord" (l. 838). The singular "accord" takes full responsibility for the supposed agreement and treats the Knight as a legal nonentity.

    Harry Bailly is acting the tyrant, a role that will prove dangerous. The tone of authority is not backed up by absolute power; his power is actually derived from the consent of the governed. When he ignores his dependence on them, he overreaches and makes himself vulnerable to rebellion, which is just what he hopes to avoid. The rest of Fragment A witnesses the erosion of his power.[31] □

In Ferster's reading, the Host emerges as a despotic ruler, one not dissimilar to the tyrants of Shakespeare's History plays. The Host as Richard III? It is certainly food for thought.

    This lengthy chapter began with a discussion of the 'new wave' of criticism which swept over Chaucer studies in the 1980s. Much of the splash, of course, was also caused by gender studies and feminist critiques of the poetry. Julian N. Wasserman and Robert Blanch, for example, speak of this in their *Introduction to Chaucer in the Eighties* (1986). Charting the varied contents of this volume, they write: ' . . . mingling of measures medieval and modern is especially evident in those essays which take up questions involving women.'[32] Approaches of this nature were even more widely applied to *The General Prologue* in the 1990s and shall, accordingly, be the main focus of the final chapter of this Guide.

CHAPTER SIX

# 'She was a Worthy Womman al hir Lyve': The 1990s

IT WAS mentioned in the Introduction to this Guide that *A Variorum Edition of the Works of Geoffrey Chaucer* was published in 1993; volume two of this edition is devoted to *The General Prologue*. In this volume, Malcolm Andrew speaks in a general way about the 'accounts of topics and approaches which have proved particularly influential and significant in writing on the *General Prologue*'.[1] Taken together, this amounts to a vast body of scholarship. This expansion has, of course, continued into the 1990s and one growth area in recent decades is that of feminist and gender-based readings of *The Canterbury Tales*. Critics have examined Chaucer's portrayal of such female characters as Virginia, Custance and Griselda from, respectively, the tales of the Physician, the Man of Law and the Clerk; and the archetypal old man/young woman relationship acted out by January and May in *The Merchant's Tale* has also been the subject of study.[2] Indeed, the notion of a 'feminist Chaucer' has even been mooted. Gayle Margherita, in her essay 'Originary Fantasies and Chaucer's *Book of the Duchess*' (1993), outlines the arguments for and against this reading of the poet's gender politics and, simultaneously, provides Chaucer's readers with a useful mini-bibliography:

■ The idea of a feminist Chaucer reflects, on the one hand, recent interest in feminist readings of Chaucer and, on the other, a simultaneous desire to exculpate Chaucer the poet on the charge of phallocentrism. Some of the more politically problematic aspects of this phenomena [sic] are discussed at length by Elaine Tuttle Hansen in her essay "Fearing for Chaucer's Good Name," *Exemplaria* 2, no. 1 (Spring 1990): 23–36. Many of Hansen's points are well taken, particularly her indictment of what she calls the "post-feminist" trend in contemporary medievalism. Her essay is, however, based on some essentializing assumptions about the relationship between "male" versus "female" reading and writing that I find difficult to accept. Hansen defines feminist criticism in terms of "an insistence that the gender of the author and reader/critic matters." This definition carries with it decidedly empiricist assumptions, most notably the idea that writing bears an immediate and unproblematic relation to the experience of gender. If the gender of the *author* is so important, how can feminist criticism address the huge corpus of anonymous works from the Middle Ages? If the gender of the *critic* determines his or her capacity to read politically or not, how can feminism become more than a single-sex discourse? How can it address the equally problematic category of masculinity? Is the gender-category of "man" to remain unproblematic, while that of "woman" remains as a site of contention, contradiction, and instability? More to the (political) point, what does Hansen's assumption promise for those of us who are *not* heterosexual, that is, who have only a vexed relationship to our culturally determined gender? These are difficult questions, questions I will not presume to answer here. I do think, however, that there is more at stake in the idea of a feminist Chaucer than merely "Chaucer's good name." For a provocative analysis of the discursive and cultural implications of gender as an epistemological category, see Nancy Armstrong, "The Gender Bind: Women and the Disciples," *Genders* 3 (Fall 1988): 1–23.[3] □

There is also the continuing, related interest in the inter-relationship of the tales of the so-called 'Marriage Group', a name coined by G.L. Kittredge in his article 'Chaucer's Discussion of Marriage'.[4] Priscilla Martin summarises Kittredge's theory as follows:

■ ... ... On this view, the Wife of Bath initiates a debate on marriage with her polemical Prologue and Tale, both stories of a wife's successful bid for 'maistrye' over her husband. Giving the lie to her complaint that no clerk will speak good of women, the Clerk retaliates with his Tale of an absolutely obedient wife. The Merchant, embittered by his own brief experience of marriage to a woman who could not be more different from Griselda, tells a savagely ironic story of female treachery and male fantasy and folly. The *Franklin's Tale* repeats the knight-wife-squire triangle but with better-natured characters and a happy outcome. It also opens quite differently, with a genuinely good marriage between unselfish people who negotiate a kind of equity. The Merchant's ironic encomium of marriage is echoed and answered in the Franklin's sincere praise. He repudiates both the Wife of Bath's doctrine of female sovereignty and the theory of male dominance embodied in the Clerk's Walter. Kittredge concludes that the Franklin offers not only the solution to the marriage debate but also Chaucer's own view on the subject and, indeed, ours: "We need not hesitate, therefore, to accept the solution which the Franklin offers as that which Geoffrey Chaucer the man accepted for his own part. Certainly it is a solution that does him infinite credit. A better has never been devised or imagined."[5] ☐

Feminist criticism of *The General Prologue* has tended, not surprisingly, to focus on the only two women described in the pilgrim portraits, the Wife of Bath and the Prioress. This approach has not, however, been without its difficulties. Like Margherita above, Elaine Tuttle Hansen, in *Chaucer and the Fictions of Gender* (1992), explains what critics are up against when they attempt to adopt feminist approaches to pre-modern texts. Chaucer's attitude is not, at least, the problem. In fact, where women are concerned his attitude is seen as enlightened:

■ . . . . . . What then, I have inquired, is the nature and function of late twentieth-century feminist analysis of . . . canonical, male-authored late medieval texts?

As I have pursued this question, I have become convinced that in Chaucer studies, the uncertain footing of any feminist approach to pre-modern works has been made even more slippery, ironically, by the unusual ease with which a prima facie case for the importance of women as characters and Woman (and gender, where the feminine is the marked position) as topic can be made. Under the influence of recent mediations [debates] in the practice of literary criticism, a growing number of scholars . . . have concluded in one way or another that the representation of women in Chaucerian fiction testifies to the poet's open-mindedness and even intentional subversion of traditional antifeminist positions. This view is sometimes part of a move to make Chaucer studies more theoretically au courant and to draw analogies between various contemporary approaches and Chaucer's insights and methods. There has been no systematic and thorough attempt to posit the evolution of the protofeminism that many have identified in Chaucer and his poetry. However, if the implications of separate studies were brought together and extended, it would be possible to see that they sketch a developmental poetics in which the female voice itself, as speaker instead of spoken about, gradually enters Chaucerian fiction, while, as one recent critic [Lee Patterson] sees it, Chaucer "abandoned his career as a poet of women."[6] ☐

Other gender-based approaches have dealt with the masculinity of the Host and the sexual orientation of the Pardoner. As early as 1948, Muriel Bowden, for example, in her pioneering work *A Commentary on the General Prologue to The Canterbury Tales* (which is discussed at length in chapter two of this Guide) posited the theory that the Pardoner was clearly portrayed as homosexual by Chaucer. She supports her argument with a close reading of this pilgrim's portrait and a consideration of his relationship with the Summoner. Bowden's views on this friendship are far from liberal:

■ ... ... The Pardoner sings a particular song [to the Summoner] ... and although he has selected a verse which may be part of some popular ditty, the suggestion is that he has not chosen at random: he addresses the words evidently to the evil Summoner, who, far from being unresponsive to depraved and unnatural advances, trumpets forth a bass accompaniment ['burdoun', l. 673] to emphasize his perverted friendship with the Pardoner. To be sure Chaucer may here be making allusion also to the generally observed connivance between many summoners and pardoners in their successful efforts to fleece the people; but it seems plain that Chaucer meant the stress to fall on the personal nature of a specific relationship. Certainly Chaucer's description of the physical attributes of the Pardoner mark this figure explicitly as the kind of person we immediately suspect him to be.[7] □

Bowden's concludes on a similarly disapproving note:

■ ... ... The Pardoner may properly be shown to be the scoundrel he is: a lying, avaricious, and shameless cheat, hawking his pigs' bones as relics, preaching eloquent sermons only to deceive, and openly singing love-ditties in his girlish voice to a diseased and wicked summoner.[8] □

A more modern exploration of the Pardoner's homosexuality and the scholarship surrounding it is Monica E. McAlpine's 'The Pardoner's Homosexuality and How It Matters' of 1980. McAlpine provides here an extremely detailed set of responses to the key questions surrounding the character of the Pardoner and she begins her article by reiterating these for the reader:

■ The famous pronouncement of Chaucer's narrator on Chaucer's Pardoner – "I trowe he were a geldyng or a mare" [l. 691] – poses several questions for modern readers. What are the options that it offers for the interpretation of the Pardoner? Why is the narrator unable to decide between them? To what extent does Chaucer maintain this indeterminacy about the Pardoner and require the reader, like the narrator, to remain forever undecided? Does Chaucer in any way lead the reader to a greater certitude? If so, what is the sexual status of the Pardoner? Finally, what is the moral significance of that status? These questions arise partly from the complexity of Chaucer's poetry and partly from present-day ignorance of medieval sexual concepts and terminology.[9] □

## 'SHE WAS A WORTHY WOMMAN AL HIR LYVE': THE 1990s

McAlpine continues:

■ The term "mare," in particular, has proved notoriously difficult for modern readers to interpret, and even when the term is glossed, the possibility that the Pardoner may be a "mare" is often ignored in favor of the belief that he is certainly a "geldyng," or eunuch. Psychological, moral, and spiritual interpretations of the Pardoner's eunuchry and of the sterility and, less accurately, the impotence with which it is associated permeate current critical treatments of this pilgrim. A faithful reading of Chaucer's line requires that the balance be restored. We need a gloss for "mare," and we need interpretations of the Pardoner's portrait and of his prologue and tale that explore the implications of his possible status as "geldyng." It is neither likely nor desirable that such a reading will replace the view of the Pardoner as eunuch; rather, it is to be hoped it will shed new light on familiar aspects of Chaucer's characterization.

As a contribution to this work, I wish to offer, in the first and longer part of this essay, a more detailed argument than has so far been attempted in favor of viewing the Pardoner as a possible homosexual. In the second part, I consider the spiritual implications of the Pardoner's sexuality by redirecting attention to his bagful of pardons and relics. The initial references to these objects occupy a significant place in the middle section of the Pardoner's tripartite portrait in the General Prologue: he is not only a "geldyng or a mare" (ll. 669–91) but also both a "pardoner" peddling false relics (ll. 692–706) and a "noble ecclesiaste" (ll. 707–14). Through an interpretation of the Pardoner as homosexual, I hope to confirm what this structure suggests: that his pardons and relics constitute the essential link, the lifeline, between this sexually anomalous Christian and his church.[10] □

As part one of McAlpine's study deals specifically with the Pardoner as he is presented in *The General Prologue* it is, accordingly, reproduced in full in the following extract:

■ For many of Chaucer's readers, the narrator's pronouncement is intimately linked with certain deservedly influential commentaries on the Pardoner's sexual status, and any reconsideration of the subject must acknowledge its debt to those studies and carefully discriminate its conclusions from theirs. In his ground-breaking review of medieval texts on medicine and physiognomy [defined in the *OED* as 'The art of judging character and disposition from the features of the face or the form and lineaments of the body generally'], **Walter Clyde Curry** [in *Chaucer and the Mediaeval Sciences* of 1926] **opened discussion of the Pardoner's physical nature. Although the point is seldom noticed,**

Curry interprets the narrator's pronouncement as offering a choice between impotence and effeminacy (p. 58). He treats the mention of these two sexual phenomena as serving to define a third possibility, underlying and unnamed, and then shows that the Pardoner's physical characteristics – long, fine hair; high voice; glaring eyes; and beardlessness – fit the descriptions of eunuchs offered by medieval doctors and physiognomists. All but one of Curry's sources, moreover, associate eunuchry with immorality, and some also insist that the congenital eunuch is more evil than the castrated eunuch. The sins attributed to eunuchs include dissoluteness, shamelessness, cunning, and viciousness. In what has proved the least convincing part of his argument, Curry contends that the other pilgrims, and Chaucer's audience, would have been able to go beyond the narrator's speculations to deduce that the Pardoner suffers from the (presumably rare) condition of congenital eunuchry.

Since in the view of the medieval experts the physical characteristics of all eunuchs are much the same, Curry's labeling of the Pardoner as a *congenital* eunuch is grounded not in unarguable physiognomical fact, as is sometimes believed, but in fallible literary interpretation. One argument appeals to the influence of source. Chaucer may have based his Pardoner, in part, on the characterization of a eunuch by the physiognomist Polemon (pp. 62–4), and Curry assumes that because Polemon's eunuch was a congenital eunuch, Chaucer's must be, too. A second argument rests on Curry's own estimate of the Pardoner's character; the depth of the Pardoner's depravity is seen as justifying his classification with the more malicious congenital eunuchs rather than with the comparatively benign castrated eunuchs (pp. 59–64). Moreover, by concentrating on the moral distinction between congenital eunuchs and castrated eunuchs, a prominent distinction in his sources, Curry distracts his readers from what he himself understands to be the different distinction in the General Prologue: that between "geldyng" and "mare." While he reveals the accuracy with which Chaucer uses the stereotype of the eunuch for some of the details of the Pardoner's portrait, Curry neither proves that the Pardoner is a congenital eunuch nor definitively exhausts the implications of the narrator's pronouncement.

The relationship of the Pardoner's eunuchry to his spiritual condition and to the larger themes of Chaucer's work was first addressed in a sophisticated way by Robert Miller [in 'Chaucer's Pardoner, the Scriptural Eunuch, and the *Pardoner's Tale*', *Speculum* 30, (1955), pp. 180–99]. Miller examines medieval biblical glosses that attempt to resolve a conflict in attitudes towards eunuchs in the Old Testament. Deuteronomy xxiii.1, reflecting a literal-minded racial and sexual perception of holiness, excludes eunuchs from the temple, while Isaiah lvi. 3–5, taking a more spiritual approach, gives assurances that righteous eunuchs are among God's people. The medieval commentators found a solution to this conflict in a statement of Christ's discriminating among congenital eunuchs, involuntary castrates, and "eunuchs who have made themselves such for the Kingdom of heaven" (Matt[hew] xix.12). Identifying the last group, the voluntary celibates in the service of God, as the eunuchs of Isaiah who will be accepted by God, the commentators go on to invent a second group of metaphorical eunuchs who will be rejected, as in Deuteronomy: those who, while capable of good works, deliberately remain spiritually sterile. Miller argues that the Pardoner's physical eunuchry is the sign of his deliberate spiritual sterility. His chosen role as *eunuchus non Dei* [eunuch not of God] is seen as bitterly satiric, since he has a special responsibility as a churchman to be a *eunuchus Dei* [eunuch of God], fruitful in good works.

If, however, Chaucer did use the Pardoner's physical condition as a sign in this way, he ran a considerable risk of undermining the very spiritual values he was attempting to communicate. Both Christ and the medieval commentators were reacting against the physical determinism of one strain of Jewish tradition. For them, involuntary eunuchry had no necessary moral significance at all; they were attempting to free the career of the soul from questions of genital competency. Miller's Pardoner, in contrast, is a static figure. While Miller rightly emphasizes the free action by which the Pardoner would have become a *eunuchus non Dei*, he does not recognize in Chaucer's characterization a continuing human potential for change. Because the immutable physical fact of eunuchry is taken as the sign of the Pardoner's spiritual status, his soul cannot be allowed its own career independent of his sexual destiny. Despite this difficulty, Miller's study has done more than any other to establish the level of seriousness on which the problem of the Pardoner's sexuality should be addressed. Moreover, the biblical materials he has brought to our attention can now be seen as documenting one kind of consideration that medieval people gave to a question central to Chaucer's characterization of the Pardoner: What is the place of sexually different, or "deviant," persons in the scheme of salvation?

Wide acceptance of the conclusions of Curry and Miller has had the unintended side effect of dulling readers' responses to the Pardoner; this pilgrim, it seems, has been fully "explained." As Donald Howard puts it in *The Idea of the Canterbury Tales*, the theory of the Pardoner's congenital and "scriptural" eunuchry has become an excuse for not taking him seriously. In his dazzling treatment of the Pardoner as a grotesque, as a "feminoid" or "hermaphroditic" male, Howard succeeds in re-creating the strangeness of this pilgrim – his power to mystify, frighten, and fascinate. Partly from motives of anger and revenge, the

Pardoner alienates himself from the community of human and divine values; in Howard's view, he becomes – like evil itself as defined in medieval philosophy, like the grotesque in manuscript illuminations, and like the very fragment of the *Canterbury Tales* in which his tale appears – something "on the periphery of the ordered world of created goodness," "marginal," "floating," "outside," "demonic" (pp. 338–41). Curiously, Howard accepts as fact the congenital and "scriptural" eunuchry that theories have attributed to the Pardoner and claims that we know the character's sexual status while the narrator and the others do not (pp. 343–5). His discussion of the Pardoner nevertheless proceeds, rightly I think, as if we share the same general perspectives as the pilgrims – that is, as if we too remain uncertain about the Pardoner's sexual status and thus experience the whole man as mysterious.

Howard fears that any interpretation of the Pardoner as homosexual would "explain" the Pardoner in the same deadening and unprofitable way as the belief in the character's eunuchry has and that the modern stereotype of the effeminate male homosexual would be anachronistically used to deny the Pardoner mystery. While I agree that the danger of another reductive reading is real, a view of the Pardoner as homosexual would not necessarily have this effect; for the danger lies not in any particular sexual definition but in the manner of relating the Pardoner's sexuality to his spirituality. Nor is the stereotype of effeminate male homosexuality an anachronism; it is as authentically medieval as it is modern. Indeed, the medieval confusion of homosexuality with effeminacy and, as we shall see, with other sexual phenomena indicates both that Chaucer's contemporaries tried to explain homosexuality to themselves and that they failed to dispel the mystery it presented to them. It is true, however, that I cannot produce a Pardoner quite so enigmatic as Howard's, but this difference arises not from our disagreement about the Pardoner's possible homosexuality but from my unwillingness to accept, with Howard (p. 351), the Pardoner's definition of himself as a "ful vicious man." By turning our attention from the standard glosses on the Pardoner's sexuality to the literary characterization itself, Howard has brought the Pardoner alive again; but in his invaluable explication of the Pardoner as grotesque, he accepts too fully the Pardoner's own tortured and theatrical self-image. While giving detailed consideration to the possibility that the Pardoner is isolated from his heterosexual and homophobic peers by a condition of homosexuality, I emphasize the Pardoner's identity as a pilgrim in the fellowship of other pilgrims, motivated, even in his cupidity, by the love they all seek and experiencing an anguished self-division not unlike what others suffer.

The first step in a reconsideration of the Pardoner's sexuality must be the establishment of a gloss for "mare." "Geldyng" and "mare" are

## 'SHE WAS A WORTHY WOMMAN AL HIR LYVE': THE 1990s

homely metaphors that must have meanings both familiar and fairly precise for Chaucer's medieval audience; modern readers, however, face difficulties in recovering those meanings. Curry's influence is registered, but often inaccurately or incompletely, in modern editions of the *Canterbury Tales*. Among recent editors, only Donald Howard glosses both "geldyng" and "mare," and he interprets the first as "castrated eunuch" and the second as "congenital eunuch." John Hurt Fisher [in *The Complete Poetry and Prose of Geoffrey Chaucer* of 1977] preserves Curry's too narrow interpretation of "geldyng" as suggesting impotence, while Albert Baugh [in *Chaucer's Major Poetry* of 1963] reflects what I think is the most common understanding of Curry's argument (and of the Pardoner's status): that "geldyng" means "eunuch" (without implying any differentiation of types) and that the Pardoner is a eunuch. Neither Fisher nor Baugh, however, repeats Curry's interpretation of "mare" as a reference to effeminacy or offers any alternative gloss for that word. Finally, while both the *Middle English Dictionary* and the *Oxford English Dictionary* fully document the use of "geldyng" as a term for "eunuch," neither includes any evidence for a meaning of "mare" relevant to Chaucer's context.

For many modern readers, the obvious possible translations for "mare" are "effeminate male" and "homosexual male." Until recently, though, there appeared to be no evidence that the word had been used in either of these senses. Then, in 1973, Jill Mann pointed to a Latin poem by the twelfth-century satirist Walter of Chatillôn in which homosexual men, also described as effeminate, are labeled "mares": "equa fit equus", "the horse becomes a mare" (*Medieval Estates Satire*, p. 146). While it is not certain that Chaucer knew Walter's works, they were relatively well known in England, and the poem does add weight to the suggestion that "mare" may mean "effeminate male" or "homosexual male" or both. But even if there were no question about Chaucer's having read the poem, one supporting text would not constitute proof of his meaning.

We need not wait for the discovery of more supporting texts, however. The details of the Pardoner's portrait and the term "geldyng" create a context that suggests criteria for glossing "mare." "Mare" must be a term commonly used in Chaucer's day to designate a male person who, though not necessarily sterile or impotent, exhibits physical traits suggestive of femaleness, visible characteristics that were also associated with eunuchry in medieval times and that were thought to have broad effects on the psyche and on character. The gloss that most satisfactorily fulfills these criteria is "a homosexual." Chaucer did not know the word "homosexual," of course, since it did not enter the language until 1869, but he might have referred to what we call homosexuality by making a biblical reference (to sodomites), a mythological reference (to Ganymede or Orpheus), a historical reference (to Julius Caesar, for example), or a philosophical reference (to sinners against nature). As we shall see, the choice of "mare" has several important and related advantages: it avoids provoking an immediate response of condemnation, which other references might have invited; it focuses attention not on sexual acts but on a type of person in whose soma [body] and psyche [mind] Chaucer apparently believed homosexuality to be deeply rooted; and it suggests an attitude on the narrator's part in keeping with his character – a mixture of sympathy, amusement, and condescension.

Since several historical accounts are available, I shall not pause to document in detail the familiarity of Chaucer's audience with male homosexuality; I should like to explore instead the situation reflected in my criteria for glossing "mare," the confusion of homosexuality with other sexual phenomena.

In using a word denoting femaleness, Chaucer reflects one ancient and widespread misunderstanding about male homosexuality, that it involves a man's becoming in some sense a woman. The concept of effeminacy provides one way of thinking about this supposed transformation, but care must be taken in interpreting references to effeminacy in the medieval setting. The *Middle English Dictionary* records only two uses of the word "effeminate," both in the sense of "self-indulgent" or "unreasonable." Satires on the fop, often described as long-haired and beardless, reflect a perception of feminization of behavior and appearance without any necessary suggestion of homosexuality (Mann, *Medieval Estates Satire*, pp. 147–8). In medieval Latin, however, *effeminatus* sometimes means "homosexual," as in the Vulgate Bible, and this sense had passed into English by the time of the King James Bible ([Derrick Sherwin] Bailey, [*Homosexuality and the Western Christian Tradition*, 1955] pp. 38–9, 48–53). There is some evidence, moreover, that the young aristocrat who aspired to fashion had to be careful to observe the boundaries that marked off effeminacy and homosexuality. At the end of a lengthy set of instructions on conduct, dress, and grooming in Guillaume de Lorris' *Roman de la rose*, for example, the God of Love tells the young lover:

> Cous tes manches, tes cheveus pigne,
> Mais ne te farde ne ne [sic] guigne:
> Ce n'apartient s'as dames non,
> Ou a ceus de mauvais renon,
> Qui amors par male aventure
> Ont trovees contre Nature.

## 'SHE WAS A WORTHY WOMMAN AL HIR LYVE': THE 1990s

> Sew your sleeves and comb your hair, but do not rouge or paint your face, for such a custom belongs only to ladies or to men of bad repute, who have had the misfortune to find a love contrary to Nature. (ll. 2169–74)

Just as not all effeminate males were suspected of homosexuality, so not all homosexual males were perceived as effeminate. In his translation of Dante's *Inferno*, Mark Musa notes the contrast between the effeminate speech patterns of the sodomitical clerks in Canto xv and the more robust manner of the sodomitical soldiers in Canto xvi. Since the substance of what constitutes effeminacy in males is culturally defined and subject to change, it is not necessary to find in the Middle Ages exact replicas of our current stereotype of effeminacy in homosexual males (including, for example, distinctive walk or hand movements); it is only necessary to show that certain types of feminized behavior and appearance in males were sometimes interpreted as evidence of homosexuality. Thus, even if the primary meaning of "mare" was "an effeminate male," a second meaning may have been a "possibly homosexual male."

Another ancient way of conceiving the male homosexual's supposed participation in the feminine was to think of him as a hermaphrodite. In Hellenic [Greek] rites and legends, the hermaphrodite is a double god, a being with the overt equipment of both sexes (i.e., male genitals and female breasts), a symbol of unity, fruitfulness, and eternal life. In Hellenistic art, however, the hermaphrodite is an extremely feminized figure, though recognizably male, representative of one ideal of homosexual beauty. Interest in this type of hermaphrodite revived during the twelfth-century resurgence of classical scholarship ([Ernst] Curtius, [*European Literature in the Latin Middle Ages, 1953*] pp. 113–6). A late and perhaps unconscious reflection of this tradition, evidence of its thorough absorption into European thinking, appears in the treatment of the story of Sodom and Gomorrah in the Middle English *Purity*, a work commonly ascribed to the *Gawain* poet. The poet describes Lot's first glimpse of the angels as they pass through the crowded streets of Sodom toward his house; they are extraordinarily beautiful young men with beardless chins, rosy complexions, and luxurious hair like raw silk (I have modernised some of the characters in the following quotation):

> As he stared into the strete, ther stout men played,
> He syye ther swey in asent swete men twyne.
> Bolde burnes wer thay bothe, with berdles chynnes,
> Royl rollande fax to raw sylk lyke,
> Of ble as the brere-flour, where-so the bare scheweed.

Ful clene was the countenance of her cler yyen;
Wlonk whit was her wede, and wel hit hem semed; (ll. 787–93)

On one level the beauty of the angels is meant to suggest a spiritual excellence superior to all considerations and distinctions of human sexuality; but as A. C. Spearing remarks, it also explains something left unexplained in the biblical text: how the men of Sodom came to desire homosexual intercourse with the angels. It seems likely that a hermaphroditic or feminoid male would have been suspected of sexual deviance.

An alternative to thinking of the male homosexual as a woman-man was to think of him as a nonman, for homosexuality was long confused with eunuchry. In Gautier de Leu's thirteenth-century fabliau "La Veuve," for example, a widow who remarries finds the vigorous sexual performance of her new husband on the wedding night nonetheless disappointing [marked omissions are McAlpine's]:

Nos avons çaiens un bruhier,
un durfeüt, un hebohet.
Ahi! Con Damerdex me het
qui fui des bons vallés aquius,
et des cortois et des gentius,
si pris cest caitif par nature.
............................................

Et cis ribaus me tient plus vil
que le femier de son cortil,
mais je sai bien, par Saint Eloi,
qu'il n'est mie de bone loi,
ains est de çaus del Mont Wimer:
il n'a a soing de dames amer.

What have we here? An impotent,
beardless ne'er-do-well! Ah me!
The Lord must hate me bitterly,
who turned away from fine young men,
well born, courteous, and then
wound up with this congenital bum!
............................................

This scoundrel shows me less regard
than he does the dungheap in the yard.
However, by Saint Loy I know
his moral code is just as low

as that of those on Mount Wimer;
for woman's love he doesn't care.

The widow equates less than heroic sexual performance with impotence, impotence with beardless eunuchry, both of these with homosexuality, and all of these with heresy, for the reference to Mount Wimer concerns a large group of *bougres* [Bulgars, here meaning homosexuals] who were burned to death for homosexuality and heresy in Champagne in 1239. The fabliau makes fun of the widow and her insatiable appetite, but the intended comedy of her speech must have depended partly on the pervasiveness of just such misunderstandings; at the same time, the poet who made comedy out of the widow's confusion must himself have been in some degree superior to it. Like the French poet, Chaucer may be seen as making artistic use of what he perceived to be common misunderstandings of sexual phenomena. The Pardoner's possible eunuchry may contribute to the portrait of a homosexual since medieval people apparently strove to understand homosexuality by identifying it with now one, now another, sexual anomaly.

Seen against this background, Chaucer's portrait of the Pardoner in the General Prologue emerges as a pastiche of allusions to the three distinct sexual phenomena with which homosexuality was often confused – effeminacy, hermaphroditism, and eunuchry – and thus very probably to homosexuality itself. In the order of their appearance in the portrait the allusions are the description of the Pardoner's hair – its length and fineness suggesting effeminacy, eunuchry, and hermaphroditism and his grooming of it suggesting effeminacy; the Pardoner's concern with fashion, implying effeminacy; the references to goats and hares, suggesting hermaphroditism; the high voice, connoting effeminacy and eunuchry; the glaring eyes, associated with eunuchry; and the beardlessness, a symptom of effeminacy, eunuchry, hermaphroditism, and homosexuality. Furthermore, the glaring eyes and references to goats, hares, and mares connote extreme lechery, which is at least as suggestive of sexual deviance as of sexual inadequacy. What this catalog shows is that most of the allusions tend to be *multivalent* [able to be read in more than one way], and the reason is that the lines between these various sexual phenomena were fluid in medieval theory. It is impossible to say whether beardlessness, for example, was more likely to suggest eunuchry or homosexuality to a medieval person. Because of this fluidity, too, references to effeminacy, hermaphroditism, and eunuchry could serve as a code for homosexuality. Finally, while the categories "effeminate," "hermaphrodite," and "eunuch" can each account for some of the Pardoner's characteristics, only the category "homosexual" can account for all of them. For example, while the Pardoner's interest in fashion can be referred directly only to effeminacy (and not to eunuchry or hermaphroditism) and the narrator's allusion to goats only to hermaphroditism, both can be referred to homosexuality through what the medieval audience regarded as the mediating concepts of effeminacy and hermaphroditism.

Thus at a minimum it seems impossible to exclude the suggestion of homosexuality from the portrait. It is also impossible for the reader not to be influenced by the opening frame for this physical description: the presentation of the Pardoner's association with the Summoner. The nature of this association has long been debated, but there is no doubt that the Pardoner is introduced to us traveling with a male "friend" and "compeer" and that the two are singing, in their contrasting voices, a love song, "Com hider, love, to me" (ll. 670–7[2]). This tableau may be read in two ways. The Pardoner may be seen as a frustrated homosexual who associates himself with the lecherous Summoner in order to deny his own impotence and to acquire symbolically the Summoner's virility; or he may be seen as a homosexual, ambivalent about disclosing his status, who nonetheless becomes suspect through the public display of this ambiguous friendship. These are the two possibilities that the narrator makes explicit, I believe, when he provides the closing frame for the physical description of the Pardoner: "I trowe he were a geldyng or a mare" [l. 691]. Thus these three parts of the Pardoner's portrait – the opening tableau, the physical description, and the closing pronouncement – fit together in a way that has not been fully appreciated. For the medieval audience, with its confused and limited lexicon of sexual terms and concepts, it was the physical description, I suspect, that was most ambiguous; the opening frame first provided implicit guidance, and the closing frame then explicit guidance, to its interpretation. Modern readers may have a different experience, since the meaning of the Pardoner's friendship with the Summoner has been clouded by controversy and the meaning of the term "mare" has long been lost. In this situation, the physical description, once it is set in the context of medieval sexual theory, seems to me to provide the strongest evidence of the Pardoner's possible homosexuality, which in turn helps us both to recognize a possible implication of his association with the Summoner and to gloss "mare."

Given, then, that Chaucer's text explicitly and implicitly raises the issue of homosexuality, the narrator's treatment of the Pardoner seems to unfold in this way. Faced with a somewhat bewildering set of indications to interpret, the narrator rather shrewdly cuts through the complexity to suggest that the Pardoner is either a nonman, that is, a eunuch, or a woman-man, a homosexual. Indeed the phrase "I trowe," which may denote either speculation or certainty, serves to dramatize the narrator in his role as interpreter, dealing confidently yet respectfully with resistant reality. There may even be an element of self-congratulation in his announced inability to decide exactly what the Pardoner's status is; the narrator may think that the double reference to eunuchry and homosexuality displays his sophistication. Actually, though, he is rather like the modern person who has not mastered the distinctions among homosexuals, bisexuals, transvestites, and transsexuals. One consequence of the narrator's characteristically limited perception is that we initially encounter the Pardoner as a kind of puzzle to be solved rather than as a pilgrim to be judged.

The animal imagery of the narrator's pronouncement also helps temporarily to isolate the Pardoner from moral judgment. The narrator perceives the Pardoner as someone conspicuously deficient in the animal sphere of perfection, lacking integrity of sexual identity, physical intactness, or procreative competency – the amoral perfections, elaborated in various cultural forms, that the narrator admires in the Monk and Harry Bailley. Though found wanting in one sphere, the Pardoner is perceived as supremely competent in another; thus the significance of the "but" as the narrator turns to the Pardoner's work in the world: "But of his craft, fro Berwyk into Ware,/Ne was ther swich another pardoner" (ll. 692–3). Sheer expertise, unrelated to its use or purpose, is one of the narrator's chief measures of value throughout the General Prologue (Mann, *Medieval Estates Satire*, p. 194), and this ideal, despite its moral limitations, has a special virtue in regard to the Pardoner since it embraces more than sexuality. For the narrator, the "pardoner" and the "noble ecclesiaste" are as important as the "geldyng" or the "mare." The narrator sets an example of not reducing the Pardoner to his sexuality, an example that at other levels of response Chaucer means us to emulate.

Nevertheless, we cannot be so content with the narrator's tentative diagnosis of the Pardoner as the narrator himself is. As viewed by the medieval church, eunuchry and homosexuality had very different moral statuses; pace [in all deference to] the doctors and physiognomists, eunuchry was not in itself regarded as sinful, while homosexual acts (the concept of a homosexual condition was not recognized by the moral theologians) were considered grave sins. From this standpoint the narrator's self-satisfied conclusion that the Pardoner is one thing or the other is quite astonishing, for it reflects an essentially secular perspective. Since, however, we must view the Pardoner as a pilgrim – that is, not only as an animal being and an expert worker but also as a moral being with a spiritual destiny – we need to know more than the narrator is able to tell us. The narrator's comment on the Pardoner's sexual status preserves immutably for all time the narrator's own uncertainty about his fellow pilgrim. It does not fix to the same degree the mystery about the Pardoner himself, although the absence of any other explicit statement about his sexuality means that a choice between "geldyng" and "mare" or any extrapolation using both terms will always be an *interpretation*. Many critics, having chosen "geldyng" have traced the implications of their choice in readings of the Pardoner's prologue and tale; while admitting that the Pardoner may be a eunuch as well, I choose to emphasize his possible status as a "mare," or homosexual . . . [11] ☐

McAlpine's suggestion above that the narrator of *The General Prologue*, whilst wary and uncertain of the Pardoner, openly admires the masculine, 'amoral perfections' of Harry Bailley supports what Susan Crane, for example, in her book *Gender and Romance in Chaucer's Canterbury Tales* (1994), says of the 'unquestioned masculinity ascribed to the host in the *General Prologue*'.[12] This comment was anticipated in 1986 by David Aers in *Chaucer*, and in the following short extract we find Aers concentrating on the aggressive masculinity demonstrated by the Host when he comes up against the confessional Pardoner and his 'troubling disclosure':

■ The Host is consistently presented as a conventional bourgeois Christian, hostile to any hints of nonconformism, proudly exhibiting the stereotyped marks of male egoism and aggression, piously sentimental (*General Prologue*, 1. 754; *Man of Law's Tale*, ll. 1943–62; *Merchant's Tale*, ll. 2419–40). Untroubled by any touch of his maker's critical imagination, he enjoys the unexamined life with gusto. His reaction to the Pardoner's troubling disclosure [at the end of his tale] is appropriate to the commonplace figure Chaucer composed. He bursts out in a self-righteous and personal attack on the Pardoner [translation of 'coillons' is provided by Aers]:

> I wolde I hadde thy coillons [balls] in myn hond
> In stide of relikes or of seintuarie.
> Lat kutte hem of, I wol thee helpe hem carie;
> They shul be shryned in a hogges toord!
> ([*The Pardoner's Tale*] ll. 952–5)

This violence allows th[e] Host to ignore the profoundly disturbing issues raised through Chaucer's poem and his Pardoner. It turns the individual Pardoner into a scapegoat for the massive problems and anxieties in the late medieval Church, ones that were to prove intractable. The Host assumes that by crushing (and castrating) the Pardoner the problems dramatised through his performance will simply disappear. This kind of response is still found in readings which fail to grasp the representative nature of the Pardoner and the manner in which the poem explores decisive contradictions and crisis in the official Church. Chaucer aligns such a limited response with the mentality figured forth in his Host. Instead of facing distressing institutional, intellectual and religious difficulties for what they are, individual scapegoats are singled out, substituted for the real problems and then destroyed. Any threat to the 'seuretee' of conventional piety must be suppressed; any voice that stimulates uncomfortable and potentially subversive reflection must be silenced; the abyss must be decently veiled with simple-minded pieties and certainties, however anomalous and remote from contemporary practices these have become. When the other pilgrims see the Pardoner attacked and silenced, they laugh ([*The Pardoner's Tale*] ll. 956–7, 961). True, the Knight asks Host and Pardoner to kiss: he too wishes to veil the abyss, preserving the precarious cohesion of the group, substituting laughter (not necessarily simple) for the meditation Chaucer's text stimulates and embodies ([*The Pardoner's Tale*] ll. 960–7). Some readers will choose to respond with the Host or the Knight; or in some variation of that response. But others will refuse that reaction. For these, Chaucer's writing continues to undermine the uncritical acceptance of authority and its self-images, the conventional separation of the 'spiritual' or 'ideal' from the social, economic and material dimensions of human being. For these readers this text is a supreme and characteristic moment in Chaucer's poetry, revealing his critical power as he works over major problems of authority in the religious practices and discourses of his culture.[13] □

Aers describes here the moment when an adversarial relationship between the Host and the Pardoner is established and concludes that through this altercation Chaucer is critiquing contemporary (to him) discourses of authority. This oppositional pairing is in stark contrast to the alignment that has been identified between the Pardoner and the Wife of Bath. They seem somehow connected at the moment when the Pardoner interjects his fulsome response to her rousing avowal in her *Prologue* that 'An housbonde I wol have – I wol not lette – /Which shal be bothe my dettour and my thral' (ll. 154–5). Some suggest that his response is an example of 'the lady doth protest too much' variety and that it reveals a man masquerading his male identity:

■ Up stirte the Pardoner, and that anon;
"Now, dame," quod he, "by God and by Seint John!
Ye been a noble prechour in this cas.
I was aboute to wedde a wyf; allas!
What sholde I byc it on my flessh so deere?
Yet hadde I levere wedde no wyf to-yeere!" (ll. 163–8) □

Interestingly, the Wife, like the Host, silences the Pardoner: '"Abyde!" quod she, "my tale is nat bigonne"' (l. 169). This may be more to do with her own egotism and exhibitionism, however, than with the type of aggression Aers identifies in the Host's response. Lee Patterson speaks of this connection between the Wife and the Pardoner in his book *Chaucer and the Subject of History* (1991). Patterson uses these two characters to illustrate his theory that in *The General Prologue* ' . . . Chaucer persistently filters into the narratorial description of each pilgrim an individualizing voice. Virtually every pilgrim is presented not only as a physical appearance and set of typical practices but also as a speaker, and the *Prologue* is full of references to their linguistic habits . . . '.[14] In the following short extract we see Patterson establishing a link between the Wife and the Pardoner on the basis of the rhetorical similarities their narratives display and the shared literary source from which they themselves derive:

■ In the *Wife of Bath's Prologue and Tale* Chaucer used the rhetoric of misogyny to construct a feminine subjectivity. In the remarkably similar *Pardoner's Prologue and Tale*, he deploys the rhetoric of penance for an analogous act of self-constitution. That the Pardoner and the Wife of Bath form an odd couple among the Canterbury pilgrims at the level of theme has been well argued by a number of critics; there are also several formal analogies that link them [see, for example, Anne Kernan, 'The Arch-Wife and the Eunuch', *ELH, A Journal of English Literary History* 41, (1974), pp. 1–25]. For one thing, both the Wife and the Pardoner find their immediate literary source in the *Roman de la Rose*, in the complementary figures of La Vieille and Faus Semblant. For another, the structure of their discourses are [sic] strikingly similar: a confessional prologue followed by a self-revealing tale, and the whole embedded in a carefully articulated dramatic context. But what is most important at the level of form is that in both cases their confessional narratives are preceded by tales that aspire to hagiographical authority: Man of Law-Wife of Bath, Physician-Pardoner.[15] □

Whilst Aers and others have pinpointed the main, 'immediate literary source' for the Wife of Bath's portrait as the *Roman de la Rose*, the *Prologue* to this character's tale responds equally to, and is virtually awash with, references to earlier anti-feminist texts. This is illustrated, for example, by Alcuin Blamires's discussion of *The Wife of Bath's Prologue* in his *Women Defamed and Women Defended: An Anthology of Medieval Texts* (1992). Blamires also makes the poem more accessible here by breaking it down into three distinct sections:

■ Chaucer was a subtle purveyor of the old wine of received classics. He also reinvigorated the antifeminist favourites by situating them in strange new contexts, as when Ecclesiasticus 7:29 becomes a bone of contention for Pluto and Proserpina while they are presiding over the *fabliau* denouement of *The Merchant's Tale*. Many of his poems also challenge consideration as narratives in defence of women. However, the Wife of Bath's speech partly fulfils that function even in the process of submerging the reader in a welter of misogynistic quotations. It therefore functions . . . as a kind of interface between readings from antifeminism and responses to antifeminism.

Her Prologue comes 'out of the blue' in *The Canterbury Tales*, so needs little introduction save to recall that she is one of only a few women participating in the pilgrimage and the story-telling competition which the pilgrims conduct. The Prologue can be divided into three main sections. The first (1–9) tackles [Saint] Jerome's argument with Jovinian about marriage and virginity, vigorously re-manipulating some of the ideas and scriptural texts which constitute their battleground. It has seemed to most that in the process she backs some conspicuous losers as well as trenchant winners: so she is shadowed by the stereotype of the intellectually flawed female. Ambivalence continues into the second section (14–33), ostensibly an account of her first three husbands but largely a brilliantly simple *riposte* to Theophrastan slurs. She indignantly retails these same slurs as the 'lies' her husbands have thrown at her (she pretends) in their drunkenness. Her tirade, as [Jill] **Mann** [in *Geoffrey Chaucer*, 1991, p.79] has said, 'thus functions simultaneously as a demonstration of female bullying and a witness to masculine oppression', demonstrating how 'each feeds off the other'. The last section comments on her other spouses and represents the combined forces of antifeminism as one huge book, *Of Wikked Wives* – recited to her daily by her fifth, clerical, husband. Suffocated by a procession of hostile androcentric [male-centred] writings, the Wife retaliates against both book and husband. She rips out three pages, once again vindicating woman only at the cost of conforming to a (male) caricature of philistine female rancour.[16] □

Eric Jager, in *The Tempter's Voice: Language and the Fall in Medieval Literature* (1993), identifies similar anti-feminist strains in the Wife's portrait and *Prologue* and, not surprisingly, he traces these attitudes to the biblical story of Eve and the Fall as can be seen in the following extract:

■ Though hardly written by outright misogynists, both *Ancrene Wisse* [a guide for anchoresses written c. 1225] and the *Livre du Chevalier* [*The Book of the Knight*, a French manual of manners and morality composed in the early 1370s] **show that the written record of Eve's faults and follies continued to multiply fruitfully after the twelfth century.** According to a medieval legend invoked in *Ancrene Wisse*, the Devil writes down everyone's sins and, on Judgment Day, will read aloud all those sins not "erased" by confession. The author accordingly warns the anchoress, "Give him as little to write as you possibly can, for there is no employment he likes better, and whatever he writes, take care to erase it completely" . . . Although most medieval antifeminists profess concern for the souls of the women whom they counsel and admonish as daughters of Eve, often they seem to be enthusiastically sharing an inkhorn with the Devil himself. Before the story of Eve, a male narrative, would make room for Eve's story, a truly female one, women had to take up the pen and write books themselves. But the traditional clerical accounts of the Fall were not seriously challenged – in writing and by women – until about the end of Chaucer's times. And even then a writer such as Christine de Pizan was able to defend Eve only by emphasizing that her sin was a *felix culpa* [fortunate fault].

In *The Canterbury Tales*, a fictional female contemporary of the chevalier's daughters affirms vigorously that antifeminist clerics used the story of Eve as their principal brief against women. The unlettered Alisoun of Bath narrates how she was "beten for a book" [l. 712] because Jankyn, her fifth husband and a cleric, used to read aloud to her at the hearth from a misogynist anthology, especially "Of Eva first, that for hir wikkednesse/Was al mankynde broght to wrecchednesse" [ll. 715–6]. In the skirmish in the battle of the sexes that follows one of Jankyn's reading sessions, Chaucer (like Christine de Pizan) suggests that antifeminist texts were not always passively received but sometimes faced resistance from the female reader – or audience [see Robert W. Hanning, 'From Eva and Ave to Eglentyne and Alisoun: Chaucer's Insight into the Roles Women Play', *Signs* 2 (1977): pp. 580–99]. When Alisoun angrily tears "thre leves" [l. 790] out of Jankyn's book – do these loosened *folia* symbolize the first chapters of Genesis? – there is an exchange of blows, one of which, to Alisoun's head, presumably makes her "somdel deef" [*GP* l. 446] thereafter to the voice of male authority. It all ends with Jankyn agreeing to burn his book and Alisoun gaining the "governance" of everything, including her husband-cleric's "tonge" and "hond" [ll. 814–5], which represent speech and writing, among other things.

In looking at Chaucer's (and Alisoun's) challenge to traditional interpretations of the Fall, we leave the thinly documented world of medieval private life and enter the even more uncertain realm of medieval poetic fiction, a realm complicated here, of course, by Chaucer's gendered ventriloquism – a male poet doing women's voices doing men's. But not all of Chaucer's women must, like Alisoun, give up an ear to gain a voice. The richly populated world of *The Canterbury Tales* also contains literate women, both story-tellers and characters, who join Alisoun (or are made to seem to do so) in challenging male assumptions about Eve, the feminine, and the Fall.[17] □

Our next extract, from Priscilla Martin's *Chaucer's Women: Nuns, Wives and Amazons* (first published in 1990 and reprinted in 1996), deals not only with the Wife of Bath but also with the other woman who joins her on the pilgrimage to Canterbury, the Prioress. Martin begins her study by charting the not at all swift rise of 'full-length studies . . . of the women in Chaucer's poetry'.[18] This seems 'strange', she argues, particularly in light of the fact that ' . . . as early as 1915 Kittredge [in *Chaucer and his Poetry*] suggested that Chaucer's problems and preoccupations were analogous to those of the twentieth century: "There is scarcely a political or social catchword of the present (even 'feminism') . . . which does not fit the fourteenth century."'[19] Martin supports Kittredge's claim through an examination of women, gender and sexuality in Chaucer's work. Of particular interest to this Guide's exploration of *The General Prologue* is chapter three of Martin's book, 'Two Misfits: The Nun and the Wife'. As is apparent from its title, this chapter offers an analysis of the two main female pilgrims, the Wife of Bath and the Prioress. It appears here in its entirety:

■ Of the 'nyne and twenty' pilgrims whom Chaucer joins for the journey to Canterbury, only three are women: the Prioress, the Second Nun and the Wife of Bath. All three tell a story, but in the *General Prologue* there are portraits only of the Prioress and the Wife. Whereas the men are defined in terms of a large number of professions – knight, innkeeper, parson, ploughman, merchant, lawyer, etc. – we see women in only two roles; the nun and the married woman. Each is defined in terms of sexuality or its renunciation, each defined, in a sense, in relation to men.

Any modern feminist would be likely to notice this contrast and to find it unjust. But how far are modern and feminist ideas about justice, equality, cultural conditioning, personal growth and self-realisation appropriate in discussing medieval literature? Are not our ideas of character and self-expression anachronistic and irrelevant, the products of romantic individualism and Victorian liberalism? Perhaps Chaucer regarded his characters primarily as performers of God-appointed roles and saw very few roles for women. Perhaps the pilgrims, men and women, are defined entirely in terms of vocation, not appreciated for unique personal qualities but assessed according to how well they fit their stations in life. The appropriate question may be not 'What sort of person is this?' but 'How well did this creature fulfil his/her obligations as monk, knight, wife, nun, etc.?' And, even within these terms, men may be permitted more variety than women. Medieval society was considered by some political theorists to consist of three estates – those who work, those who fight and those who pray – and women were sometimes lumped together as a fourth estate.

The two portraits in the *General Prologue* exemplify the two major roles for women in fourteenth-century England.[20] Neither woman fits her role perfectly. This may suggest that women are depraved or that the roles are constricting and deforming. The Prioress is described as 'nat undergrowe' (I 156). Perhaps she would feel it cramping to compress herself within her role. The Wife of Bath knows much about 'wandrynge by the weye' (467), as if she were straying beyond the outlines of hers. Behind the nun and the wife stand the archetypal figures of Mary and Eve, model and reproach. Between them many contrasts are implied. The two women are as different as they could be – one of many reasons why only two portraits can say so much – but the differences are not between poverty, chastity and obedience in the nun and contented marital love, family life and motherhood in the wife. We do not see the nun in private prayer or the wife caring for a husband and children.

Contrasts and criticisms are implied, not stated. Chaucer does not overtly judge the characters he describes in the *General Prologue*. Or, in as far as he judges, his verdicts are nearly always ostensibly favourable. Most of the pilgrims are described as 'gentil', 'worthy' or the best examples of their kind that you could meet. It is left to the audience to evaluate the character from the apparently haphazard collection of attributes reported by the narrator. The narrator, indeed, seems so naive that critics sometimes treat 'Chaucer the pilgrim' as another fictional character on the pilgrimage and quite distinct from 'Chaucer the poet'.

The portrait of the Prioress is a study in role-playing and a joke against it. The standard accounts analyse how she falls short as a nun, though the pilgrims, including the narrator, find her attractive as a woman. She breaks the rules of her order by indulging in personal adornment, by keeping pets, and, indeed, by going on the pilgrimage. But before we consider the conflicting roles of nun and lady, let me suggest that Chaucer has deftly exposed something more fundamental: the Prioress is playing the role of being a woman. It seems obvious now that 'masculinity' and 'femininity' are largely socially constructed. Chaucer almost certainly believed that they were innate. But he does not depict them as natural, in the sense of being spontaneous or taken for granted. Masculinity and femininity carry great charges of anxiety and power in his poems. They are not merely maleness and femaleness but are attributes that men and women can cultivate and parade. The Prioress is a virtuoso performer. She is one of those women who seem to be engaged in a continuous act of female impersonation.

## 'SHE WAS A WORTHY WOMMAN AL HIR LYVE': THE 1990s

The first point made in the description is that her smile is 'symple and coy' [l. 119]. 'Symple', here, is an example of the first set of definitions of the word in the *OED*: 'Free from duplicity, dissimulation or guile, innocent and harmless; undesigning, honest, open, straightforward . . . Free from . . . ostentation or display; unpretentious . . . Free from elaboration or artificiality; artless; unaffected; plain; unadorned.' But if a smile is described as unaffected, its naturalness comes into question. Later details in the portrait ('peyned hire to counterfete cheere/Of court, and to been estatliche of manere/And to ben holden digne of reverence' [ll. 139–41]) suggest that Madame Eglantyne is striving for effect.

'Coy' is another double-edged word. Derived ultimately from the Latin *quietus*, it may mean only 'quiet, still', but it may be beginning to slide into implications of affectation and flirtatiousness. Here is the *OED* definition: 'Of a person: displaying modest backwardness or shyness (sometimes with emphasis on the displaying); not responding readily to familiar advances; now *esp.* Of a girl or young woman.' The Host seems to think the adjective proper only for women. He tells the Clerk, 'Ye ryde as coy and stille as dooth a mayde' (iv 2) when he wants to spur him into some manly self-assertion. Soon it will suggest not only femininity but contrivance. There is also an idiom, 'to make it coy', which the *OED* first cites in 1529 and defines: 'to affect reserve, shyness or disdain.' The combined connotations of 'symple and coy' range from suggesting a silent, self-denying, celibate withdrawal from the world and a self-conscious, consciously feminine, almost flirtatious concern with it. John Livingstone Lowes has investigated the occurrences of the phrase in other medieval poetry and finds 'simple et coie' particularly common in French pastoral.[21] The genre, like the Prioress, is dedicated to the artifice of innocence. She seems like the religious equivalent of a china shepherdess.

The portrait continues to suggest coyness in the modern sense with its praise of the Prioress's ladylike oath, 'St. Loy' [l. 120], and the details of her fastidious table manners. Consideration for others can hardly be wrong and the medieval imagination . . . had found a place for courtesy in Christianity. Yet it seems incongruous to single out neatness at table as a salient characteristic of one who has renounced the world and to give it more space in the description than any other feature. It contributes to an air of 'gentility' (also in the modern sense) about the portrait of the bourgeois lady, with her East London French 'after the scole of Stratford atte Bowe' (l. 125), who tries to 'counterfete cheere of court' (139–40) and follow the most fashionable models. I described her mild expletive as 'ladylike' but, if Hotspur's sense of social nuance two centuries later is relevant here ('Swear me, Kate, like a lady, as thou art,/A good mouth-filling oath' – 1 *Henry V* III

251–2), it also places her as genteel, fitting to neither court nor convent. The encomium on her table manners may have had amorous, as well as worldly, associations for its audience. Its source is a passage in the *Romance of the Rose* [ll. 13408–32] where a young lady is advised on how to behave fetchingly in order to attract a suitor.

The Prioress certainly attracts the narrator. She is pretty, polite, friendly and sweet-natured. But is she not altogether too charming? Adjectives and adverbs used in the portrait include 'symple and coy' (119), 'ful semely' (123, 136), 'faire and fetisly' (124), 'ful plesaunt, and amyable of port' (138), 'charitable' (143), 'pitous' (143). The words have worldly connotations or are ambiguous or are applied in unexpected ways. Continually the suggestion is of a daintiness, a preoccupation with effect, a fondness for worldly objects unbecoming to a religious. She has a flair for dress which can make even her nun's habit stylish. Her rosary, of fine coral with a gold pendant, doubles as a bracelet. Her wimple, 'ful semyly . . . pynched' (151), becomes more decorative than decorous: contrary to the rules, it reveals her high forehead, a particularly admired feature in this period. Her looks are described in the stock vocabulary of romantic poetry: 'hir nose tretys, her eyen greye as glas' (152). Her mouth is small, like that of a heroine of romance, and her lips are not only red but (a moment of quite inappropriate fantasy!) 'softe' (153). Her fragrant name might come from a love poem. The entry to the new life of the religious is symbolised by the assumption of a new name. We should expect a saint's name, not 'Madame Eglantyne', for a nun who has renounced her worldly identity. Details such as these are commonplace in medieval satire against nuns but Chaucer does not include the slur of unchastity which usually accompanies them. The Prioress is compromising rather than committing major sin. She herself seems hardly conscious of her deviations from the austere path of perfection. The ambiguities of the description dramatise her self-deception. Her singing of the divine service is 'semely': appropriate for the worship of God or becoming in the eyes of men? Her sensitivity to the sufferings of animals is her version of Christian qualities of 'conscience' and 'tendre herte'. The ambiguities culminate in the emblem on her rosary: *Amor Vincit Omnia* (Love conquers all) – human love or divine?

In an excellent essay on the images of women in Chaucer, Hope Phyllis Weissman argues that the Prioress has made the wrong choice of the two approved role models available, the courtly lady and the Madonna.[22] I think that the portrait is yet more complex. The Prioress is her own work of art and, like greater artists in the later Middle Ages, she produces a synthesis of human and divine. She does model herself on the Madonna and her comic confusions are nourished by the contemporary emphasis on the humanity of Mary. Madame

## 'SHE WAS A WORTHY WOMMAN AL HIR LYVE': THE 1990s

Eglantyne is described in terms used in lyrics which might be secular or religious, since the same vocabulary expresses the adoration of mistress or of Madonna. The visual arts contribute to the effect. Her 'symple' (artless?) smile is fashionable in the spiritual sphere: the tender smile on the face of the Madonna develops in the sculpture of the fourteenth century. Jill Mann has demonstrated that nuns were positively recommended to view their vocation in a romantic light, that there was a 'tradition of translating the role of the courtly heroine into a religious sphere'. This translation occurs in sermons as well as in satires. 'In the serious ideal . . . Christ, in his role as the nun's heavenly Bridegroom . . . is discussed in terms appropriate to a courtly lover.'[23]

The Prioress manifests the loving kindness and ready emotions of late medieval piety, though her objects are not the conventional ones. She has a prized spiritual talent, the gift of tears, but she weeps if her dogs are beaten or killed, rather than over the scourging and passion of Christ. She should not have had pets at all, much less weep over them or spoil them with expensive food when people were starving. But we can understand why she did. Pets were forbidden in religious houses and the authorities waged war against them for centuries in vain. The dogs and cats always got back. They must have met some emotional needs for a large number of people who were in religious orders but had no religious vocation. The Prioress is clearly one of these. On the sternest view, her dogs arouse idolatrous devotion which should be offered to God.[24] A more humane response is that they are a godsend to her affectionate nature. They are surrogates for the children she cannot have. This aspect of the Prioress, her yearnings and the limitations in her experience, finds expression in her Tale.

The *Prioress's Tale* is the only Canterbury Tale whose central character is a child. It begins with a prayer. The first stanza is addressed to the Lord, whose glory is exalted not only by great men but by babes and sucklings, as it will be by the boy in her Tale, living and dead. The rest of the Invocation extols the Virgin, 'the white lylye flour/Which that the bar and is a mayde alway' (VII 461–2). In the last lines the speaker casts herself as an infant, 'as a child of twelf month oold, or lesse,/That can unnethes any word expresse' (484–5), too weak to bear the weight of praising the Virgin and needing her guidance in telling the story.

The Tale is about the murder of a Christian child by a community of Jews in Asia. The boy is seven years old and the son of a widow. He is taught the hymn *'Alma Redemptoris'* by an older schoolboy, who cannot explain the Latin words but knows that it is sung in honour of the Virgin. The younger child memorises the hymn and sings it as he walks through the Jews' street on his way to and from school. Satan inspires the Jews to kill him and throw his body into a cesspit. His mother, distracted with grief, searches for him and asks the Jews in vain if they have seen him. But the child's body, with its throat cut, miraculously continues to sing the *'Alma Redemptoris'* from the pit. The crime is thus discovered and the Jews are tortured and executed. The boy's body continues to sing, until a grain placed on his tongue by the Virgin Mary at the moment of death is removed and she releases his soul and takes it to her.

This story evidently has considerable sentimental appeal for the Prioress. Just as in the Invocation she could regard the Virgin Mary as model and mother, so in the Tale she can identify with both the anguished widow and the innocent child. She is entranced by the pathos of the murder and the vulnerable charm of the young boy, whom she repeatedly describes as 'litel'. His ignorance makes him even sweeter, a kind of holy fool, singing a sacred hymn of which he does not understand the words. Childishness and sanctity merge in his song, unstoppable in the street of the Jews, unquenchable by death. He exemplifies the Christian promise that the humble shall be exalted by his triumph over death. The heavenly mother takes him to her and he follows the Lamb in the New Jerusalem with the white procession of virgin martyrs. He makes vivid the meaning of the Christian command to become as little children. His legend has the power of simplicity with its absolutes of black and white, its wicked Jews inspired by Satan and its pure little hero supported by the Virgin Mother, its total poetic justice. The pilgrims are silent with emotion when it ends.

It is obviously a highly dangerous story. The *Canterbury Tales* are full of sex and violence but the gentle Prioress tells the only story that could seriously corrupt anybody. Beside her Tale the cynical Pardoner's account of his avaricious sharp practices seems harmless. My reaction is inevitable for a late twentieth-century reader and it may be anachronistic. But it probably is not. The Church has prohibited dissemination of rumours of ritual murders of Christian children by Jews. The Tale not only relates an event which took place once upon a time far away in Asia but brings it up to the moment with its final prayer to 'yonge Hugh of Lincoln, slayn also/With cursed Jewes, as it is notable,/For it is but a litel while ago' (VII 684–6).

The Prioress's allusions to Jewish tradition seem to emphasise her inability to grasp the implications of her narrative. Her comparison of the Virgin Mary to the 'bussh unbrent, brennynge in Moyses sight' (468) is a traditional piece of typology, which Chaucer also uses in the *ABC*, but the remainder of God's revelation to Moses seems at odds with her description of the Jewish heart as the wasp's nest of Satan (558–9). The grieving mother is also presented in an Old Testament figure: She is a 'newe Rachel'. The story of Rachel prefigures the

# 'SHE WAS A WORTHY WOMMAN AL HIR LYVE': THE 1990s

*Prioress's Tale* and recalls Herod's Slaughter of the Innocents. But that massacre was of *Jewish* children, though they were to be co-opted as the first Christian martyrs, and re-enactments of it were fomented by stories such as these. Ironically, the story advocates the 'eye for an eye, tooth for a tooth' ethic that Jesus wanted to amend. The provost remarks 'Yvele shal have that yvele wol deserve' (632) before putting the Jews to death.

I am presenting an interpretation which is, in more than one sense, partial. I am emphasising the negative aspect of the Tale, its cruelty and prejudice. Other critics have been moved, like the pilgrims, by its pathos and devotion. It belongs to the spiritual tradition of 'affective piety', playing on profound emotions for the purposes of awe and prayer. It could be argued that the other purposes to which these emotions have been roused are irrelevant to Chaucer's poem. I am also dwelling on the dramatic aspect of the Tale, viewing it as an expression of the Prioress's charm and limitation. The relationship of story to narrator is certainly variable throughout the *Canterbury Tales*: sometimes it is obviously close and significant, sometimes apparently perfunctory. All readers would agree that this miracle of Our Lady is a generally apt Tale for the Prioress; not all would wish to analyse its details for what they yield about her psychology. Some critics have used the dramatic approach in defence of the Tale. It has been described as a kind of fairy-story, appropriate to the child-like nature of its teller. This, of course, is precisely what is wrong with it. If we are tempted to think of it as taking place in Never-neverland remote from actual life, the closing reference to Hugh of Lincoln jolts us back into the horrors of the actual world. And this is what the Prioress knows little about. She is in some ways not 'worldly' enough. She lives at a level of moral theory to which no adult is entitled. This emotional immaturity is not necessarily due to the convent or to the Christian ideal of virginity. It is inseparable from the cultivation of ignorance as delectably intrinsic to femininity.

The *Prioress's Tale* may be wicked but the Prioress is not. Like the child in her story, who sings a song which he does not understand, she is not exactly conscious of what she is expressing: affection and affectation, religious grace and social graces, love human, divine and animal. These are certainly different aspects of *Amor* but the lesser versions are imperfect rather than evil. The Prioress is, probably through no fault of her own, in the wrong kind of life. She has adapted her role until she can play it prettily and even be applauded for it.

One moral we can draw from the contrast between the Prioress and the Wife of Bath will be more unpalatable to the feminist than to the sexist. Gentle sabotage will get you further than open rebellion. This, though not a very moral moral, has some psychological truth. As the

## THE GENERAL PROLOGUE

narrator of the *Franklin's Tale* suggests, the distinction between self-sacrifice and self-interest may not be absolute: 'Pacience is a heigh vertue . . . For it venquysseth . . . Thynges that rigor sholde nevere atteyne' (V 773–5). So perhaps patience, rather than honesty, is the best policy. The Prioress quietly bends all the rules and no one even notices. The pilgrims, including apparently the narrator, think she is lovely. She inspires even the bossy Host to courtesy; her story, so horrific to modern sensibilities and probably also to informed contemporary opinion, unites the noisy bickering pilgrims in awed silence. The Wife of Bath questions the rules and assorted clerics in her audience – Friar, Pardoner, Clerk and Parson – close ranks against her.

The Prioress is indeed extremely 'feminine'. She emanates an excess of misplaced femininity, though in a very sexist society no one is likely to complain of that. Ironically, she is considerably more seductive than the much-married Wife of Bath. The Wife seems, like many feminists, not very 'feminine'. In her own Prologue she gives the astrological explanation: she was born under the contradictory influences of Venus and Mars. Venus contributed her 'likerousnesse', Mars her 'hardynesse' (III 609–12). In the portrait in the *General Prologue* her martial qualities are very evident and compromise her conventional feminine attributes: spinning, dressing smartly and husband-hunting. Like the Virtuous Woman of the Book of Proverbs, she spins and makes fine linen, but this traditional female skill is presented in terms of capitalism and competition, not service and self-abnegation. She is a successful businesswoman, surpassing even the renowned cloth-makers of the Low Countries, and so proud of herself that she is out of all charity if anyone takes precedence over her in church. She has evidently taken a lot of trouble and spent a lot of money on her outfit – a traditional female vanity, according to the satirists – but the general effect is more strident than seductive. Despite her nun's habit, there is something gauzy about that Prioress. The Wife's attire seems loud ('Hir hosen weren of fyn scarlet reed'– I 456), heavy ('Hir coverchiefs . . . weyden ten pound'– 454), and abrasive ('spores sharpe' – 473). Unlike the Prioress with her 'coy' smile, the Wife talks and laughs freely. Whereas the Prioress strains ('peyned hire'– 139) to comport herself correctly, the Wife is vulgarly relaxed and sits 'esily' (469) on her ambler. The effect of masculinity is reinforced by her hat, 'As brood as is a bokeler or a targe' (471), and her vast experience in 'wandrynge by the weye' (467). She is a parody of a knight-errant. The narrator exclaims over the *weight* of her headdress as one might over a soldier's armour or equipment.

'Wandrynge by the weye' has further implications. Has the Wife been on too many pilgrimages, married too many times, done too much, seen too much, thought too much? The Prioress, by contrast, despite the blurring of her Rule, is inexperienced: she knows the French of Stratford-at-Bow but has never been to Paris. At the beginning of her Prologue the Wife backs experience against authority. She is a latter-day Eve, repeating the original sin of intellectual curiosity when she should comply in obedience. She deviates rather than following a straight and narrow path. And her intellectual presumption leads her into direct conflict with the masculine exponents of orthodoxy, the clerks. We are told in the *General Prologue* that she is 'somdel deef' (446) and learn in her own Prologue that it is a result from a blow from her fifth husband, an ex-clerk. She is also partly deaf – not absolutely – to the voice of authority.

The five marriages suggest more than intellectual desires. She is 'gat-tothed' (468), a physiognomic sign of a lecherous nature, and there is the suggestion, in her 'wandrynge by the weye' (467) and knowledge of 'the olde daunce' (476) that she has also been adulterous. The narrator does not commit himself on this point. 'Withouten oother compaignye in youthe' (461) is ambiguous. It may mean that she did have lovers in youth or that she did not. The next line, 'But therof nedeth nat to speke as nowthe' (462) is usually taken to be incriminating. I think that the second line may compound, rather than dissolve, the ambiguity of the couplet. We learn at the opening of the Wife's own Prologue that she was first married at twelve, the earliest age according to canon law. She was sold off to a rich husband at the first opportunity. Was she therefore cheated out of a normal romantic life at the proper stage? Does the narrator drop the subject because the poet is to complicate it further in the Wife's own Prologue?

The two portraits of women in the *General Prologue* say a great deal. But there is one major female experience which is absent. Neither woman is a mother. The Prioress, a celibate, has an imaginary child while she tells her Tale. The Wife of Bath, though she has been married five times, seems to be childless. If she has had children, surely she would say so. She says almost everything else. She knows about 'remedies of love' (I 475), which may suggest contraceptive practices. The frank enjoyment of sex described in her Prologue shows that her intentions are by orthodox standards perverse, that, like Chaunticleer [in *The Nun's Priest's Tale*] she makes love 'moore for delit than world multiplye' (VII 3345). In her Prologue she quotes God's command to increase and multiply as a literal justification for sex and marriage (III 28) without clinching her argument by adducing the evidence of children. There could be a natural explanation: her first three marriages were to old men and by the time she was free to marry the younger husbands of her choice she was middle-aged herself. The abuse she puts into the mouths of her first three husbands suggests literal as well as metaphorical barrenness:

> Thou liknest wommenes love to helle,
> To bareyne lond, ther water may nat dwelle.
> Thou liknest it also to wilde fyr;
> The moor it brenneth, the moore it hath desir
> To consume every thyng that brent wol be. (III 371–5)
>
> In contrast to the Madonna's virgin motherhood, which the Prioress likens to the bush that burned and was not consumed (VII 468), the Wife fears that her barren sexuality resembles wild fire, destructive and insatiable. Both women, the nun and the wife, seem in their totally different ways, to be doing what they can with roles that have proved unfulfilling.
>
> The oldest profession – prostitution – is not represented on the pilgrimage. We may note, however, in passing, that the Shipman's boat is called 'Maudelayne'. An ambiguity to rank with *Amor Vincit Omnia*.[25] □

Martin's analysis of the female 'misfits' of *The General Prologue* is useful in two ways. First, and most obviously, it provides us with an example of a detailed feminist critique of the poem, something different to set against the other types of approaches presented in previous chapters of this Guide. It also, however, explores, in relation to the Nun and the Wife, a topic long seen as central to an understanding of the connection between *The General Prologue* and *The Canterbury Tales* as a whole; that topic being the relationship between the teller and the tale. Thus, Martin argues that the child-like qualities, sentimental yearnings and excessive femininity attributed to the Prioress in her portrait are very much in evidence in the tale she goes on to tell. Martin does, however, caution us not to adopt this as a blanket approach when she points out, above, that 'the relationship of story to narrator is certainly variable throughout the *Canterbury Tales*: sometimes it is obviously close and significant, sometimes apparently perfunctory'.

Before we leave our discussion of Priscilla Martin's *Chaucer's Women: Nuns, Wives and Amazons* it is worth citing an observation she makes in her 'Preface to the 1996 Reprint' of this volume. In a short discussion of the relatively recent bibliography of books on women in Chaucer's poetry, she concludes that 'despite our different approaches and conclusions we all concur in seeing gender as a locus of anxiety in Chaucer's work and in seeing the work as about gender'.[26] Martin acknowledges here that the debate concerning Chaucer's treatment of gender and, more generally, his 'sexual politics' has become a wide-ranging one. This is seen quite clearly, for example, in Jane Chance's *The Mythographic Chaucer: The Fabulation of Sexual Politics* of 1995, an innovative examination of the poet's use of mythography and how it exposes (if this is the right word) the sexual politics at work in his writing. She begins by contextualising the issue in her Preface:

## 'SHE WAS A WORTHY WOMMAN AL HIR LYVE': THE 1990s

■ The concealment of embarrassing secrets, often sexual in nature, and the burden of political alliances and strategies – what together might be termed sexual politics – motivated Chaucer in much of his work (an idea long evident but for the most part ignored by Chaucer critics). Because Chaucer had treated Criseyde (and therefore all women) so shamefully in the *Troilus* through his misogynistic depiction of her as fickle, he was accused of having abrogated courtly norms of decorum. Having well documented his offense in the *Prologue* to the *Legend of Good Women*, Chaucer proscribed as poetic penance for himself (through the authority of the God of Love) the writing of the legends of good women, a task that he never completed and that was exchanged for the more inviting task of constructing the drama of class subversion in the *Canterbury Tales*.

Although he never finished either project, Chaucer learned well from his offense. Even in his mostly classical legendary and mythological tales, women are not merely manipulated *as tales* (something that critics have only recently begun to observe); that is, if as a consequence of the Fall woman is linked by the cleric with desire and the body, and if reading a text literally rather than figuratively implies a prohibited carnal reading, then allegorical reading leaves women out of the text. Therefore Chaucer avoids allegory in most of his later writing. But he also returns the female, and the "female" – the essentialized ideal of the female as different, other, alien – to the text. What remains the same in all phases of Chaucer's developing poetic, despite the social and political demands placed upon him, is his abiding interest in the use of mythological imagery as a means of protection for the helpless from charges such as misogyny, immorality, or treason.

Mythography, focused as it is upon moral theology in the tradition of medieval poetic, is indeed a political technique... ...*The Mythographic Chaucer* analyzes [then] mythological references, images, and characters throughout Chaucer's poetry in the light of the medieval mythographic tradition, with the goal of clarifying those truths hidden within the text, whether for literary, social, or political reasons. Medieval mythographers are generally well known for their moralizing and allegorizing penchants; Chaucer, in contrast, often inverts typically allegorical signification for psychological or political or ironic purposes.[27] □

Chance applies this unique approach to *The General Prologue* in chapter five of her book, 'Zephirus, Rape, and St. Thomas à Becket: The Political Vernacular'.[28] A substantial portion of this chapter provides the material for our next set of extracts:

■ The tension between pagan and Christian forms what might be termed the idea of the *General Prologue* as it functions on its two levels, literal (natural, physical, pagan, feminine) and figurative (supernatural, spiritual, Christian, masculine). Although Chaucer refers to many classical gods throughout the dream visions, the *Troilus*, and some of the tales of the *Canterbury Tales*, he mentions only one pagan figure in the whole of the *General Prologue* – the West Wind, or Zephirus, in line 5. The dependent clause in the first half of the *reverdie* indicating the time when Zephirus most influences the natural world (5–9; that is, "*Whan* Zephirus eek with his sweete breeth/Inspired hath in every holt and heeth/The tendre croppes, *and* the yonge sonne/Hath in the Ram his half cours yronne,/*And* smal foweles maken melodye") is succeeded in the second half (12–8) by an independent clause indicating the temporal consequence of Zephirus's influence on humankind ("*Thanne* longen folk to goon on pilgrimages,/*And* palmeres for to seken straunge strondes" [ll. 12–13]).

For the alternation of Christian and classical, Chaucer may have drawn on the idea of the Latin pastoral debate poem *Ecloga Theoduli*, which similarly juxtaposes classical myth with Old Testament story to create an effect similar to that which he achieves here and elsewhere in his poems, including the classical epic parody in the moralistic *Nun's Priest's Tale* and the conjunction of the mythological fable in the *Manciple's Tale* with the Christian homily in the *Parson's Tale* at the end of the *Canterbury Tales*. Chaucer's political interest in veiling "abominations" through the use of classical mythology in his composition of narrative "chaff", particularly as filtered through his own subjectivity, is also embedded in his only short poem with a mythological image – like the General Prologue, an image seamed with scriptural (and Old Testament) referentiality.[29] □

Chance then moves on to an analysis of Chaucer's lyric 'The Former Age' and some of its possible continental sources. One of these texts, 'the important twelfth-century commentary on the *Ecloga Theoduli* by Bernard of Utrecht', is also cited as a possible influence on *The General Prologue*.[30] A more detailed discussion of the *Prologue* follows:

■ Chaucer's deployment of Zephirus in the *General Prologue* . . . warns against heresy and tyranny, through a series of mythological and literary associations chiefly drawn from Dante's *Paradiso* [from *The Divine Comedy*] . . . Both Chaucer and Dante bend the conventional mythographic significations of Zephirus as the West Wind and as metonymy [change of name] for spring's fructifying breezes, he is a harbinger and messenger, a fructifier of the world in spring. In many of the earliest medieval mythographic poems and tracts, Zephirus as a rejuvenating force is also linked with the World Soul, in which the individual human soul was believed, in microcosm, to share. From this early association, the figure of Zephirus gradually accumulates a potency suggestive of psychological then Christian renewal. In the *General Prologue* especially, but also in most of his other works, Chaucer's use of Zephirus depends upon the conception of the fructifying West Wind as a masculinized poetic correlative for spiritual renewal, as developed in the Latin mythographic tradition and in Dante . . .

Chaucer draws on both these Italian interpretations [those of Dante and of Boccaccio in his *Genealogia deorum gentilium*] in his use of a classical ("pagan") image within a Christian context, to defuse artistically that dramatic tension between the desires of the world and those for the next from which humankind suffers and which is amply demonstrated in the pilgrims on the Canterbury journey. In addition, Chaucer here demonstrates how the vernacular poetical context subverts and colors, controls, the rigid clerical Latin mythographic tradition. Chaucer lifts from the patristic mythographic tradition a much-glossed figure, Zephirus, to use within a passage about an English martyr; he also borrows, I am arguing, from contemporary vernacular imagery associated with the birthplace of the author of the Dominican Inquisition. The English rebel-martyr Thomas, in helping to protect the hegemony of the church is, in this sense, like the Spanish Saint Dominic.

The beginning as well as the ending of life for the soul is linked with Zephirus in several classical and medieval literary texts by means of the Greek concept of Zephirus as the breath of human life, in part because the World Soul, according to Stoic belief, was a macrocosmic equivalent of the human soul and responsible for its engendering. Zephirus's power over life translates into psychological and spiritual power over the human microcosm and within the cosmic macrocosm . . .
. . . In Chaucer's *General Prologue*, too, the West Wind appropriately signals the return of life to the English countryside, awakening it from the "death" of winter and human mortality and suffering. Thematically, the arrival of the West Wind in the *Prologue* also signals a "marriage" – of the body and the soul, Cupid and Psyche, or, within the eighteen lines of the *reverdie*, the natural urge of the birds to mate, in the first eleven lines, so to speak, coupled with the supernatural urge of the pilgrims to travel for penance, in the last seven.

Prior to Chaucer, the association of Zephirus with spiritual life in a specifically Christian context involving renewal of the soul occurs in a ninth-century passage from Rabanus Maurus's *De universo*. Rabanus uses as a basis for his allegorical reading the more usual associations of Zephirus with the West Wind as fructifier of seed and flowers . . . In addition, Zephirus's appearance in spring, the time of year in which Christ died, carries with it the seeds of all virtue and good works that are born in the world . . . Rabanus, however, focuses only on . . .

Zephirus as a rejuvenator of the human soul, an idea used by Chaucer in the *Book of the Duchess* to suggest psychological renewal of the soul without any necessary and explicit Christian renewal, in contrast to the more explicit relationship celebrated in the *reverdie* of the *General Prologue*.

In the *General Prologue* and at the end of the *Canterbury Tales*, Chaucer seems to use Zephirus anagogically, within the church militant, to typify Saint Thomas as a catalytic rejuvenator of the church in his empowerment of male sanctity – ironically, one that is achieved through a feminizing posture, of martyrdom as political "rape," or else one that subverts hierarchy and order through its displacement of secular authority. But this image evolves into the rich and complex vernacular treatment of Zefiro by Dante in the twelfth canto of the *Paradiso*, a text that I believe Chaucer was familiar with and that he used in part as a model for the literary roles of Zephirus in the *General Prologue*. The Dantesque associations of Zefiro with the Spanish-born Saint Dominic also acts as an analogue, in Chaucer, for the English martyr Saint Thomas à Becket, whose resistance to the king's secular authority led to his homicide and whose shrine, symbolically as well as literally and anagogically, is the pilgrims' goal – the "thanne" – of the syntactical diagram in the opening lines. Such syntactical patterning invites an identification of the inspiration of the topos of leaves by Zephirus's "sweete breeth" with that of the pilgrims traveling to Canterbury, to echo the natural process of growth suggested by the mythic action with a more supernatural one – the "inspiration," or longing, of the pilgrims to visit Canterbury.

. . . . . . The reference to Zephirus may also exemplify the underlying satiric theme contemporary with Chaucer of corruption – impotence – in the church fighting against the state and thus the need for renewal: just as Zephirus announces what might be seen as a pagan "marriage," in the first eleven lines, of a feminine and passive earth, or the roots, sap vessels, and flowers of lines 2–5, to the masculine and active heavens, of the showers and Wind of April of lines 1, 5–6, so also Zephirus anticipates the analogous analogical revivification of the church, not by her ostensible leaders, the Prioress, Monk, or Friar, but by the truly Christian Parson and his brother the Plowman, in echo of Saint Thomas.

The power of Zephirus to transform the church through his anthropomorphized "breath" has been explained by Boccaccio in *Genealogia* through the sexual relationship of Zephirus and Flora, goddess of flowers – the gendering of nature [according to some classical sources, Zephirus raped the nymph Chloris, a name later changed to the Roman Flora] . . . . . . In its harsh emphasis on masculine violence, the rape belies the seeming gentleness of Chaucer's Zephirus and his "sweet breath." The gender associations in the mythography of the figure assume, in Chaucer, a more politicized role involving church and state, a signification that can be teased through Zephirus's genealogy and his kinship with the Titans. According to the First Vatican Mythographer, the Greek Zephirus is one of four winds, including the North Wind Boreas, the East Wind Eurus, and the South Wind Auster, who, according to the Second Vatican Mythographer, were born as a result of the mythical coupling of Astraeus, one of the Titans who bore arms against the gods, with Aurora the dawn, and who are . . . ruled by the king Aeolus, father of the winds. The mythological family connections of the winds reveal ties to those same Titans conjoined in Bernard of Utrecht in his gloss on castrating Jupiter and tyrannous Nimrod – both involved in political and cosmic subversion, a social rape.

But Zephirus's patristic mythography is employed by Chaucer to suggest a *remedium* for social rape, for the violence of Henry II toward Saint Thomas, by means of the healing of England through pilgrimage, or the marriage of Zephirus and Flora (which, of course, does not actually happen on this pilgrimage) . . . . . . The association of a powerful, masculine Zephirus with weak, passive, abducted or raped female figures in all the sources . . . culminates here [in *The General Prologue*] in the images of a passive feminized Nature and a potent masculinized English church, but a church whose power springs from its independence, its rebellion by martyrs, its vernacularism, and not its tradition, its obedience, its Latinate ties. This model is one that Chaucer will find especially congenial in those mythologized Canterbury Tales whose sexual politics demand the concealment afforded by such fabulation. To Canterbury the rebels of 1381 [the year of the Peasants' Revolt], led by dissident preacher John Ball, also headed, according to Jean Froissart's *Chronique* account, where they damaged Christ Church Cathedral and whose archbishop, Simon Sudbury, they later beheaded.[31] ☐

Like the above extracts from Chance's work, much of the secondary material cited in this chapter sets out to scrutinise the more subversive, radical and political aspects of *The General Prologue*: the notion of masquerade – how a pilgrim 'acts out' his or her gender role – has been particularly foregrounded on several occasions. Many of these ideas are brought together, indeed, anticipated, by John M. Ganim, in *Chaucerian Theatricality*. I say 'anticipated' as this book was published in 1990, and, thus, before the other extracts presented in our discussion of the criticism of the 1990s. As the final extract of this Guide will show, Ganim observes within the poem a world of 'subcultures' all with their own 'definitions of performance' and possibilities for subversion of the 'official' consensus: a world of mirror images. Here, *The General Prologue* meets *Alice through the Looking Glass*:

■ ... the "literary" theme in the General Prologue reflects the social and ethical patterns that also operate in it. We begin with an assumption of a cohesive literary tradition and a description of members of groups who might differ in purpose but share values. As the portraits move on, however, we become aware of startlingly different versions of the use of language, speech and literature. Indeed, this difference begins almost immediately and becomes increasingly stark. Moreover, we become aware that the "official" consensus is only the tip of the iceberg, and that beneath the surface, worlds of simultaneously thriving subcultures, have their own languages and their own definitions of performance.

It is precisely that pluralism which the Host's plan attempts to control and which, quite against his intention, he encourages. He sets the game in motion and thereby immediately compromises his goal of a harmonious social group and controllable literary standards. Harry thus epitomizes the dilemma, not of "medieval" culture, but of bourgeois and "modern" culture. The means by which he attempts to establish order are in fact the forces of constant change and relative perspectives, which thereby undermine absolute values.[32] □

It is hoped that the extracts presented throughout this Guide have equally given the reader an insight into the many thriving critical (sub)cultures generated by *The General Prologue*. If the sheer volume and plurality of response is anything to go by, critics, for any variety of reasons, should continue to travel the road to Canterbury well into the new millennium.

# APPENDIX

Table of the relative popularity of Chaucer's poems at different times.

(i)
*Order up to* 1700.

|  | Approximate No. of refs. |
|---|---|
| Troilus | 115 |
| Cant. Tales (as a whole) | 53 |
| General Prol. C.T. | 33 |
| Nonne Preestes T. | 26 |
| Knight's T. | 23 |
| W. of Bath's Prol. | 20 |
| H. of Fame | 18 |
| Clerke's T. | 17 |
| Sir Thopas | 16 |
| Marchant's T. | 15 |
| W. of Bath's T. | 15 |
| Squieres T. | 13 |
| Rom. of Rose | 13 |
| Legend | 13 |
| Pardoneres T. | 12 |
| Astrolabe | 8 |

(ii)
*Order up to* 1750.

| Troilus | 124 |
|---|---|
| Cant. Tales | 59 |
| General Prol. C.T. | 42 |
| Knight's T. | 29 |
| Nonne Preestes T. | 26 |
| W. of Bath's Prol. | 25 |
| House of Fame | 24 |
| Clerke's T. | 18 |
| Marchant's T. | 17 |
| Rom. of Rose | 17 |
| Sir Thopas | 17 |
| Squieres T. | 13 |
| Pardoneres T. | 12 |
| Astrolabe | 8 |

# THE GENERAL PROLOGUE

### (iii)
### *Order from* 1750 *to* 1800.

| | |
|---|---:|
| Cant. Tales | 19 |
| General Prol. C.T. | 11 |
| Knight's T. | 10 |
| Squieres T. | 8 |
| W. of Bath's Prol. | 5 |
| Troilus | 5 |
| House of Fame | 5 |
| Sir Thopas | 4 |
| Nonne Preestes T. | 4 |
| Pardoneres T. | 2 |
| Rom. of Rose | 2 |

### (iv)
### *Order from* 1700 *to* 1800.

| | |
|---|---:|
| Cant. Tales | 24 |
| General Prol. C.T. | 17 |
| Knight's T. | 16 |
| Troilus | 13 |
| H. of Fame | 11 |
| W. of Bath's Prol. | 10 |
| Squieres T. | 8 |
| Rom. of Rose | 6 |
| Sir Thopas | 4 |
| Nonne Preestes T. | 4 |
| Pardoneres T. | 2 |

### (v)
### *Order from the beginning up to* 1800.

| | |
|---|---:|
| Troilus | 129 |
| Cant. Tales | 78 |
| General Prol. C.T. | 50 |
| Knight's T. | 39 |
| W. of Bath's Prol. | 30 |
| Nonne Preestes T. | 30 |
| House of Fame | 29 |
| Sir Thopas | 24 |
| Squieres T. | 24 |
| Clerkes T. | 20 |
| Rom. Of Rose | 19 |
| Marchantes T. | 18 |
| Pardoneres T. | 14 |
| Astrolabe | 9 |

# NOTES

## INTRODUCTION

1 Malcolm Andrew, Charles Moorman & Daniel J. Ransom, eds., *A Variorum Edition of the Works of Geoffrey Chaucer*, vol. 2 (London: University of Oklahoma Press, 1993), p. xv.
2 Andrew, Moorman & Ransom, p. xvi.
3 Larry D. Benson, ed., *The Riverside Chaucer* (Oxford: Oxford University Press, 1987), p. xxv.
4 Dolores Warwick Frese, *An Ars Legendi for Chaucer's Canterbury Tales* (Gainesville: University of Florida Press, 1991), p. 100.
5 Charles A. Owen, Jr., ed., *Discussions of the Canterbury Tales* (Westport, Connecticut: Greenwood Press, 1961), p. 4.

## CHAPTER ONE

1 Caroline F. E. Spurgeon, ed., *Five Hundred Years of Chaucer Criticism and Allusion: 1357–1900* [Chaucer Society 1908–1917] 3 vols. (Cambridge: Cambridge University Press, 1925; New York: Russell and Russell, 1960), p. lxxvi.
2 William Thynne's Chaucer of 1532 was the first edition of the poet's collected works. It was circulated again in 1561 with numerous additions by John Stowe. Thynne's edition was re-edited in 1598 by Speght; in 1602 a second edition of Speght's Chaucer was published and this was reprinted in 1687. Thomas Tyrwhitt was the first to produce an edition of *The Canterbury Tales* (1775–78) on its own; its second edition was published in 1798. As Thomas R. Lounsbury explains: 'Tyrwhitt's edition of the "Canterbury Tales" – the only work of Chaucer he ever edited – appeared in four volumes in March, 1775. A fifth volume, containing a glossary to all the poet's writings, followed in 1778. In the preparation of this work Tyrwhitt collated twenty-six manuscripts, to five of which he attached a special value.' (*Studies in Chaucer: His Life and Writings*, 3 vols. (New York: Harper and Brothers, 1892), I, p. 301).
3 Thomas Tyrwhitt, ed., *The Canterbury Tales of Chaucer (to which are added an essay on his Language and Versification, and an introductory discourse together with notes and glossary)*, second edition (Oxford: At the Clarendon Press, 1798), p. iv.
4 David Williams, *The Canterbury Tales: A Literary Pilgrimage* (Boston: Twayne, 1987), pp. 10–11.
5 Ann Thompson, *Shakespeare's Chaucer: A Study in Literary Origins* (Liverpool: Liverpool University Press, 1978), p. 6, where the source of this phrase is given as 'Quoted by Spurgeon, i. 104'.
6 Thompson (1978), p. 7, where Thompson gives the following information regarding Harrington's *Apologie for Poetrie*: 'Reprinted in G. G. Smith (ed.), *Elizabethan Critical Essays* (Oxford University Press, 1904), ii. 215'.
7 Thompson (1978), p. 7, where the source of this phrase is given as 'Quoted by Spurgeon, i. 137–8'.
8 Thompson (1978), pp. 6–7.
9 See also the earlier, related study by Georgia Ronan Crampton, *The Condition of Creatures: Suffering and Action in Chaucer and Spenser* (London: Yale University Press, 1974).
10 Judith H. Anderson, 'Narrative Reflections: Re-envisaging the Poet in *The Canterbury Tales* and *The Faerie Queene*' in Theresa M. Krier, ed., *Refiguring Chaucer in the Renaissance* (Gainesville: University Press of Florida, 1998), p. 87. Quotation from Spenser is given by Anderson (p. 101, note 1) as: '*The Faerie Queene*, IV.ii.34. All references to Spenser's Poetry are to the *Variorum Spenser* . . . '.
11 Anderson (1998), p. 101, f.n.6.
12 [*Anderson's Note*, p. 101:] In the main, I am following – and indebted to

157

– the reading of Leicester, *Disenchanted Self*, 383–417, here 397–98, 400–05. But see also [David] Lawton, *Chaucer's Narrators*, [*Chaucer Studies* 13. Cambridge: Brewer, 1985] 1–8, 102; and Donaldson's classic essay 'Chaucer the Pilgrim'.
13 Anderson (1998), pp. 89–90.
14 Anderson (1998), p. 90.
15 Anderson (1998), p. 92.
16 Anderson (1998), p. 92. See also p. 102, note 15, which states: 'Bialostosky's statement is taken from an unpublished paper cited in Graff's *Professing Literature*, 257, 303 n.'
17 Anderson (1998), p. 97.
18 Owen (1961), p. viii.
19 Joseph A. Dane, *Who is Buried in Chaucer's Tomb?: Studies in the Reception of Chaucer's Book* (Ann Arbor: Michigan State University Press, 1998), p. 2.
20 Owen (1961), p. viii.
21 Dane (1998), p. 163.
22 Dryden in Owen (1961), p. 4.
23 Thomas A. Kirby, 'The General Prologue' in Beryl Rowland, ed., *Companion to Chaucer Studies* (Oxford: Oxford University Press, 1968; Revised ed. 1979), pp. 245–6.
24 Dane (1998), p. 2.
25 Tyrwhitt (1798), p. 73.
26 Tyrwhitt (1798), p. 73.
27 Tyrwhitt (1798), pp. 77–8.
28 Charles A. Owen, Jr., *Pilgrimage and Storytelling in the Canterbury Tales* (Norman: University of Oklahoma Press, 1977), p. 41.
29 Owen (1977), pp. 41, 45.
30 Owen (1977), p. 217.
31 Sir Arthur T. Quiller-Couch, *The Age of Chaucer* (London: J.M. Dent & Sons Ltd., 1926), p. 119.
32 Tyrwhitt (1798), p. 75.
33 Tyrwhitt (1798), p. 76, note 6.
34 Williams (1987), p. 11.
35 Williams (1987), p. 11.
36 Arnold in Owen (1961), p. 7.
37 Arnold in Owen (1961), p. 6. Apart from Matthew Arnold, another nineteenth-century poet who was moved enough by the Chaucer of *The Canterbury Tales* to write of him, this time in verse, was the American Henry Wadsworth Longfellow. His sonnet 'Chaucer', taken here from *The Poetical Works of Longfellow* (London: Oxford University Press, 1934, p. 711), of 1874, which projects a heavily idealised image of not only the mediaeval poet but the Middle Ages as a whole, reads as follows:

An old man in a lodge within a park;
   The chamber walls depicted all
      around
   With portraitures of huntsmen,
      hawk, and hound,
And the hurt deer. He listeneth to
      the lark
Whose song comes with the sunshine
      through the dark
   Of painted glass in leaden lattice
      bound;
He listeneth and he laugheth at the
      sound,
Then writeth in a book like any
      clerk.
He is the poet of the dawn, who wrote
   The Canterbury Tales, and his old
      age
   Made beautiful with song; and as I
      read
I hear the crowing cock, I hear the
      note
   Of lark and linnet, and from every
      page
   Rise odors of ploughed field or
      flowery mead.
38 Arnold in Owen (1961), p. 8.

CHAPTER TWO

1 Lounsbury (1892), pp. xi–xii.
2 Owen (1961), p. vii.
3 Owen (1961), p. vii.
4 See especially Terry Jones, *Chaucer's Knight: The Portrait of a Medieval Mercenary* (London: Eyre Methuen, 1980, pbk. ed. 1982).
5 Lounsbury (1892), vol. 1, pp. 92–3. The debate over whether or not any of

# NOTES

Chaucer's pilgrims were based upon real people is discussed more generally by John Livingstone Lowes in *Geoffrey Chaucer: Lectures Delivered in 1932 on the William J. Cooper Foundation in Swarthmore College* (Oxford: At the Clarendon Press, 1934, rpt. 1949), p. 162: '... Are they real persons ... Or are they purely Chaucer's creations ... ? The question has been lately raised in a brilliant and provocative volume, *Some New Light on Chaucer* [1926], by one of the most distinguished of Chaucerian scholars, Professor [J. M.] Manly, who has argued, on the basis of newly gathered facts, that in several figures of the *Prologue* Chaucer did have definite persons in mind. There was, as has long been known, a Harry Bailley of Southwark who kept an inn, and thanks to recently discovered records we know more. There are reasons, curious and tantalizing, which lead one to suspect that in the Reeve of Baldeswell Chaucer may have paid his respects to a rascally reeve whom he personally knew. And there were for the Man of Law, and the Franklin and Shipman besides, contemporary figures who offer more or less striking parallels. Were these figures, therefore, Chaucer's prototypes?'

6 Lounsbury (1892), vol. 3, pp. 349–50.
7 William Benzie, *Dr. F. J. Furnivall: Victorian Scholar Adventurer* (Norman, Oklahoma: Pilgrim Books, 1983), p. 163.
8 Examples of the characteristically eccentric Prefaces of Furnivall are found throughout Benzie (1983).
9 F. J. Furnivall, *A Temporary Preface to the Six-Text Edition of Chaucer's Canterbury Tales, Part I (Attempting to Show the True Order of the Tales and the Days and Stages of the Pilgrimage, Etc. Etc.)* (London: Published for the Chaucer Society by N. Trubner & Co., 1868), p. 3.
10 Sheila Sullivan, *Critics on Chaucer* (Coral Gables, Florida: University of Miami Press, 1970), p. 10. See also Derek Brewer, ed., *Chaucer: The Critical Heritage, volume 2 1837–1933* (London: Routledge & Kegan Paul, 1978), p. 33: 'The great contribution to Chaucer studies from the USA begins with [Ralph Waldo] Emerson, man of letters and transcendentalist, who refers to Chaucer several times.'
11 Furnivall (1868), p. 89.
12 Furnivall (1868), pp. 89–90.
13 Benzie (1983), p. 170. The full title of Thomas Milner's work of 1882 is *The Gallery of Nature: a pictorial and descriptive tour through creation, illustrative of the wonders of astronomy, physical geography, and geology*.
14 Benzie (1983), p. 162. For another early example of the application of this trend to Chaucer scholarship see Ewald Flügel, 'Some Notes on Chaucer's Prologue', *The Journal of English and Germanic Philology*, 1 (1897), pp. 118–35.
15 Edwin Ford Piper, 'The Miniatures of the Ellesmere Chaucer', *Philological Quarterly*, 3 (1924), p. 255.
16 Charles A. Owen, Jr., *The Manuscripts of the Canterbury Tales*, Chaucer Studies 17 (Cambridge: D. S. Brewer, 1991), pp. 13–14.
17 Martin Stevens, 'The Ellesmere Miniatures as Illustrations of Chaucer's Canterbury Tales', *Studies in Iconography*, 7–8 (1981–82), p. 113.
18 Frederick Tupper, 'The Quarrels of the Canterbury Pilgrims', *The Journal of English and Germanic Philology*, 14 (1915), p. 270.
19 Tupper (1915), pp. 257–8.
20 Umberto Eco, *Art and Beauty in the Middle Ages*, trans. Hugh Bredin (London: Yale University Press, 1986, rpt. 1989), p. 116.
21 Henry Barrett Hinckley, *Notes on Chaucer: A Commentary on the Prolog and Six Canterbury Tales* (Northampton, Massachusetts: The Nonotuck Press, 1907), p. 1.
22 Hinckley (1907), pp. 1–3.
23 [*Thompson's Note:*] The most comprehensive overview to date has been that of Donald McGrady, 'Chaucer and

the *Decameron* Reconsidered', *Ch*[*aucer*] *R*[*eview*], 12, 1977, pp. 1–26.
24 [*Thompson's Note:*] . . . R. A. Pratt, ed., *The Tales of Canterbury* (Boston: Houghton Mifflin Co., 1966, rpt. 1974), accepts that one of the sources of Chaucer's realism lay 'probably in the influence of the *Decameron*', p. xvii . . .; Jill Mann, *Chaucer and Medieval Estates Satire* (Cambridge: Cambridge University Press, 1973), posits influence (p. 46), and influence is assumed by D. R. Howard, *Chaucer and the Medieval World* (London: Weidenfeld and Nicolson, 1987), p. 261.
25 N. S. Thompson, *Chaucer, Boccaccio and the Debate of Love: A Comparative Study of the Decameron and The Canterbury Tales* (Oxford: Clarendon Press, 1996), pp. 1–3.
26 George Lyman Kittredge, *Chaucer and his Poetry* (Cambridge, Massachusetts: Harvard University Press, 1915, rpt. 1939), p. 149.
27 Kittredge (1939), pp. 147–8, 150.
28 Brewer (1978), p. 305.
29 Kittredge (1939), pp. 154–6. See also Lowes (1949), p. 164: 'The tales are not isolated entities. They stand in intimate relation to all that Chaucer in the Prologue has revealed about their tellers, and also to the give and take of dialogue which in the linking narrative leads up to them and follows them. The *Canterbury Tales*, even though their plan remains a splendid torso only, are an organic whole, and that whole is essentially dramatic. "Dialogue and action, gesture, costume and scenery, as in real life" – all are there. Long before Balzac Chaucer conceived and exhibited the Human Comedy.'
30 Kittredge (1939), pp. 158–60.
31 Alexander W. Allison, Herbert Barrows, *et al.*, eds., *The Norton Anthology of Poetry* (London: W. W. Norton & Co., 1970, rpt. 1983), p. 1000.
32 Hugh Kenner, *The Invisible Poet: T. S. Eliot* (London: Methuen & Co., 1959, rpt. 1979), p. 135.

33 Christopher Ricks, *T. S. Eliot and Prejudice* (London: Faber and Faber, 1988, rpt. 1994), p. 176. See also Linda Tarte Holley, 'Chaucer, T. S. Eliot, and the Regenerative Pilgrimage', *Studies in Medievalism*, 2:1 (1982), pp. 19–33. Holley, p. 30, concludes here that: 'To move along the thoroughfare of literary tradition that connects Chaucer and Eliot is to apprehend their quest for purification of the language of experience in the present moment with the symbols of past wisdom and so to participate in a regenerative pilgrimage.'
34 Sullivan (1970), p. 10.
35 Virginia Woolf, *The Common Reader* (London: Hogarth Press, 1925, 5th ed., 1945), pp. 24–5.
36 Woolf (1945), pp. 24–6, 28, 32–3.
37 Lowes (1949), p. 164.
38 G. K. Chesterton, *Chaucer* (London: Faber & Faber, 1932), pp. 164–5.
39 Benjamin B. Wainwright, 'Chaucer's Prioress Again: An Interpretative Note', *Modern Language Notes*, 48 (1933), pp. 34–7.
40 Carleton Brown, 'The Squire and the Number of the Canterbury Pilgrims', *Modern Language Notes*, 49 (1934), pp. 216–22.
41 B. J. Whiting, 'The Miller's Head', *Modern Language Notes*, 52 (1937), pp. 417–19.
42 Joe Horrell, 'Chaucer's Symbolic Plowman', *Speculum*, 14 (1939), pp. 82–92.
43 Muriel Bowden, *A Commentary on the General Prologue to the Canterbury Tales* (London: Collier-Macmillan Ltd., 1948, rev. ed., 1967), p. 1.
44 Bowden (1967), p. 2.
45 [*Bowden's Note:*] Miss Rosemond Tuve (*M*[*odern*] *L*[*anguage*] *N*[*otes*], 52, pp. 9–16) shows that Chaucer includes all the elements which make up the long and elaborate tradition of the spring setting.
46 Bowden (1967), pp. 19–21.
47 Edward I. Condren, *Chaucer and the Energy of Creation: The Design and the*

*Organization of the Canterbury Tales* (Gainesville: University Press of Florida, 1999), pp. 2–3, 14–17.
48 Bowden (1967), p. 22.

## CHAPTER THREE

1 George J. Firmage, ed., *e. e. cummings: Complete Poems: 1904–1962* (New York: Liveright Publishing Corporation, 1991), p. 661.
2 J.S.P. Tatlock, *The Mind and Art of Chaucer* (Syracuse: Syracuse University Press, 1950), p. 92.
3 Tatlock (1950), p. 92.
4 [*Malone's Note:*] But note [J.M.] Manly's cautious comment in his school edition of the *Canterbury Tales* (p. 522): "Here it is doubtful whether Chaucer represents the cook merely as being especially skilful or as being brought by the tradesmen for the express purpose of cooking their meals on the pilgrimage."
5 [*Malone's Note:*] The canon, like the squire, had a yeoman in his service, but the canon can hardly be reckoned one of the pilgrims, and he and his servant parted company almost as soon as they joined the pilgrims.
6 Kemp Malone, *Chapters on Chaucer* (Baltimore: Johns Hopkins Press, 1951), pp. 146–9.
7 Derek Pearsall, *The Life of Geoffrey Chaucer: A Critical Biography* (Oxford: Blackwell, 1992), p. 251.
8 R.T. Lenaghan, 'Chaucer's General Prologue as History and Literature', *Comparative Studies in Society and History*, 12 (1970), p. 82.
9 E. Talbot Donaldson, 'Chaucer the Pilgrim', *Publications of the Modern Language Association*, 69 (1954), pp. 928–9.
10 Bernard F. Huppé, *A Reading of the Canterbury Tales* (Albany: SUNY, 1964, rpt. 1967), p. 43.
11 Huppé (1967), pp. 47–8. See also Arthur W. Hoffman, 'Chaucer's Prologue to Pilgrimage: The Two Voices', *ELH, A Journal of English Literary History*, 21 (1954), pp. 1–16.
12 Rosemary Woolf, 'Chaucer as Satirist in the General Prologue to the Canterbury Tales', *The Critical Quarterly*, 1 (1959), p. 150.
13 Woolf (1959), pp. 150–6.
14 Owen (1961), p. vii.
15 J.V. Cunningham, *Tradition and Poetic Structure: Essays in Literary History and Criticism* (Denver: Alan Swallow, 1960), pp. 64–5.
16 Robert M. Jordan, *Chaucer and the Shape of Creation: The Aesthetic Possibilities of Inorganic Structure* (Cambridge, Massachusetts: Harvard University Press, 1967), p. 118.
17 See Jordan, p. 123: ' . . . [R.M.] Lumiansky's *Of S[o]ndry Folk* of 1955 establishes "The Dramatic Principle of the *Canterbury Tales*" and elucidates "the dramatic techniques by means of which the Pilgrims are kept as the center of focus throughout the *Tales*." Furthering our absorption in the "reality" of the roadside drama is this critic's manner of speaking of the tales as "performances" by actor-pilgrims.'
18 Jordan (1967), pp. 118–20.
19 Jordan (1967), p. 120.
20 D.W. Robertson, *A Preface to Chaucer: Studies in Medieval Perspectives* (Princeton: Princeton University Press, 1963), p. 242.
21 [*Robertson's Note:*] Details of the miller's physiognomy are discussed by W.C. Curry, *Chaucer and the Medieval Sciences* (New York, [Oxford University Press] 1926), pp. 81–9. For the bagpipe, see Edward A. Block, "Chaucer's Millers and their Bagpipes," *Speculum*, 29 (1954), pp. 239–42.
22 Robertson (1963), pp. 242–4.
23 Robertson (1963), p. 245.

## CHAPTER FOUR

1 William Spencer, 'Are Chaucer's Pilgrims Keyed to the Zodiac?', *The Chaucer Review*, 4 (1970), pp. 147–70.

2 R.T. Lenaghan, 'Chaucer's General Prologue as History and Literature', *Comparative Studies in Society and History*, 12 (1970), pp. 73–82.
3 Lenaghan (1970), p. 73.
4 Lenaghan (1970), pp. 79–80.
5 Lenaghan (1970), p. 82.
6 Lenaghan (1970), p. 82.
7 Lenaghan (1970), p. 81.
8 H. Marshall Leicester, Jr., *The Disenchanted Self: Representing the Subject in the Canterbury Tales* (Oxford: University of California Press, 1990), pp. 383–4.
9 Jill Mann, *Chaucer and Medieval Estates Satire: The Literature of Social Classes and the General Prologue to the Canterbury Tales* (Cambridge: At the University Press, 1973), p. 1.
10 Mann (1973), pp. 1–2.
11 Mann (1973), p. 2.
12 Mann (1973), pp. 3–4.
13 [*Mann's Note:*] 'Chaucer's Pilgrims' reprinted in [E.] Wagenknecht [ed. Chaucer: *Modern Essays in Criticism*, Oxford: Oxford University Press, 1959], p. 23. Cf. Clawson, 'The Framework of the Canterbury Tales', reprinted in Wagenknecht, p. 13, 'Chaucer's group of pilgrims is not schematically representative of English society, but covers well enough the main social elements', and H.R. Patch, *On Rereading Chaucer* [Cambridge, Massachusetts: Harvard University Press, 1939], pp. 176–7. [P.F.] Baum takes exception to Hulbert's statements on the grounds that 'society is too complex to be generalised so easily' (Chaucer, *A Critical Appreciation* [Durham, North Carolina: Duke University Press, 1958], p. 68) – to which it might be replied that society itself is complex but people's schematic ideas of it are far simpler.
14 [*Mann's Note:*] [B.H. Bronson,] *In Search of Chaucer* [Toronto: Toronto University Press, 1960], p. 60.
15 [*Mann's Note:*] *Chaucer and the French Tradition*, [Berkeley and Los Angeles: University of California Press, 1964,] p. 170. Muscatine is referring to the portrait-gallery form.
16 [*Mann's Note:*] *The Mind and Art of Chaucer* [Syracuse: Syracuse University Press, 1950], p. 92.
17 [*Mann's Note:*] Clawson, 'Framework of the Canterbury Tales', Wagenknecht, p. 14. Northrop Frye's general comment on satire has relevance here: The romantic fixation which revolves around the beauty of perfect form, in art or elsewhere, is . . . a logical target for satire. The word satire is said to come from *satura*, or hash, and a kind of parody of form seems to run all through its tradition . . . A deliberate rambling digressiveness . . . is endemic in the narrative technique of satire . . . An extraordinary number of great satires are fragmentary, unfinished, or anonymous (*Anatomy of Criticism*, pp. 233–4).
18 Mann (1973), pp. 4–7.
19 Mann (1973), pp. 9–10.
20 Mann (1973), pp. 201–2.
21 John Norton-Smith, *Geoffrey Chaucer* (London: Routledge & Kegan Paul, 1974), p. 80.
22 Norton-Smith (1974), p. 97.
23 Lee Patterson, *Chaucer and the Subject of History* (Madison: University of Wisconsin Press, 1991), p. 19.
24 Alice Miskimin, *The Renaissance Chaucer* (London: Yale University Press, 1975), pp. 2,3.
25 Miskimin (1975), p. 93.
26 Miskimin (1975), p. 12.
27 Miskimin (1975), p. 257.
28 E. Talbot Donaldson, *The Swan at the Well: Shakespeare Reading Chaucer* (London: Yale University Press, 1985), p. 2.
29 Owen (1977), p. 47.
30 Owen (1977), p. 65.
31 Owen (1977), p. 66.
32 Owen (1977), pp. 48–51.
33 Owen (1977), pp. 85–6.
34 Laura Kendrick, *Chaucerian Play: Comedy and Control in the Canterbury Tales* (London: University of California Press, 1988), p. 133.

35 Kendrick (1988), pp. 2–3.
36 Loy D. Martin, 'History and Form in the General Prologue to the *Canterbury Tales*', *ELH, A Journal of English Literary History*, 45 (1978), p. 2.
37 Martin (1978), p. 3.
38 Martin (1978), p. 3. [*Martin's Note*, p. 16:] This concept is not unusual in the late Middle Ages. For its use in both philosophical and political contexts, see Ernst Kantorowicz, *The King's Two Bodies* (Princeton, [Princeton University Press,] 1957), esp. Chap. VI.
39 [*Martin's Note:*] Probably the most penetrating perception of the significance of the opening passage in these terms is that of Arthur W. Hoffman, 'Chaucer's Prologue to Pilgrimage: The Two Voices,' in *Chaucer, Modern Essays in Criticism*, ed. Edward Wagenknecht (New York, 1959), pp. 30–45. See also Raymond Preston, *Chaucer* (London, 1952), p. 30.
40 Martin (1978), pp. 4–6.
41 Martin (1978), p. 7.
42 Martin (1978), pp. 11–12.
43 [*Martin's Note*, p. 17:] Ruth Nevo makes this observation and develops it at length in 'Chaucer: Motive and Mask in the *General Prologue*', *Modern Language Review*, 58 (1963), 1–9.
44 H. Marshall Leicester, 'The Art of Impersonation: A General Prologue to the *Canterbury Tales*', Publications of the Modern Language Association, 95 (1980), p. 213.
45 Donald R. Howard, *The Idea of the Canterbury Tales* (London: University of California Press, 1978), pp. 3–4.
46 Howard (1978), p. 141.
47 Howard (1978), pp. 148–9.
48 Howard (1978), pp. 156–8.
49 Judith Ferster, *Chaucer on Interpretation* (Cambridge: Cambridge University Press, 1985), p. 150.

CHAPTER FIVE

1 Alastair J. Minnis, 'Chaucer and Comparative Literary Theory', Donald M. Rose, ed., *New Perspectives in Chaucer Criticism* (Norman, Oklahoma: Pilgrim Books, 1981), p. 69.
2 Minnis in Rose (1981), p. 53.
3 Minnis in Rose (1981), p. 54.
4 Minnis in Rose (1981), p. 54.
5 Howard (1978), p. 231.
6 Leicester (1980), p. 214.
7 Leicester (1980), p. 216.
8 Leicester (1980), pp. 216–17.
9 Leicester (1980), p. 223.
10 Ferster (1985), p. 151.
11 Ferster (1985), p. 4.
12 [*Leicester's Note:*] See Rosemary Woolf, 'Chaucer as Satirist in the General Prologue to the *Canterbury Tales*', *Critical Quarterly*, 1 (1959), pp. 150–7.
13 Leicester (1980), pp. 219–22.
14 Barbara Nolan, '"A Poet Ther Was": Chaucer's Voices in the General Prologue to *The Canterbury Tales*', Publications of the Modern Language Association, 102 (1986), p. 154.
15 Nolan (1986), p. 154.
16 Nolan (1986), p. 154.
17 Nolan (1986), p. 156.
18 Nolan (1986), p. 156.
19 Nolan (1986), pp. 157–8.
20 Nolan (1986), pp. 161, 165, 166.
21 Julian N. Wasserman & Robert Blanch, eds., *Chaucer in the Eighties* (Syracuse: Syracuse University Press, 1986), p. xvi.
22 Wasserman & Blanch (1986), p. xv.
23 [*Higgs's Note:*] Morgan places too much emphasis on social status in the Prologue when he insists that the pilgrims are strictly ordered by Chaucer 'in accordance with social rank.' He explicitly excludes the 'moral nature' of the pilgrims as a significant organizing principle. [Gerald] Morgan, 'The Design of the *General Prologue* [to *The Canterbury Tales*]', *English Studies*, 59 (1978), pp. 484, 485.
24 [*Higgs's Note:*] Although one cannot prove whether Chaucer had planned the prologues to the tales of these three when he wrote the General Prologue, it

must be admitted that the prologues of the Wife of Bath and the Pardoner, at least, are consistent extensions of their portraits in the General Prologue. There is therefore some justification for referring to the links and individual prologues when one is analyzing the initial portraits.

25 Elton D. Higgs, 'The Old Order and the "Newe World" in the General Prologue to the *Canterbury Tales*', *The Huntington Library Quarterly*, 45 (1982), pp. 155–73.
26 Jones (1980), p. 1.
27 Jones (1980), p. 27.
28 Jones (1980), pp. 221–2.
29 Ferster (1985), pp. 139–40.
30 Ferster (1985), p. 140.
31 Ferster (1985), p. 144.
32 Wasserman & Blanch (1986), p. xvi.

CHAPTER SIX

1 Andrew, Moorman & Ransom (1993), II, p. xvi.
2 See, for example, Daniel M. Murtagh, 'Women and Geoffrey Chaucer', *English Literary History*, 38 (1971), pp. 473–92; Hope Phyllis Weissman, 'Antifeminism and Chaucer's Characterizations of Women', George D. Economou, ed., *Geoffrey Chaucer: A Collection of Original Articles* (New York: McGraw-Hill, 1975), pp. 93–110; A. Diamond, 'Chaucer's Women and Women's Chaucer', A. Diamond and L. R. Edwards, eds., *The Authority of Experience* (Amherst: University of Massachusetts Press, 1977), pp. 66–88.
3 Gayle Margherita, 'Originary Fantasies and Chaucer's Book of the Duchess', Linda Lomperis and Sarah Stanbury, eds., *Feminist Approaches to the Body in Medieval Literature* (Philadelphia: University of Pennsylvania Press, 1993), p. 141.
4 G. L. Kittredge, 'Chaucer's Discussion of Marriage', *Modern Philology*, IX (1911–12), pp. 435–67.
5 Priscilla Martin, *Chaucer's Women: Nuns, Wives and Amazons* (London: Macmillan, 1990, rpt. 1996), p. 122.
6 Elaine Tuttle Hansen, *Chaucer and the Fictions of Gender* (Oxford: University of California Press, 1992), pp. 11–12.
7 Bowden (1948), p. 274.
8 Bowden (1948), p. 286.
9 Monica E. McAlpine, 'The Pardoner's Homosexuality and How it Matters', *Publications of the Modern Language Association*, 95 (1980), p. 8.
10 McAlpine (1980), p. 8.
11 McAlpine (1980), pp. 8–14.
12 Susan Crane, *Gender and Romance in Chaucer's Canterbury Tales* (Princeton: Princeton University Press, 1994), p. 115.
13 David Aers, *Chaucer* (Brighton: Harvester, 1986), pp. 50–1.
14 Patterson (1991), p. 27.
15 Patterson (1991), p. 367.
16 Alcuin Blamires, *Women Defamed and Women Defended: An Anthology of Medieval Texts* (Oxford: Clarendon Press, 1992), p. 198.
17 Eric Jager, *The Tempter's Voice: Language and the Fall in Medieval Literature* (London: Cornell University Press, 1993), pp. 238–9.
18 Martin (1996), p. xii.
19 Martin (1996), p. xii.
20 [*Martin's Note:*] Studies of the portraits include Muriel Bowden, *A Commentary on the General Prologue to the Canterbury Tales* (London [: Methuen], 1948) pp. 92–104, 214–29; R. M. Lumiansky, *Of Sondry Folk: The Dramatic Principle in The Canterbury Tales* (Austin, Texas, 1955) pp. 79–83, 117–29; H. F. Brooks, *Chaucer's Pilgrims* (London, 1962) pp. 15–19, 31–3. In light of Martin's citation, it is useful here to quote Brooks, pp. 31–3: 'The Wife of Bath, like the Shipman, is from the west. She rounds off the middle-class group [in *The General Prologue*] by making it end as it began, with someone belonging to the world of trade and industry . . . Apart from the Shipman, she and the Knight are the great travellers among

the pilgrims, and even the Shipman has not been so far afield: but while the Knight's campaigns were undertaken in the spirit of Christian chivalry, her pilgrimages do not express any analogous ideal of piety, still less of penitence. It is the Prioress, however, whose portrait is the companion-piece to hers. These are the only two portraits of women, and they represent female nature at the opposite poles of fastidious sensibility and elemental vitality. In the temperament of the Prioress, feeling predominates; but her feelings are in part sublimated and in part deflected . . . The Wife of Bath, a Molly Bloom of the fourteenth century, is rooted in the senses. From that instinctive and physical source there arises her magnificently uninhibited appetite for experience, which she has satisfied so abundantly in travel as well as with lovers and husbands. There is a paradoxical relationship between her temperament and the religious institution of the pilgrimage, as between that of the Prioress and the religious institution of the cloister; with her, the institution is made to serve the temperament, with the Prioress the temperament is fitted, incompletely, to the institution. In the whole series of portraits, these two, though there is satire in them, are Chaucer's masterpieces of appreciative humour: one sympathetic and delicate, the other broad and rollicking.'

21 [*Martin's Note:*] J.L. Lowes, 'Simple and Coy: A Note on Fourteenth-Century Poetic Diction', *Anglia*, 33 (1910) pp. 440–51.

22 [*Martin's Note:*] Hope P. Weissman, 'Antifeminism and Chaucer's Characterization of Women', in *Geoffrey Chaucer*, ed. George D. Economou (New York, 1975) pp. 93–110.

23 [*Martin's Note:*] Jill Mann, *Chaucer and Medieval Estates Satire: The Literature of Social Classes and the General Prologue to the Canterbury Tales* (Cambridge 1973) pp. 134–7, discusses 'spiritual courtesy . . . the ladylike aspect of the spiritual life' (p. 134).

24 [*Martin's Note:*] A characteristically harsh appraisal of the Prioress as 'a particularly striking exemplar of false courtesy' is made by D.W. Robertson, Jr., *A Preface to Chaucer* (Princeton, New Jersey, 1963) p. 246. A similar judgement is made on the basis of a detailed examination of the semiology of the portrait by Chauncey Wood, 'Chaucer's Use of Signs in the Portrait of the Prioress', in *Signs and Symbols in Chaucer's Poetry*, ed. John P. Hermann and John J. Burke, Jr. (University of Alabama, 1977) pp. 81–101.

25 Martin (1996), pp. 30–9.

26 Martin (1996), p. xi.

27 Jane Chance, *The Mythographic Chaucer: The Fabulation of Sexual Politics* (London: University of Minnesota Press, 1995), pp. xix, xx.

28 Chance (1995), pp. 171–83.

29 Chance (1995), p. 171.

30 Chance (1995), p. 172.

31 Chance (1995), pp. 173, 174, 180–3.

32 John M. Ganim, *Chaucerian Theatricality* (Princeton: Princeton University Press, 1990), p. 129.

# SELECT BIBLIOGRAPHY

## Editions of *The General Prologue*, *The Canterbury Tales* and Chaucer's Collected Works:

Andrew, Malcolm, Moorman, Charles, and Ransom, Daniel J., eds. *A Variorum Edition of the Works of Geoffrey Chaucer*. Vol. II. *The Canterbury Tales. The General Prologue*. London: University of Oklahoma Press, 1993.

Benson, Larry D., ed. *The Riverside Chaucer*. Oxford: Oxford University Press, 1987. This widely used paperback edition is the authoritative text used in this Guide.

Blake, N.F., ed. *The Canterbury Tales, edited from the Hengwrt manuscript*. York Medieval Text. Second Series. London: Edward Arnold, 1980.

French, Robert D., ed. *Canterbury Tales*. Crofts Classics. New York: Appleton-Century-Crofts, 1948. This selection includes *The General Prologue* and the tales of The Wife of Bath, The Friar, The Pardoner, The Prioress, The Poet and The Nun's Priest.

Mack, Peter, and Walton, Chris, eds. *General Prologue to the Canterbury Tales*. Oxford Student Texts. Oxford: Oxford University Press, 1994.

Manly, John Matthews, ed. *Canterbury Tales*. London: Harrap, 1929.

Pollard, Alfred W., ed. *Chaucer's Canterbury Tales: the Prologue*. Macmillan's English Classics. Basingstoke: Macmillan Education, 1976.

Robinson, F.N., ed. *The Works of Geoffrey Chaucer*. 2nd. ed. Boston: Houghton, 1957.

Tyrwhitt, Thomas, ed. *The Canterbury Tales of Chaucer (to which are added an essay on his Language and Versification, and an introductory discourse together with notes and a glossary)*. Oxford: At the Clarendon Press, 1798.

Winny, James, ed. *The general prologue to the Canterbury Tales*. Selected tales from Chaucer. Cambridge: Cambridge University Press, 1965.

Wyatt, A.J., ed. *Canterbury Tales: The Prologue and the Squire's Tale*. The University Tutorial Series. English Classics. London: W.B. Clive, the University Tutorial Press, 1904.

## Journals

*Chaucer Review*
*Studies in the Age of Chaucer*

## Articles

Adams, George R. 'Sex and Clergy in Chaucer's *General Prologue*'. *Literature and Psychology*, 18 (1968), pp. 215–22.

Andrew, Malcolm. 'Chaucer's Prologue to the *Canterbury Tales*'. *Explicator*, 43:1 (1984), pp. 5–6.

# SELECT BIBLIOGRAPHY

Armstrong, Nancy. 'The Gender Bind: Women and the Disciplines'. *Genders*, 3 (1988), pp. 1–23.

Block, Edward A. 'Chaucer's Millers and their Bagpipes'. *Speculum*, 29 (1954), pp. 239–42.

Brown, Carleton. 'The Squire and the Number of the Canterbury Pilgrims'. *Modern Language Notes*, 49 (1934), pp. 216–22.

Conrad, Bernard R. 'The Date of Chaucer's *Prologue*'. *Notes and Queries*, 152 (1927), p. 385.

Danby, John F. 'Eighteen Lines of Chaucer's *Prologue*'. *Critical Quarterly*, 2 (1960), pp. 28–32.

Donaldson, E. Talbot. 'Chaucer the Pilgrim'. *Publications of the Modern Language Association*, 69 (1954), pp. 928–36.

Farina, Peter M. 'The Twenty-Nine Again: Another Count of Chaucer's Pilgrims'. *Language Quarterly*, 9 (1971), pp. 29–31.

Flügel, Ewald. 'Some Notes on Chaucer's Prologue'. *Journal of English and Germanic Philology*, 1 (1897), pp. 118–35.

Garbaty, Thomas. 'Chaucer's Guildsmen and their Fraternity'. *Journal of English and Germanic Philology*, 59 (1960), pp. 691–709.

Green, Eugene. 'The Voices of the Pilgrims in the *General Prologue* to the *Canterbury Tales*'. *Style*, 9 (1975), pp. 55–81.

Greenlaw, Edwin A. 'A Note on Chaucer's Prologue'. *Modern Language Notes*, 23 (1908), pp. 142–4.

Hanning, Robert W. 'From *Eva* and *Ave* to Eglentyne and Alisoun: Chaucer's Insight into the Roles Women Play'. *Signs*, 2 (1977), pp. 580–99.

Hansen, Elaine Tuttle. 'Fearing for Chaucer's Good Name'. *Exemplaria*, 2 (1990), pp. 23–36.

Hart, James A. '"The Droghte of March": A Common Misunderstanding'. *Texas Studies in Language and Literature*, 4 (1962), pp. 525–9.

Higgs, Elton D. 'The Old Order and the "Newe World" in the General Prologue to the *Canterbury Tales*'. *The Huntington Library Quarterly*, 45 (1982), pp. 155–73.

Hoffman, Arthur W. 'Chaucer's Prologue to Pilgrimage: The Two Voices'. *ELH, A Journal of English Literary History*, 21 (1954), pp. 1–16.

Holley, Linda Tarte. 'Chaucer, T. S. Eliot, and the Regenerative Pilgrimage'. *Studies in Medievalism*, 2:1 (1982), pp. 19–33.

Horrell, Joe. 'Chaucer's Symbolic Plowman'. *Speculum*, 14 (1939), pp. 82–92.

Kellogg, Alfred. 'An Augustinian Interpretation of Chaucer's Pardoner'. *Speculum*, 26 (1951), pp. 465–81.

Kernan, Anne. 'The Arch-Wife and the Eunuch'. *ELH, A Journal of English Literary History*, 41 (1974), pp. 1–25.

Kimpel, Ben. 'The Narrator of the *Canterbury Tales*'. *ELH, A Journal of English Literary History*, 20 (1953), pp. 77–86.

Kittredge, G. L. 'Chaucer's Discussion of Marriage'. *Modern Philology*, 9

(1911–12), pp. 435–67.

Leicester, H. Marshall, Jr. 'The Art of Impersonation: A General Prologue to the *Canterbury Tales*'. *Publications of the Modern Language Association*, 95 (1980), pp. 213–24.

Lenaghan, R.T. 'Chaucer's *General Prologue* as History and Literature'. *Comparative Studies in Society and History*, 12 (1970), pp. 73–82.

Lowes, John Livingstone. 'Simple and Coy: A Note on Fourteenth-Century Poetic Diction'. *Anglia*, 33 (1910), pp. 440–51.

Major, John M. 'The Personality of Chaucer the Pilgrim'. *Publications of the Modern Language Association*, 75 (1960), pp. 160–2.

Martin, Loy D. 'History and Form in the General Prologue to the *Canterbury Tales*'. *ELH, A Journal of English Literary History*, 45 (1978), pp. 1–17.

McAlpine, Monica E. 'The Pardoner's Homosexuality and How it Matters'. *Publications of the Modern Language Association*, 95 (1980), pp. 8–22.

McGrady, Donald. 'Chaucer and the *Decameron* Reconsidered'. *Chaucer Review*, 12 (1977), pp. 1–26.

Miller, Robert. 'Chaucer's Pardoner, the Scriptural Eunuch, and the Pardoner's Tale'. *Speculum*, 30 (1955), pp. 180–99.

Morgan, Gerald. 'The Design of the *General Prologue* to the *Canterbury Tales*'. *English Studies*, 59 (1978), pp. 481–498.

Murtagh, Daniel M. 'Women and Geoffrey Chaucer'. *ELH, A Journal of English Literary History*, 38 (1971), pp. 473–92.

Nathan, Norman. 'The Number of the Canterbury Pilgrims'. *Modern Language Notes*, 67 (1952), pp. 533–4.

Nevo, Ruth. 'Chaucer: Motive and Mask in the *General Prologue*'. *Modern Language Review*, 58 (1963), pp. 1–9.

Nitzsche, J.C. 'Creation in Genesis and Nature in Chaucer's *General Prologue* 1–18'. *Papers on Language and Literature*, 14 (1978), pp. 459–64.

Nolan, Barbara. '"A Poet Ther Was": Chaucer's Voices in the General Prologue to *The Canterbury Tales*'. *Publications of the Modern Language Association*, 102 (1986), pp. 154–69.

Page, Barbara. 'Concerning the Host'. *Chaucer Review*, 4 (1970), pp. 1–13.

Piper, Edwin Ford. 'The Miniatures of the Ellesmere Chaucer'. *Philological Quarterly*, 3 (1924), pp. 241–56.

Rogers, P. Burwell. 'The Names of the Canterbury Pilgrims'. *Names*, 16 (1968), pp. 339–46.

Rowland, Beryl. 'Animal Imagery and the Pardoner's Abnormality'. *Neophilologus*, 48 (1964), pp. 56–60.

Sedgewick, G.G. 'The Progress of Chaucer's Pardoner, 1880–1940'. *Modern Language Quarterly*, 1 (1940), pp. 431–58.

Stevens, Martin. 'The Ellesmere Miniatures as Illustrations of Chaucer's *Canterbury Tales*'. *Studies in Iconography*, 7–8 (1981–2), pp. 113–34.

Swart, J. 'The Construction of Chaucer's *General Prologue*'. *Neophilologus*, 38 (1954), pp. 127–36.

Tatlock, John S.P. 'Boccaccio and the Plan of Chaucer's *Canterbury Tales*'. *Anglia*, 37 (1913), pp. 69–117.
Tupper, Frederick. 'The Quarrels of the Canterbury Pilgrims'. *Journal of English and Germanic Philology*, 14 (1915), pp. 256–70.
Tuve, Rosemund. 'Spring in Chaucer and Before Him'. *Modern Language Notes*, 52 (1937), pp. 9–16.
Wainwright, Benjamin B. 'Chaucer's Prioress Again: An Interpretative Note'. *Modern Language Notes*, 49 (1934), pp. 34–7.
Whiting, B.J. 'The Miller's Head'. *Modern Language Notes*, 52 (1937), pp. 417–19.
Woolf, Rosemary. 'Chaucer as Satirist in the General Prologue to *The Canterbury Tales*'. *Critical Quarterly*, 1 (1959), pp. 150–7.
Wurtele, Douglas. 'Some Uses of Physiognomical Lore in Chaucer's *Canterbury Tales*'. *Chaucer Review*, 17 (1982), pp. 130–41.

## Chapters in books

Anderson, Judith H. 'Narrative Reflections: Re-envisaging the Poet in *The Canterbury Tales* and *The Faerie Queene*'. Theresa M. Krier, ed. *Refiguring Chaucer in the Renaissance*. Gainesville: University Press of Florida, 1998.
Arnold, Matthew. *The Study of Poetry*. Charles A. Owen, Jr., ed. *Discussions of the Canterbury Tales*. Westport, Connecticut: Greenwood Press, 1961, rpt. 1978.
Braswell, Mary Flowers. 'Penitential Irony: A Look at Chaucer's Prologues'. *The Medieval Sinner: Characterization and Confession in the Literature of the Middle Ages*. London: Associated University Presses, 1983.
Diamond, A. 'Chaucer's Women and Women's Chaucer'. A. Diamond and L.R. Edwards, eds. *The Authority of Experience*. Amherst: University of Massachusetts Press, 1977.
Dryden, John. 'Preface' to *Fables*. Charles A. Owen, Jr., ed. *Discussions of the Canterbury Tales*. Westport, Connecticut: Greenwood Press, 1961, rpt. 1978.
Kirby, Thomas A. *'The General Prologue'*. Beryl Rowland, ed. *Companion to Chaucer Studies*. Oxford: Oxford University Press, 1968, rev. ed. 1979.
Margherita, Gayle. 'Originary Fantasies and Chaucer's *Book of the Duchess*'. Linda Lomperis and Sarah Stanbury, eds. *Feminist Approaches to the Body in Medieval Literature*. Philadelphia: University of Pennsylvania Press, 1993.
Minnis, Alastair. 'Chaucer and Comparative Literary Theory'. Donald M. Rose, ed. *New Perspectives in Chaucer Criticism*. Norman, Oklahoma: Pilgrim Books, 1981.
Weissman, Hope Phyllis. 'Antifeminism and Chaucer's Characterizations of Women'. George D. Economou, ed. *Geoffrey Chaucer: A Collection of Original Articles*. New York: McGraw-Hill, 1975.
Woolf, Virginia. 'The Pastons and Chaucer'. *The Common Reader*. London: The Hogarth Press, 1925, 5th ed. 1945.

------. 'The Pastons and Chaucer'. Sheila Sullivan, ed. *Critics on Chaucer*. Coral Gables: University of Miami Press, 1970.

## Books

Aers, David. *Chaucer*. Brighton: Harvester, 1986.
Baum, P. F. *Chaucer: A Critical Appreciation*. Durham, North Carolina: Duke University Press, 1958.
Benzie, William. *Dr. F. J. Furnivall: Victorian Scholar Adventurer*. Norman, Oklahoma: Pilgrim Books, 1983.
Blamires, Alcuin, ed. *Woman Defamed and Woman Defended: An Anthology of Medieval Texts*. Oxford: Clarendon Press, 1992.
Boitani, Piero and Jill Mann, eds. *The Cambridge Chaucer Companion*. Cambridge: Cambridge University Press, 1986.
Bowden, Muriel. *A Commentary on the General Prologue to the Canterbury Tales*. London: Collier-Macmillan Ltd., 1948, rev. ed., 1967.
Brewer, Derek. *Chaucer: The Critical Heritage, volume 2 1837–1933*. London: Routledge & Kegan Paul, 1978.
Bronson, B. H. *In Search of Chaucer*. Toronto: Toronto University Press, 1960.
Brooks, Harold F. *Chaucer's Pilgrims: The Artistic Order of the Portraits in the Prologue*. London: Methuen & Co. Ltd., 1962.
Bryan, W. F., ed. *Sources and Analogues of Chaucer's Canterbury Tales*. Atlantic Highlands, New Jersey: Humanities Press, 1941.
Chance, Jane. *The Mythographic Chaucer: The Fabulation of Sexual Politics*. London: University of Minnesota Press, 1995.
Chesterton, G. K. *Chaucer*. London: Faber & Faber, 1932.
Coghill, Nevill. *The Poet Chaucer*. London: Oxford University Press, 1949.
Condren, Edward I. *Chaucer and the Energy of Creation: The Design and Organization of the Canterbury Tales*. Gainesville: University Press of Florida, 1999.
Crampton, Georgina Ronan. *The Condition of Creatures: Suffering and Action in Chaucer and Spenser*. London: Yale University Press, 1974.
Cunningham, J. V. *Tradition and Poetic Structure: Essays in Literary History and Criticism*. Denver: Alan Swallow, 1960.
Curry, W. C. *Chaucer and the Medieval Sciences*. New York: Oxford University Press, 1926.
Dane, Joseph A. *Who is Buried in Chaucer's Tomb?: Studies in the Reception of Chaucer's Book*. Ann Arbor: Michigan State University Press, 1998.
Donaldson, E. Talbot. *The Swan at the Well: Shakespeare Reading Chaucer*. London: Yale University Press, 1985.
Eckhardt, Caroline D. *Chaucer's General Prologue to the Canterbury Tales: An Annotated Bibliography, 1900–1982*. London: University of Toronto Press, 1990.
Eco, Umberto. *Art and Beauty in the Middle Ages*. Trans. Hugh Bredin. London: Yale University Press, 1986, rpt. 1989.

## SELECT BIBLIOGRAPHY

Ferster, Judith. *Chaucer on Interpretation*. Cambridge: Cambridge University Press, 1985.

Frese, Dolores Warwick. *An Ars Legendi for Chaucer's Canterbury Tales: A Reconstructive Reading*. Gainesville: University of Florida Press, 1991.

Furnivall, F.J. *A Temporary Preface to the Six-Text Edition of Chaucer's Canterbury Tales, Part I (Attempting to Show the True Order of the Tales and the Days and Stages of the Pilgrimage, Etc. Etc.)*. London: Published for the Chaucer Society by N. Trubner & Co., 1868.

Ganim, John M. *Chaucerian Theatricality*. Princeton: Princeton University Press, 1990.

Gardner, John. *The Poetry of Chaucer*. Carbondale: Southern Illinois University Press, 1977.

Hansen, Elaine Tuttle. *Chaucer and the Fictions of Gender*. Oxford: University of California Press, 1992.

Hinckley, Henry Barrett. *Notes on Chaucer: A Commentary on the Prolog and Six Canterbury Tales*. Northampton, Massachusetts: The Nonotuck Press, 1907.

Howard, Donald R. *The Idea of the Canterbury Tales*. London: University of California Press, 1976. pbk. ed. 1978.

———. *Chaucer and the Medieval World*. London: Weidenfeld and Nicholson, 1987.

Huppé, Bernard F. *A Reading of the Canterbury Tales*. Albany: SUNY, 1964, rpt. 1967.

Hussey, Maurice; Spearing, A.C. and Winny, James. *An Introduction to Chaucer*. Cambridge: At the University Press, 1965.

Jager, Eric. *The Tempter's Voice: Language and the Fall in Medieval Literature*. London: Cornell University Press, 1993.

Jones, Terry. *Chaucer's Knight: The Portrait of a Medieval Mercenary*. London: Eyre Methuen, 1980, pbk. ed. 1982.

Jordan, Robert M. *Chaucer and the Shape of Creation: The Aesthetic Possibilities of Inorganic Structure*. Cambridge, Massachusetts: Harvard University Press, 1967.

Kantorowicz, Ernst. *The King's Two Bodies*. Princeton: Princeton University Press, 1957.

Kendrick, Laura. *Chaucerian Play: Comedy and Control in the Canterbury Tales*. London: University of California Press, 1988.

Kenner, Hugh. *The Invisible Poet: T.S. Eliot*. London: Methuen & Co., 1959, rpt. 1979.

Kiser, Lisa. *Truth and Textuality in Chaucer's Poetry*. London: University Press of New England, 1991.

Kittredge, George Lyman. *Chaucer and his Poetry*. Cambridge, Massachusetts: Harvard University Press, 1915, rpt. 1939.

Knapp, Peggy. *Chaucer and the Social Contest*. London: Routledge, 1990.

Lambdin, Linda C. and Robert T., eds. *Chaucer's Pilgrims: An Historical Guide to the Pilgrims in the Canterbury Tales*. London: Greenwood Press, 1996.

Lawton, David. *Chaucer's Narrators.* Chaucer Studies 13. Cambridge: D.S. Brewer, 1985.
Leicester, H. Marshall, Jr. *The Disenchanted Self: Representing the Subject in the Canterbury Tales.* Oxford: University of California Press, 1990.
Lindahl, Carl. *Earnest Games: Folkloric Patterns in the Canterbury Tales.* Bloomington: Indiana University Press, 1987.
Lounsbury, Thomas R. *Studies in Chaucer: His Life and Writings,* 3 vols. New York: Harper and Brothers, 1892.
Lowes, John Livingstone. *Geoffrey Chaucer: Lectures Delivered in 1932 on the William J. Cooper Foundation in Swarthmore College.* Oxford: At the Clarendon Press, 1934, rpt. 1949.
Lumiansky, R.M. *Of Sondry Folk: The Dramatic Principle in the Canterbury Tales.* Austin: University of Texas Press, 1955.
Malone, Kemp. *Chapters on Chaucer.* Baltimore: Johns Hopkins University Press, 1951.
Manly, John Matthews. *Some New Light on Chaucer.* New York: P. Smith, 1926, rpt. 1952.
Mann, Jill. *Chaucer and Medieval Estates Satire: The Literature of Social Classes and the General Prologue to the Canterbury Tales.* Cambridge: At the University Press, 1973.
———. *Geoffrey Chaucer.* Hemel Hempstead: Harvester Wheatsheaf, 1991.
Martin, Priscilla. *Chaucer's Women: Nuns, Wives and Amazons.* London: Macmillan, 1990, rpt. 1996.
Miskimin, Alice. *The Renaissance Chaucer.* London: Yale University Press, 1975.
Muscatine, Charles. *Chaucer and the French Tradition: A Study in Style and Meaning.* Berkeley: University of California Press, 1957.
Myles, Robert. *Chaucerian Realism.* Chaucer Studies 20. Cambridge: D.S. Brewer, 1994.
Norton-Smith, John. *Geoffrey Chaucer.* London: Routledge & Kegan Paul, 1974.
Owen, Charles A., Jr. *Discussions of the Canterbury Tales.* Westport, Connecticut: Greenwood Press, 1961.
———. *Pilgrimage and Storytelling in the Canterbury Tales.* Norman: University of Oklahoma Press, 1977.
———. *The Manuscripts of the Canterbury Tales.* Chaucer Studies 17. Cambridge: D.S. Brewer, 1991.
Patch, H.R. *On Rereading Chaucer.* Cambridge, Massachusetts: Harvard University Press, 1939.
Patterson, Lee. *Chaucer and the Subject of History.* Madison: University of Wisconsin Press, 1991.
Pearsall, Derek. *The Life of Geoffrey Chaucer: A Critical Biography.* Oxford: Blackwell, 1992.
Preston, Raymond. *Chaucer.* London: Sheed & Ward, 1952.
Quiller-Couch, Sir Arthur T. *The Age of Chaucer.* London: J.M. Dent & Sons Ltd., 1926.

# SELECT BIBLIOGRAPHY

Ricks, Christopher. *T. S. Eliot and Prejudice*. London: Faber, 1988, rpt. 1994.

Robertson, D. W. *A Preface to Chaucer: Studies in Medieval Perspectives*. Princeton: Princeton University Press, 1963.

Robinson, Ian. *Chaucer and the English Tradition*. Cambridge: Cambridge University Press, 1972.

Schaar, Claes. *The Golden Mirror: Studies in Chaucer's Descriptive Technique and its Literary Background*. Lund: C.W.K. Gleerup, 1967.

Spurgeon, Caroline F. E., ed. *Five Hundred Years of Chaucer Criticism and Allusion: 1357–1900*. Chaucer Society 1908–1917. 3 vols. Cambridge: Cambridge University Press, 1925; New York: Russell and Russell, 1960.

Sullivan, Sheila, ed. *Critics on Chaucer*. Coral Gables: University of Miami Press, 1970.

Tatlock, John S. P. *The Mind and Art of Chaucer*. Syracuse: Syracuse University Press, 1950.

Thompson, Ann. *Shakespeare's Chaucer: A Study in Literary Origins*. Liverpool: Liverpool University Press, 1978.

Thompson, N. S. *Chaucer, Boccaccio and the Debate of Love: A Comparative Study of the Decameron and The Canterbury Tales*. Oxford: Clarendon, 1996.

Wagenknecht, Edward, ed. *Chaucer: Modern Essays in Criticism*. Oxford: Oxford University Press, 1959.

Wasserman, Julian N. and Blanch, Robert, eds. *Chaucer in the Eighties*. Syracuse: Syracuse University Press, 1986.

Williams, David. *The Canterbury Tales: A Literary Pilgrimage*. Boston: Twayne, 1987.

# ACKNOWLEDGEMENTS

The editor and publisher wish to thank the following for their permission to reprint copyright material: Oxford University Press (for material from *The Riverside Chaucer*); *PMLA* (for material from: 'Chaucer the Pilgrim'; 'The Art of Impersonation: A General Prologue to the *Canterbury Tales*'; 'The Pardoner's Homosexuality and How it Matters'; and '"A Poet Ther Was": Chaucer's Voices in the General Prologue to *The Canterbury Tales*'); *Journal of English and Germanic Philology* (for material from 'Some Notes on Chaucer's Prologue'); *The Huntington Library Quarterly* (for material from 'The Old Order and the "Newe World" in the General Prologue to the *Canterbury Tales*'); *ELH* (for material from: 'Chaucer's Prologue to Pilgrimage: The Two Voices'; and 'History and Form in the General Prologue to the *Canterbury Tales*'); *Comparative Studies in Society and History* (for material from 'Chaucer's General Prologue as History and Literature'); *Critical Quarterly* (for material from 'Chaucer as Satirist in the General Prologue to *The Canterbury Tales*'); University Press of Florida (for material from: 'Narrative Reflections: Re-envisaging the Poet in *The Canterbury Tales* and *The Faerie Queene*', in *Refiguring Chaucer in the Renaissance*; and *Chaucer and the Energy of Creation: The Design and the Organization of the Canterbury Tales*); Greenwood Press (for material from *Discussions of the Canterbury Tales*); University of Pennsylvania Press (for material from 'Originary Fantasies and Chaucer's *Book of the Duchess*', in *Feminist Approaches to the Body in Medieval Literature*); Harvester Press (for material from *Chaucer*); Clarendon Press (for material from: *Woman Defamed and Woman Defended: An Anthology of Medieval Texts*; and *Chaucer, Boccaccio and the Debate of Love: A Comparative Study of the Decameron and The Canterbury Tales*); Macmillan (for material from: *A Commentary on the General Prologue to the Canterbury Tales*; and *Chaucer's Women: Nuns, Wives and Amazons*); Methuen (for material from: *Chaucer's Pilgrims: The Artistic Order of the Portraits in the Prologue*; and *Chaucer's Knight: The Portrait of a Medieval Mercenary*); University of Minnesota Press (for material from *The Mythographic Chaucer: The Fabulation of Sexual Politics*); Alan Swallow (for material from *Tradition and Poetic Structure: Essays in Literary History and Criticism*); Michigan State University Press (for material from *Who is Buried in Chaucer's Tomb?: Studies in the Reception of Chaucer's Book*); Cambridge University Press (for material from: *Chaucer on Interpretation*; and *Chaucer and Medieval Estates Satire: The Literature of Social Classes and the General Prologue to the Canterbury Tales*); University of California Press (for material from: *Chaucer and the Fictions of Gender*; and *The Idea of the Canterbury Tales*); SUNY (for material from *A Reading of the Canterbury*

# ACKNOWLEDGEMENTS

*Tales*); Harvard University Press (for material from *Chaucer and the Shape of Creation: The Aesthetic Possibilities of Inorganic Structure*); Cornell University Press (for material from *The Tempter's Voice: Language and the Fall in Medieval Literature*); Johns Hopkins University Press (for material from *Chapters on Chaucer*); University of Oklahoma Press (for material from *Pilgrimage and Storytelling in the Canterbury Tales*); University of Wisconsin Press (for material from *Chaucer and the Subject of History*); Princeton University Press (for material from *A Preface to Chaucer: Studies in Medieval Perspectives*); Syracuse University Press (for material from *The Mind and Art of Chaucer*); Liverpool University Press (for material from *Shakespeare's Chaucer: A Study in Literary Origins*); Twayne (for material from *The Canterbury Tales: A Literary Pilgrimage*).

There are instances where we have been unable to trace or contact copyright holders before our printing deadline. If notified, the publisher will be pleased to acknowledge the use of copyright material.


J.-A. George wishes to acknowledge the following colleagues at the University of Dundee who, in various ways, offered fun and friendship during the writing of this Guide: Kasia Boddy, Alison Chapman, Richard Dunphy, Linda Hartley, Tracey Herd, John Low, Juan Carlos Olmos Alcoy, David Robb, Victor Skretkowicz, Anna Spackman, Jim Stewart, Vero Wechtler and Keith Williams.

For Jane Roberts, Dan Kempton and Alan Fletcher, my scholarly role models.




J.-A. George is a graduate of Vassar College and holds a PhD from the University of London (King's College). She has lectured in the Republic of Ireland and is currently a member of the English Department at the University of Dundee, where she also runs the Mediaeval Drama Group.

# INDEX

Aers, David
　Host/Pardoner 134–5
　masculinity 134, 135, 136
aesthetics, mediaeval/modern 28, 38–9, 40, 60–2
allusion 61, 131–2
American critics 9, 25
anatomical approach 84–5
anchoresses 137–8
*Ancrene Wisse* 137–8
Anderson, Judith H.
　narrator 13–14
　poststructural analysis 14–15
Andrew, Malcolm 119
angels 130
anonymous authors 120
anti-feminists 138
apology 15, 24, 70, 76
Armstrong, Nancy 120
Arnold, Matthew 9, 20–1
artistry, unimpersonated 88–9
astrolabe 26
Augustine, Saint 55–6, 79, 97, 105
author, gender 120

Bailey, Derrick Sherwin 128
Bailley, Harry (Host)
　in control 52, 86, 113, 118
　Ferster 117
　function 28, 30, 32–3, 59
　masculinity 121, 134, 135, 136
　and narrator 41, 90, 117, 134
　and Pardoner 134–5
　real person 159 n5
　story-telling 96, 154
　voice 95
Ball, John 153
barrenness 147–8
Baugh, Albert 127
Benedict, Saint 105
Benson, Larry D. 7–8
Bernard of Cluny 57
Bernard of Utrecht 150
Bialostosky, Don H. 15
Blake, William 20
Blamires, Alcuin 136–7
Blanch, Robert 118
Bloomfield, Morton W. 88

Boccaccio, Giovanni 78, 151, 152
　*Decameron* 28, 29–30
Boethius 114, 116
*Book of the Duchess* 152
Bowden, Muriel A. 9
　Knight 115
　Nature 38, 115
　Pardoner 121–2
Brewer, Derek 31
Bronson, Bertrand 52–3, 69
Brooke, Christopher 105
Brooks, Harold F. 111
Brown, Carleton 38

Canon's Yeoman 40, 41, 100, 104–6
Canterbury 153
*The Canterbury Tales* 61, 85, 161 n17
　Dryden on 15–16
　early editions 11, 17–18, 20, 22–4, 26–7, 157 n2
　Ellesmere manuscript 26–7
　and *The General Prologue* 7, 18, 37–8
　as Human Comedy 31–2
　as influence 12, 13
　opposites 44
　sources 13, 30–1
　structure 60–2, 73, 117
　tellers 16, 160 n29
catalogue device 40–1, 52, 79–80, 81
Caxton, William 11
Chance, Jane
　mythography 148–9
　Zephyrus 150–3
characterisation of pilgrims
　autonomy 76
　individuals 16, 32, 38, 54–5, 74–5
　naïve narrator 56
　real people 29
　satire 54–5
　self-revelation 56, 61
Chaucer, Geoffrey 8, 39–40
　female characters 119, 121
　gender politics 119–20, 148
　as influence 12, 13, 15–16
　irony 15, 51–2, 93
　literary canon 9, 12, 16, 20, 21, 58, 84
　modernity 95
　morality 13, 36, 74, 103
　Nature 34–6, 38, 75
　as Pilgrim 41, 50–1, 52–5, 57, 62, 66, 75, 91–4, 140

# INDEX

as Poet 50–1, 52–3, 62, 87, 91, 93–4, 140
Renaissance readings 73–4
as Reporter 51–2, 116
satire 53–8, 66
self-reflexivity 14, 15, 117
*see also* narrator
Chaucer, Geoffrey (work) 8, 11, 22–4, 26–7, 155–6, 157 n2
*Book of the Duchess* 152
*Chaucers Wordes unto Adam, His Owne Scriveyn* 84
'The Former Age' 150
*The House of Fame* 84
*The Legend of Good Women* 31, 51
*The Parlement of Foules* 79–80, 81, 82
*Troilus and Criseyde* 11, 12, 39, 84, 93, 95, 149
*see also* The Canterbury Tales; The General Prologue
Chaucer Society 26
*Chaucers Wordes unto Adam, His Owne Scriveyn* 84
Chesterton, G.K. 37–8
Child, F.J. 25
Christ Church Cathedral, Canterbury 153
Christianity 101, 102, 124–5, 149–50
Christine de Pizan 138
Clarendon Press edition 22–4
class
  conflict 86
  feudalism 98–9
  grouping of pilgrims 100
  hierarchy 70
  satire 27, 67–8
  *see also* estates satire
clergy/laity 70
Clerk of Oxenford 82
  as ideal 98, 106–7
  learning 101, 113
  marriage 120
*The Clerk's Tale* 37, 41
Coghill, Nevill 97–8
Coleridge, Samuel Taylor 20
common good 102–3, 110, 111, 113–14
commons 101, 102
Condren, Edward I.
  cataloguing 40–1
  creation 41–3
  grammatical analysis 43, 44
  narrator/Harry Bailley 41

confessions 110, 136
Cook 16, 49, 108
  appearance 56
  craft 101, 161 n4
  and Manciple 27
Corinthians, First 102
corruption 152
Craig, Cairns 34
Crane, Susan 134
creation device 41–3
critics 8–9, 10
  American 9, 25
  feminist 10, 118, 120, 121
crusades 115
cummings, e.e. 46
Cummings, H.M. 30
Cunningham, J.V. 59–60, 79–80
Curry, Walter C. 112–13, 123–4, 127
Curtius, Ernst 129

Dane, Joseph A. 15–16
Dante Alighieri 151
  and Chaucer 20
  *Divine Comedy* 129, 150, 152
David, Alfred 98, 99
decorum 13, 70, 149
Derrida, Jacques 89–90
Deschamps, Eustache 9, 12
*discordia* 63
Dominic, Saint 152
Donaldson, E. Talbot 9, 41, 89
  Chaucer as Pilgrim/Poet 50–2, 62, 66–7, 91
  Chaucer/Shakespeare 74
dream visions
  *The General Prologue* 79–81, 86–7
  *The Parlement of Foules* 78–80, 81, 82
  *Romance of the Rose* 59–60, 78–83
Dryden, John 10, 15–16, 21, 31, 59

Ecclesiasticus 137
Eco, Umberto 28
effeminacy 124, 126, 127, 128, 129, 132
elements and opposites 42
Eliot, T.S., *The Waste Land* 34
Ellesmere manuscript 26–7
English society 16–17, 66, 162 n13
Enlightenment readings 16, 17–18
equinoxes 25–6
estates
  stereotypes 71–2

177

three 66, 67–8, 98, 100, 102, 140
  *see also* class
estates literature 17, 67–9, 71–2
estates satire 17, 67–8, 82–3
eunuchry 127
  Christian view 124–5
  congenital/castrated 124, 127
  homosexuality 130–1
  impotence/effeminacy 123, 124, 127
  Jewish tradition 125
  'mare'/'geldyng' terms 123, 126–8
  Pardoner 112–13, 122–3, 125–6, 131
Eve 137–9

*fabliau* 130–1, 137
Fall myth 138–9
femininity 146
feminist criticism 10, 118, 120, 121
feminisation 128, 129
Ferster, Judith 90, 116–18
feudalism
  class 98–9
  groupings of pilgrims 100
  rural–urban migration 105
  undermined 98, 101
Fisher, John Hurt 127
Flora 152–3
Fowler, Alastair 79
framing device 28–9, 30, 37, 40
Franklin 56, 82, 101, 107–8
*The Franklin's Tale* 120–1
Frese, Dolores Warwick 8–9
Freud, Sigmund 78
Friar 82, 96
  appearances 100, 104–6
  colloquialisms 55–6
  self-justifying 75
  and Summoner 27, 112
friars 55, 105–6
Froissart, Jean 153
Frye, Northrop 162 n17
Furnivall, F.J. 24–6

Ganim, John M. 153–4
Garbaty, Thomas 108
Gautier de Leu 130–1
Gaylord, Alan T. 117
Geertz, Clifford 78
'geldyng' term 126–8
gender 119–20, 139–40, 148, 153–4
  *see also* femininity; masculinity

gender studies 118
*The General Prologue* 7, 11, 95–6, 119
  as *aide-mémoire* 87, 100
  and *The Canterbury Tales* 7, 18, 37–8
  cataloguing device 40, 52, 79–80, 81
  criticism 8–9, 10, 25, 118, 120, 121
  divisions 47–8, 49–50, 86
  dream vision 79–81, 86–7
  Enlightenment readings 16, 17–18
  estates literature 17, 67–9, 71–2
  framing device 28–9, 30, 37, 40
  irony 15, 51–2, 93
  meanings 8–9, 19
  modernity 47, 95
  paganism/Christianity 149–50
  poststructuralist analysis 14–15
  quarrels 27–8
  Ram debate 25–6
  realism 19, 29, 61–2, 76–7, 85
  representing England 16–17, 66, 162 n13
  social changes 69, 97–8, 106
  Spring opening 38, 40, 47, 95
  structure 59–60, 78
  styles 47–8
  themes 101–2
  time/space 75–6, 79, 80, 82–3
  voicing 66–7, 95–6
  *see also* narrator; pilgrims
genres 79, 141
Gower, John 73
  *Confessio Amantis* 28
grammatical analysis 43, 44
Guido delle Colonne, *Historia Destructionis Troiae* 39
Guildsmen 101, 108

Hanning, Robert W. 138
Hansen, Elaine Tuttle 119–20, 121
Harrington, Sir John 13
Henry II 153
Henry IV 23–34
hermaphrodites 129, 132
Higgs, Elton D. 17, 97–114
Hilton, H. 102
Hinckley, Henry Barrett 28–9, 30–1
homosexuality 122
  effeminacy 124, 126, 127, 128, 129, 132
  eunuchry 130–1
  feminisation 128, 129
  'mare' term 127

## INDEX

mediaeval view 128, 132
  Pardoner 121–2, 123, 132–3
  punished 131
Horrell, Joe 38
Host: *see* Bailley, Harry
*The House of Fame* 84
Howard, Donald R. 83–4
  anatomical approach 84–5
  class 98–100
  disordered society 98–100
  dream vision 86–7
  'geldyng'/'mare' terms 127
  Pardoner as eunuch 125–6
  'unimpersonated artistry' 88–9
Huizinga, Johan 78
Hulbert, J.R. 69
Human Comedy 31–2
Huppé, Bernard F. 52–3

iconography 63–4
ideal standard 57, 86, 98–9
  Clerk 98, 106–7
  Knight 82, 96, 98, 99, 106, 113
  Parson 98, 99, 113, 114
  Ploughman 71, 98, 99
identity
  masquerade 135
  textuality 90
illusion-breaking 61
illustrations, Ellesmere manuscript 26–7
impotence 123, 124, 127
informality 47–9
intellectual world 106–10, 114
inter-textuality 23
irony 15, 51–2, 93

Jager, Eric 137–9
James, Henry 60–1
Jewish tradition 125, 144–5
John of Gaunt 23
Jones, Terry 114–16
Jordan, Robert M. 59, 60–2
Juvenal 56

Keats, John 20
Kendrick, Laura 77–8
Kenner, Hugh 34
Kernan, Anne 136
Kirby, Thomas A. 16–17
Kittredge, G.L. 25, 89, 139
  Chaucer as Pilgrim 51

Human Comedy 31–2
Knight/Harry Bailley 32–3
Marriage Group 120–1
sources for *The Canterbury Tales* 30–1
Klein, Melanie 78
Knight
  appearances 104–6
  chivalry 37
  feudalism 100
  as ideal 82, 96, 98, 99, 106, 113
  Jones 114–16
  Martin, L.D. 81–2
  origins 23–34
  role 32–3, 70, 71
*The Knight's Tale* 63, 116
knowledge: *see* learning
Krier, Theresa M. 13

laity/clergy 70
Langland, William 97
  *Vision of Piers Plowman* 29, 57, 68
learning 101, 106–10, 113
  misused 107–9
lechery 131, 147
*The Legend of Good Women* 31, 51
Leicester, H. Marshall Jr. 14
  Chaucer as narrator 92–4
  Chaucer the Pilgrim 91–2
  dramatic model 89–90
  Ferster on 90
  and Howard 83
  Monk 92–3
  'unimpersonated artistry' 88–9
  voice/presence 66–7, 89–90
Lenaghan, R.T. 50, 65–6, 83
Lepley, Douglas L. 116
Lerner, Robert E. 106
literary theory, mediaeval 88
*Livre du Chevalier* 137–8
Longfellow, Henry Wadsworth 158 n37
Lorris, Guillaume de 128–9
Lounsbury, Thomas R. 22–4, 157 n2
Lowes, John Livingstone 25, 36–7, 61, 141
Lumiansky, R.M. 89

McAlpine, Monica E.
  eunuchry 123–5
  hermaphroditism 129–30
  homosexuality 126–9, 130–2
  narrator on Pardoner 133–4
  Pardoner 113, 122–7, 132–3

179

Major, John M. 92
Malone, Kemp 9
  characterisation 55
  groupings of pilgrims 49–50, 55, 99
  pronouns 48–9
  style 47–8
Man of Law 82, 84, 101, 105, 107
Manciple 27, 56, 101, 111–12
manipulation 101–2
Manly, J. M. 25
  estates 67
  Knight 115
  pilgrims/real people 159 n5
  society 69
Mann, Jill
  Chaucer's morality 103
  estates literature 68, 71–2
  estates satire 66–70, 82
  homosexuality 127, 128
  nuns 143
  subjectivity 72–3
  Wife of Bath 137
manners manual 137–8
'mare' term 123, 126–8
Margherita, Gayle 119
Marriage Group 8, 120–1, 137
Martin, Loy D.
  dream visions 78–81
  estates satire 82–3
  Knight 81–2
  pilgrimage frame 103
  social changes 113–14
Martin, Priscilla
  gender in mediaeval society 139–40
  marriage theme 120–1
  Prioress 140–6, 147
  Wife of Bath 146–8
martyrdom 152
Marxist critiques 65–6
masculinity 121, 134, 135, 136
masquerade
  identity 135
  pilgrimage 153–4
material/social world 73
mediaeval aesthetics 28, 38–9, 40, 60–2
mediaeval view
  anti-feminism 138
  class hierarchy 70
  homosexuality 128, 132
  literary theory 88
  memory 87

natural history 39–40
Nature 38
*persona* 53
pilgrimages 43–5
society 139–40
mediaevalism, post-feminist 119–20
memory 84–6, 87, 100
men, status 70
Merchant 114
  appearances 100, 104–6
  locale 82
  marriage 120
  trade 101
  wealth 76, 106
*The Merchant's Tale* 63, 119, 137
meta-fictional readings 77–8
Miller 16, 32, 37
  evil 57
  physicality 37, 63–4, 110–11
  physiognomy 161 n21
  and Reeve 27, 76
  rural service 101
Miller, Robert 124–5
Milner, Thomas, *Gallery of Nature* 26
Minnis, Alastair J. 88
Miskimin, Alice 73–4
Miskimin, Harry A. 101, 106
misogyny 136
modernity 47, 95
modes of writing 79
Mohl, Ruth 68
money economy 106, 111
Monk 15, 92–3
  appearances 56, 100
  and Knight 115–16
  self-justifying 75
*The Monk's Tale* 73, 116
morality
  apology 24
  Chaucer 13, 36, 74, 103
  ideal standard 57
  Miller and Pardoner 57
Morell, Thomas 11
Morgan, Gerald 163 n23
Musa, Mark 129
Muscatine, Charles 69, 89
mythography 148, 149

narrator
  Anderson 13–14
  *Decameron* 30

# INDEX

and Harry Bailley 41, 90, 117, 134
memory 87
naïve 56, 66–7, 92, 94, 140
omniscient 85
and Pardoner 132–4
and Prioress 142
role 14–15, 50, 75
satire 58
self-reflexivity 14–15
sophistication 92, 94
*see also* Chaucer, as Pilgrim
national consciousness 17
natural history 39–40
Nature 34–6, 38, 75
Nevo, Ruth 83, 111
*New York Review of Books* 83–4
nobility 101, 102
Nolan, Barbara 94–7
Norton-Smith, John 73
*nouveaux riches* 108
nuns 55, 143
Nun's Priest 18–19

opposites 42, 44
originality 28, 40
Owen, Charles A. Jr.
    Chaucer's influences 58–9
    Chaucer's role 75–7
    Ellesmere manuscript 26–7
    story-telling 74, 77
    structure 18–19, 74–5

paganism/Christianity 149–50
Pardoner 32, 75, 82, 111, 114
    appearance 96, 123–4
    craft 101, 133
    depravity 27, 57, 105, 112–13, 124–6
    as eunuch 112–13, 122–3, 125–6, 131
    and Harry Bailley 134–5
    homosexuality 121–2, 123, 132–3
    McAlpine 122–7
    and narrator 132–4
    as scapegoat 134–5
    self-revelation 61, 110
    and Summoner 122, 132
    and Wife of Bath 135–6
*The Pardoner's Tale* 135
*The Parlement of Foules* 79–80, 81
Parson 15
    as ideal 98, 99, 113, 114
    rural service 101

pastoral, French 141
Patterson, Lee 73, 121, 136
Paul, Saint 102
*persona* 53, 90
personal poetry 87
*The Philological Quarterly* 26
physical world 104–6, 114
Physician 56, 101, 105, 108, 109
physiognomy 123, 124, 161 n21
Piaget, Jean 78
pilgrimages
    masquerade 153–4
    mediaeval view 43–5
    spiritual/worldly 43–5, 86, 96–7
pilgrims 103
    appearances 56, 82, 100, 104–6
    autonomy 76–7
    characterisation 16, 29, 32, 38, 54–5, 56, 61, 74–5, 76
    common good 113–14
    confessions 110, 136
    English society 66, 162 n13
    groupings 49–50, 99–102, 104–13, 114, 163 n23
    ideal standard 57, 71, 82, 86, 96, 99, 106–7, 113–14
    intellectual world 106–10
    Marriage Group 120–1
    occupations 72
    real people 159 n5
    social factors 32–3, 65–6, 100
    spiritual world 110–13
Piper, Edwin Ford 26
Plague 28–9, 105, 110
play 78, 96
Plowman 70, 114
    as ideal 71, 98, 99
    rural service 101, 110
Polemon, physiognomist 124
Postan, M. M. 105
postfeminism 119–20
poststructuralist analysis 14–15
presence/voice 66–7, 89–90, 91
Preston, Raymond 17
Priests 18
Prioress 100, 139, 165 n24
    appearance 104–6
    class 70
    emotional immaturity 145
    femininity 146, 165 n20
    gentility 16, 141–2

## THE GENERAL PROLOGUE

iconography 64
loving kindness 143
Martin, P. 140–6, 147
narrator 142
role-playing 140–1, 145–6
self-deception 142
*The Prioress's Tale* 143–6
pronouns
   first and second person 48–9
   first person 54, 95
*Purity* 129–30

quarrels 27–8
Quiller-Couch, Sir Arthur T. 19

Rabanus Maurus 151–2
Ram debate 25–6
rape 152–3
readers 48, 138
realism 19, 61–2, 76–7, 85
   Chaucer 29, 39–40
   in fiction 50
   Tyrwhitt 19–20
reality/ideal 98–9
Reeve 16, 37, 82, 111
   manipulation 101
   and Miller 27, 76
   subversive 112
Reidy, John 111
Renaissance readings of Chaucer 73–4
reporting 51–2, 62, 116
rhetoric/voicing 95–6
Richard II 23, 24, 74
Ricks, Christopher 34
Robertson, D. W. 9, 62–4
Robinson, F. N. 115
*Romance of the Rose* 27, 59–60, 64, 128–9, 136, 142
Root, Robert Kilburn 25
Rowland, Beryl 17
Ruggiers, Paul 89
rural–urban migration 105

satire
   Chaucerian 53–8, 66
   class 27, 67–8
   classical authors 56, 57–8
   estates satire 17, 67–8, 82–3
   Frye 162 n17
Scottish Chaucerians 12
self-reflexivity 14, 15, 117
self-revelation 56, 61, 110

Sercambi of Lucca, Giovanni, *Novelle* 28–9, 31
sexuality
   barrenness 147–8
   female pilgrims 139
   masculinity 35, 121, 134, 136
   virginity 137
   *see also* homosexuality
Shakespeare, William 12, 74
Shipman 82, 101, 108–9
Sidney, Sir Philip 12
Skeat, Walter 23, 26
social changes 69, 97–8, 106
social order
   breaking down 112, 113
   *The General Prologue* 69–70
sociological readings 65–6
Sodom and Gomorrah 129–30
Spearing, A. C. 130
Speght, Thomas 11, 13, 157 n2
Spencer, William 65
Spenser, Edmund 12, 14
   *The Faerie Queene* 14, 15
spiritual world 107, 110–13, 114
Spring opening 38, 40, 47, 95
Spurgeon, Caroline F. E. 11
Squire 56, 82, 100, 104–6
stereotypes 71–2, 137
Stevens, Martin 26
story-telling
   Ferster 117
   Harry Bailley 96, 154
   mediaeval tradition 31
   memory 84–5
   Nolan 96–7
   Owen 74, 77
   structure 35, 74, 96–7, 117
Stowe, John 11, 157 n2
subjectivity 72–3
Sudbury, Simon 153
Sullivan, Sheila 25
Summoner 15, 37, 111
   appearance 57
   and Friar 27, 112
   manipulation 101
   and Pardoner 112, 122, 132

tales/tellers 16, 37, 135, 160 n29
Tatlock, J. S. P. 9, 25, 52
   class 70
   mediaeval tradition 38–9
   modernity 46–7

# INDEX

Tennyson, Alfred, Lord 35
textuality 89–90, 91
Thomas à Becket, Saint 33, 40, 151, 152, 153
Thompson, Ann 13, 73–4
Thompson, N. S. 29–30
three estates 66, 67–8, 98, 100, 102, 140
Thynne, William 11, 13, 14, 157 n2
time/space 75–6, 79, 80, 82–3
town/country 35, 105
*Troilus and Criseyde* 84
    Criseyde 93, 149
    literary criticism 11
    psychological complexity 95
    Shakespeare 12
    sources 39
Tupper, Frederick 27–8
Tyrwhitt, Thomas
    on Caxton 11
    *Decameron* 28
    edition of *The Canterbury Tales* 17–18, 20, 157 n2
    Ram/Bull debate 25
    realism 19–20

'unimpersonated artistry' 88–9
Urry, John 11

*Variorum* edition 7, 119
vernacular text 95–6
virginity 137
voice
    *The General Prologue* 66–7, 95–6
    Nolan 94–5
    presence 66–7, 89–90, 91
    rhetoric 95–6

Wainwright, Benjamin B. 38
Walter of Chatillon 127
Wasserman, Julian N. 118
Weissman, Hope Phyllis 142–3
Whiting, B.J. 38
Wife of Bath 32, 82, 114, 164–5 n20
    barrenness 147–8
    class 70
    and Clerk 109–10
    craft 101
    deafness 138
    femininity 146
    intellectual curiosity 147
    marriage debate 40, 41, 96, 120–1
    marriages 147
    Martin, P. 146–8
    and Pardoner 135–6
    *Prologue* 137
    role-playing 140
    self-revealing 61
Williams, David 11–12, 13, 16, 20
women
    estates literature 69
    mediaeval society 139–40
    roles 140
    status 70
    *see also* gender
Woolf, Rosemary 53–8
Woolf, Virginia 34–6, 38
Worde, Wynkyn de 11
Wordsworth, William 35, 51

Yeoman 40, 41, 100, 104–6

Zephirus 150–3